'As the founder of Schema Therapy, I am excited to see the paradigm expanded into new territories. This is the first book to explore how Schema Therapy can be applied – both theoretically and clinically – to working with individuals experiencing psychosis and bipolar conditions. Given the complexity of such presentations, it is clear that modifications of our therapeutic techniques are needed. This book fully demonstrates these through detailed case studies. What sets this book apart is the authors' ability to bridge theory and practice seamlessly. Rhodes and Vorontsova have not only added a vital chapter to the Schema Therapy approach but have also opened doors to a more compassionate and effective treatment for individuals facing the challenges of psychosis and bipolarity.'

Jeffery Young, *founder of Schema Therapy and co-director of Schema Therapy Institute of New York and New Jersey*

'This book offers something many have long waited for: how to apply Schema Therapy, and techniques from Schema Therapy, in chronic psychosis and in bipolar disorder. Schema Therapy is a particularly effective treatment for personality disorders and chronic depression. The authors of this book describe how the theory and practice of Schema Therapy can also be applied to these challenging problem areas. Clinicians will benefit greatly from this work.'

Arnoud Arntz, *professor at the Department of Clinical Psychology, University of Amsterdam, Amsterdam, The Netherlands*

'A masterful text on the application of Schema Therapy to Psychosis and Bipolarity. Chapters cover the value of a part-selves conceptualisation as well as creative adaptations to change techniques, brought to life by rich clinical accounts. A must read for anyone working in these clinical areas.'

Helen Startup, *director of Schema Therapy School, UK*

Schema Therapy Adapted for Psychosis and Bipolarity

This book explores how Schema Therapy and its underlying theory might be used in work with clients who suffer from psychosis, bipolarity and related symptoms.

The first part of the book presents in-depth qualitative research featuring first-person testimonies that describe the self-states or 'modes' of a person with psychosis or bipolarity. These self-states involve a range of features, such as emotions, thoughts, motivations and behaviours, which manifest as patterns. The second part proposes the adaptation and application of Schema Therapy, a transdiagnostic approach working with emotion and interpersonal functioning for clinical work with these two groups.

Offering unique insights, this text will appeal to a range of practicing clinicians, such as psychologists, therapists, psychiatrists and those with a special interest in psychosis or bipolarity.

John Rhodes is a consultant clinical psychologist and a visiting lecturer at the University of Hertfordshire, and research fellow at Birkbeck, University of London. He wrote *Narrative CBT: Distinctive Features* (2014) and *Psychosis and the Traumatised Self* (2022), and co-authored *Narrative CBT for Psychosis* (2009). He has published articles in the areas of psychosis, trauma and depression.

Natasha Vorontsova is a senior clinical psychologist in early intervention for psychosis at the NHS in the UK. She specialises in advancing psychological understandings of psychosis, particularly regarding the roles of emotional difficulties and trauma. Her research concerns improving psychological therapies, and she teaches at University College London and King's College London.

Schema Therapy Adapted for Psychosis and Bipolarity

Exploring the Multi-Self

John Rhodes and Natasha Vorontsova

With contributions from:

Nicola Airey, Katherine Berry, Georgie Paulik and
Christopher D. J. Taylor

LONDON AND NEW YORK

Designed cover image: *Circles in a Circle* (1923) by Vasily Kandinsky
Philadelphia Museum of Art: The Louise and Walter Arensberg
Collection, 1950 The Louise and Walter Arensberg Collection, 1950,
1950-134-104

First published 2025
by Routledge
4 Park Square, Milton Park, Abingdon, Oxon OX14 4RN

and by Routledge
605 Third Avenue, New York, NY 10158

Routledge is an imprint of the Taylor & Francis Group, an informa business

British Library Cataloguing-in-Publication Data
A catalogue record for this book is available from the British Library

Library of Congress Cataloging-in-Publication Data
Names: Rhodes, John, 1955- author. | Vorontsova, Natasha, 1986- author. |
Airey, Nicola, author. | Berry, Katherine, author. | Paulik, Georgie,
author. | Taylor, Christopher D. J., author.
Title: Schema therapy adapted for psychosis and bipolarity : exploring the
multi-self / John Rhodes, Natasha Vorontsova ; with contributions from
Nicola Airey, Katherine Berry, Georgie Paulik and Christopher D.J. Taylor.
Description: Abingdon, Oxon ; New York, NY : Routledge, 2025. | Includes
bibliographical references and index. |
Identifiers: LCCN 2024006673 (print) | LCCN 2024006674 (ebook) | ISBN
9781032396224 (hbk) | ISBN 9781032396217 (pbk) | ISBN 9781003350583 (ebk)
Subjects: MESH: Psychotic Disorders--therapy | Bipolar Disorder--therapy |
Schema Therapy
Classification: LCC RC480.5 (print) | LCC RC480.5 (ebook) | NLM WM 200 |
DDC 616.89/1--dc23/eng/20240528
LC record available at https://lccn.loc.gov/2024006673
LC ebook record available at https://lccn.loc.gov/2024006674

ISBN: 978-1-032-39622-4 (hbk)
ISBN: 978-1-032-39621-7 (pbk)
ISBN: 978-1-003-35058-3 (ebk)

DOI: 10.4324/9781003350583

Typeset in Times New Roman
by SPi Technologies India Pvt Ltd (Straive)

Contents

Acknowledgements   *ix*

1   Modes, psychosis and bipolarity   1

2   Exploring modes in psychosis   15

3   Exploring modes in bipolarity   36

4   Developing the concept of modes in psychosis and bipolarity   58

5   Adapting Schema Therapy for psychosis and bipolarity   77

6   Attachment, schemas and imagery focused therapy for psychosis (iMAPS)   91
NICOLA AIREY, KATHERINE BERRY AND CHRISTOPHER D. J. TAYLOR

7   Imagery rescripting in trauma-affected voice hearers   111
GEORGIE PAULIK

8   Psychosis and Schema Therapy   128

9   Bipolarity and Schema Therapy   144

Index   *161*

Acknowledgements

John Rhodes
I would like to thank Vartouhi Ohanian for her inspiring supervision in Schema Therapy and Dave Harper, Zoe Williams and Hannah Whitehead for their contributions to the research in Chapters 2 and 3.

I wish to express my appreciation of those who support me, Natan and friends.

Natasha Vorontsova
I would like to thank all of the participants of our research, who kindly shared their time and their experiences in the hope that they could help others. I also want to thank all of my loved ones for their patience and support, particularly Giles Barrett.

Chapter 1

Modes, psychosis and bipolarity

Contemporary psychological therapies for psychosis and bipolar conditions have evolved through waves of behavioural and cognitively focused models, and more recently have given greater attention to the importance of emotional and interpersonal domains. Clinicians and researchers alike have noted histories of early trauma, extreme negative appraisals of self and others, and attachment disturbances accompanying the presentations of those who we see entering psychotic and extreme mood states. We came to the ideas in this book by way of the question: how can we better understand and help people with such interpersonal and emotional difficulties, when these seem to precede, predict and perpetuate the indicative symptoms of the 'serious mental illnesses' with which our clients have been diagnosed? In this book we explore how Schema Therapy and its underpinning theory, including the concept of modes, may advance our understanding of these areas. We present an exploration of the schema mode concept as applied to the experiences of people with psychosis or bipolar diagnoses, presenting newly analysed qualitative data from direct report of participants. We then set out a framework for clinical applications and illustrate how such approaches have been pursued in therapy, with detailed case examples.

This first chapter explains the concept of modes as used within Schema Therapy, briefly considering evidence supporting the model and summarising the case for why we think it might be useful for working with psychosis and bipolarity. Next, we describe how the presence of modes in those with psychosis and bipolar diagnoses was investigated using qualitative research, the results of which will be presented in Chapters 2 and 3.

Schema Therapy and modes

Schema Therapy evolved from the evidence-based tradition of the Cognitive Behavioural Therapies (CBT) and is built around understandings of attachment and the impacts of early adversity on identity, emotional and relational functioning. The model at first relied on conceptualising and working with schemas, meaning 'self-defeating emotional and cognitive patterns that begin

DOI: 10.4324/9781003350583-1

early in our development and repeat throughout life' (Young et al., 2003), influencing emotions, perceptions, sensations and behavioural responses. For example, an individual might frequently feel extreme distress at perceived abandonment, responding disproportionately to the magnitude of triggering events, such as a partner going away on a short work trip or a friend being unavailable for a social event. Over time, it was found that individuals with very difficult backgrounds and multiple current struggles tended to show evidence of a large number of maladaptive early schemas, some perhaps becoming more active and visible in certain situations and shifting over time. This presented a challenge for the original Schema Therapy model, as formulations including so many schemas were cumbersome and might be overwhelming for clients. The schema mode concept was developed in order to simplify the approach to Schema Therapy case conceptualisation for clients with complex presentations, including those who had received a diagnosis of personality disorder.

To better meet the needs of clinical work with this group, Young et al. (2003) set out the schema mode framework as a simplified set of pervasive and persistent subsections of the self or personality, which may play certain roles in responding to daily situations, and may interact with each other, as well as manifesting in interactions with other people. Each mode is linked to sets of early maladaptive schemas in particular ways, but functions as a fluctuating state of self rather than a stable trait. This 'multi-self' mode framework, as an open and flexible system conceptualising multiple self-states, has been found to have great clinical utility in working with complexity in the presentations of people diagnosed with personality disorders, but has not yet been applied to those with psychosis or bipolar conditions.

Schema mode framework

The ten modes originally set out by Young et al. (2003) were grouped into child modes, dysfunctional parent modes, maladaptive coping modes and the healthy adult mode. All modes with exception of the healthy adult and healthy child are linked with the activation of maladaptive early schemas or with particular coping styles related to them. The framework describes mode categories and suggests the different sorts of features often found in each type of mode, contrasting for example the helpless feelings of the vulnerable child mode against the harsh criticism of the punitive parent mode. It is understood that each individual person's modes will have a specific selection of features related to the general description of that mode type, but that these will vary between individuals. In actual clinical practice, the mode categories function as guidelines, suggesting the sorts of possible mode types that may operate; the therapist aims to work with the particular states of self described by the individual, naming them using the preferred words of the client. Here we briefly summarise each mode type in line with Young et al.'s framework and introduce their thera-peutic use.

Child modes

Child modes comprise four types: three dysfunctional child modes – the vul-nerable child, angry child, impulsive or undisciplined child – and the healthy child. The dominance of one or more of the dysfunctional child modes in adulthood would be expected to result from certain unmet core emotional needs in early life. Young et al. presented these descriptions based on clinical observations made while working with a wide range of clients in therapy. They reported that clients entering a child mode would sometimes report 'feeling like a child' in that state, but this would not always be the case. Others have simplified the mode names, referring simply to vulnerable, angry and impulsive or undisciplined modes (e.g. Lazarus & Rafaeli, 2023). As with all modes, in clinical practice the aim would be to select a personalised name for each of a person's specific self-states, reflecting its particularities and their personal pref-erences. Here we initially present Young et al.'s mode categories using their original names, for clarity. In the research presented in our subsequent chap-ters, however, we will use simplified terms.

The vulnerable child mode is characterised by feelings of anxiety, fearful-ness, loneliness, helplessness and sadness. There is a sense of defencelessness that can be accompanied by a desperate yearning to be looked after by a caring or parental figure of some kind. Young et al. suggested subtypes correspond-ing to different early emotional adversities, including the abandoned child, abused child, deprived child and defective child. The vulnerable child modes are linked to most of the maladaptive early schemas and are the core target for healing in Schema Therapy.

The angry child mode, too, is linked with unmet early emotional needs, but instead of vulnerability and help-seeking, presents anger or rage, becomes furi-ous, can yell and may lash out. The individual in an angry child mode may feel abused, abandoned, deprived or subjugated, and can have a subjective sense of losing control of their feelings and behaviour. Their reactions may appear to others as being out of proportion to the triggering circumstance and can pres-ent as dysregulated demanding, venting, aggression and even violence.

The impulsive or undisciplined child mode acts on impulse to attain desires or seek pleasure, without regard for limits or consequences. Young et al. described this as representing the child in a 'natural,' uninhibited state. This child mode is linked with intolerance of frustration and an inability to delay gratification for the sake of longer-term goals. A person in this mode may come across to others as being spoiled, lazy, impatient or careless, and may give up easily when faced with frustrating or boring tasks.

The happy child mode represents the absence of any maladaptive schema activation, and it is associated with the child's core emotional needs being met adequately. The happy child feels contented and loved, fulfilled, worthwhile, competent, safe, resilient, adaptable, optimistic and spontaneous.

Dysfunctional parent modes

Two common types of dysfunctional parent modes were proposed by Young et al.: the punitive parent mode and the demanding parent mode. Both were conceptualised typically as arising from internalisations of a parent or caregiver from the individual's early life, although they might also relate to later experiences with authority figures or bullying from peers. Young et al.'s original naming of the dysfunctional parent modes reflects their clinical observation regarding the frequent connections between the activities of these modes and the individual's earlier experiences with a parent; others, however, have subsequently spoken simply of critical or demanding modes (e.g. Lazarus & Rafaeli, 2023). Clinically, it would be recommended to use the language that best fits each individual client's experience of their modes or self-states. We describe the modes here using Young et al.'s original names, for clarity.

The punitive parent mode is typically blaming, shaming, subjugating, harsh and unforgiving, attacking the self and inflicting pain. Individuals with activation of this mode may have been punished for expressing normal needs early in life. When activated, the punitive parent mode can induce self-loathing, self-denial and self-criticism, and might lead into self-injury, suicidal thoughts and self-destructive behaviours. Therapeutically, an aim would be to set limits on the activation of the punitive parent mode, while understanding its origins but not condoning its destructive manifestations. At times, a Schema Therapy approach may seek to banish this mode entirely.

The demanding parent mode, in contrast to the punitive parent, is not characterised by self-hate or explicit self-attack, but rather pushes and pressures the self to reach exacting high standards. In this mode, there may be a focus on perfection, overachievement, efficiency, avoidance of wasting any time, or extreme humility and always putting the needs of others before one's own. There is a sense of striving for self-improvement and being a 'good person,' but with such a pressured approach and such perfectionistic standards that one's efforts never feel enough, and ongoing distress is generated. We would typically expect that clients with activation of this mode were treated in demanding and perfectionistic ways by early caregivers, or on the other hand may have been parentified in childhood in relation to a vulnerable or isolated caregiver who was unable to contain the child's distress and to maintain the role of a parent. Within clinical work in Schema Therapy, there may be a negotiation with this demanding mode in relation to how it effects or influences the person, seeking to arrive at a more balanced, flexible and reasonable approach to striving for goals or attending to moral standards.

Coping modes

The maladaptive coping modes presented by Young et al. were of three types: the compliant surrender, detached protector and the overcompensator. Each of these corresponds to a style of basic psychological strategy that a child might have used to adapt to living in a threatening environment with unmet emotional needs: acquiescence, avoidance and overcompensation, respectively. Each of these types of coping can be understood as having been adaptive or functional at least in some ways at the time of becoming established; however, when relied upon inflexibly in adult life, each can become unhelpful in particular ways. In Schema Therapy, an aim would be to reduce the need for maladaptive coping by meeting the needs of the more vulnerable parts of the person, but the coping modes might also be worked with directly using techniques such as empathic confrontation.

The compliant surrender mode acts in accordance with maladaptive schemas, functioning to avoid further mistreatment by submitting to the will of others, potentially accepting adversity or abuse, and failing to take steps to get healthy needs met, instead prioritising the avoidance of conflict, rejection or retaliation. Individuals with compliant surrender mode activation may come across as passive and submissive, and may experience themselves as helpless in the face of a more powerful figure, having no choice but to try to appease the other for fear of the consequences otherwise.

The detached protector modes use avoidance as a coping style in relation to the person's maladaptive schemas, and this often involves forms of social disconnection. Psychological and emotional distancing is used, sometimes accompanied by behavioural withdrawal, and individuals affected may feel numb or empty, coming across to others as aloof, disinterested or cynical. A form of this mode may rely on self-stimulating or self-soothing activities to escape from painful feelings, and this can be associated with addictive or compulsive behaviour patterns such as workaholism, problem gambling, drug abuse, overeating, playing excessive computer games or spending great lengths of time watching television. The detached protector modes tend to have felt very helpful for individuals at some point in their lives, perhaps even been crucial to survival in adverse environments, and they may have become so heavily relied upon that they feel automatic.

The overcompensator modes use a coping style that involves acting as if the opposite of maladaptive schemas were true. For example, extravagant attention-seeking might be used to overcompensate for underlying loneliness and worthlessness, or perfectionism and expressed superiority could be used to cope with an underlying sense of defectiveness. Types of overcompensatory response could also include self-aggrandizement, perfectionistic or paranoid over-control, or even bullying and aggression towards others. When an individual is in an overcompensating mode, others tend to feel dominated, controlled, or under attack by them.

Healthy adult mode

The healthy adult mode, alongside the healthy child mode, represents an absence of maladaptive schema activation. Individuals in the healthy adult mode are able to attend to strategic and organisational functions in relation to themselves and the other modes, and can engage in healthy adult behaviours such as parenting, working, health maintenance, sex, intellectual, aesthetic and cultural pursuits. The healthy adult can nurture and protect the vulnerable child, can set limits for the angry, impulsive or undisciplined child, and can moderate or confront the dysfunctional parent and maladaptive coping modes. Schema Therapy seeks to strengthen and support the healthy adult mode to perform its executive functions and regulate the operation of the other modes and the multi-self as a whole.

Effectiveness and acceptability

Schema Therapy has demonstrated effectiveness in a number of clinical trials, mostly with groups of people experiencing chronic depression or with diagnoses of personality disorders (Bakos et al., 2015; Körük & Özabacı, 2018). A review of the existing trials applying Schema Therapy to people with anxiety disorders has also recently shown promising results, although authors note that more research is needed (Peeters et al., 2022). As a transdiagnostic approach attending to underlying issues with attachment, emotional and interpersonal functioning, it makes sense that Schema Therapy can be of use to individuals with a wide range of clinical presentations, especially those with relatively longstanding issues.

The high acceptability of Schema Therapy to clients has been noted in trial reports, which have found very low drop-out rates (Renner et al., 2016), including in comparison to those of treatment as usual (Bamelis et al., 2014) or psychotherapy for the same groups of clients (Giesen-Bloo et al., 2006). It may be that the focused emphasis early on in Schema Therapy on building a strong therapeutic relationship protects against drop-out to some extent. We would propose, based on clinical experience, that the schema mode model carries particular advantages conceptually in relation to acceptability. Namely, the central concept of the multi-self, meaning a plurality of states of self within individuals, and the mode mapping associated with it, is a distinctive feature facilitating insight into the complexity of self-states interacting with each other and changing over time, as well as effective empathic confrontation of dysfunctional parts or patterns, and collaboration around change. Dysfunctional and maladaptive processes can be attributed to just a mode or part of the self, rather than the self as a whole, maintaining the individual's connections to their resourceful healthy sides and reducing the potential for defensiveness or feeling pathologised. Our observation from clinical experience is that the model is intuitive and relatively easy to connect with experientially for many clients.

Rationale for application to psychosis

The difficulties for which Schema Therapy was developed are common in people experiencing psychosis: attachment disruptions, early trauma, interpersonal difficulties and issues with emotion regulation all show high prevalence in groups given schizophrenia-spectrum diagnoses (Addington & Addington, 2008; Gumley et al., 2014; Livingstone et al., 2009; Stanton et al., 2020). Seeing these difficulties co-occurring so prevalently with psychosis would serve as a sufficient basis to seek to address them. The case has also been made, however, that they have causal effects feeding into psychotic symptoms.

Early trauma and adversity have repeatedly been found by meta-analyses to be strongly predictive of the subsequent onset of psychosis (Bonoldi et al., 2013; McKay et al., 2021; Van Winkel et al., 2013; Varese et al., 2012), with prospective cohort studies notably supporting the causal link running from trauma to psychosis, rather than the reverse (Arseneault et al., 2011; Cutajar et al., 2010). Theoretical models have conceptualised the pathways of effect (Hardy, 2017; Hardy et al., 2016), highlighting emotion regulation issues and extreme negative beliefs about self and others, alongside memory disruptions, as processes by which the impacts of trauma feed into the form and content of psychotic symptomatology. Based on this theoretical framework, a randomised controlled trial of trauma focused therapy for people with psychosis is currently ongoing (Peters et al., 2022), with sections of the intervention addressing each hypothesised pathway of effect from trauma to psychosis.

Among the types of traumatic events in the histories of people experiencing psychosis, interpersonal traumas have been associated with the occurrence and severity of positive psychotic symptoms, as well as with attachment disturbances, negative core beliefs (Humphrey et al., 2022) and social dysfunction (Stain et al., 2014). This pathway parallels the theoretical basis of Schema Therapy, which posits that unmet early emotional needs contribute to the formation of maladaptive schemas and the emergence of dysfunctional mode states, whose interactions both within the individual and with other people then manifest in emotional and relational dysregulation (Young et al., 2003). The clinical implication of seeing a similar sequence of issues leading up to and predicting people's experiences of psychosis is that addressing these sequelae of trauma – disruptions in emotion regulation, schematic beliefs and interpersonal functioning – with a therapy targeting them specifically, such as Schema Therapy, has the potential not only to ameliorate these elements of the client's experience, but to have an impact in addition on the occurrence of psychotic symptoms.

Cognitive Behavioural Therapy for psychosis (CBTp) as recommended by NICE (National Collaborating Centre for Mental Health (UK), 2014) has proven effectiveness in the treatment of psychotic symptoms, but its effectiveness remains limited, demonstrating small to medium effect sizes, and showing high drop-out rates in clinical practice (Gould et al., 2004; Lincoln et al., 2014;

Wykes et al., 2008). CBTp originally was not explicitly formulated to address emotional and interpersonal difficulties directly: emotions and core beliefs (sometimes referred to as schematic beliefs) were included in the formulations, but the focus of the interventions was very much on ameliorating the impacts of positive psychotic symptoms, using practical coping skills, behavioural exposure principles and cognitive appraisals as therapeutic targets and mechanisms of change. In striving to improve both the accessibility and outcomes of psychological therapies for people who have experienced psychosis, more recent protocols of CBTp and adjacent therapies such as Compassion Focussed Therapy (CFT) have placed increasing emphasis on components seeking to directly target schematic beliefs and emotional and relational processes (e.g. Freeman et al., 2021; Heriot-Maitland et al., 2019; Peters et al., 2022). Analogously to the rationale for the original development of Schema Therapy, which sought to target longstanding and recurrent difficulties that were not amenable to standard CBT, we wish to address for people with psychosis the interpersonal and emotional struggles that sit outside the remit of traditional symptom-focused CBTp. Initial investigations into the application of Schema Therapy concepts to this group have found a range of early maladaptive schemas reported by participants experiencing psychosis (Taylor & Harper, 2017), but research on modes has not yet been done. We suggest that the multi-self concept conveyed by the schema mode model has a particular power to improve both clinicians' understanding of the dynamics of psychotic symptomatology and also the therapeutic engagement of clients.

Rationale for application to bipolarity

Like psychosis, bipolar disorder was historically often seen as essentially a biological illness, presumed to have a genetic basis, with which sufferers should learn to cope. Psychological therapies initially targeted circadian rhythm regulation and stress management, essentially seeking to behaviourally stabilise the manifestations of mood fluctuation using techniques with clear links to physiology (Lam, 1999; Lam et al., 2010). Subsequently, a more cognitive perspective was applied, and a range of features such as maladaptive assumptions and rules for living identified as drivers of mood ascent and descent cycles (Mansell et al., 2007). More recent protocols have sought to attend to social and interpersonal rhythms in the lives of clients with bipolar diagnoses (Crowe et al., 2020; Steardo et al., 2020); however, the focus has remained largely on skills and understandings centrally connected to the regulation of mood, with the aim of trying to keep its fluctuations within a narrower range.

Studies assessing attachment disruptions and early trauma in groups of people with bipolar diagnoses have found striking prevalence of both (Dualibe & Osório, 2017; Harnic et al., 2014; Kefeli et al., 2018; Morriss et al., 2009), although the studies are more scant than with psychosis. Severity of trauma history and attachment disruption have been found to be correlated with later symptom severity and dysfunction (Aas et al., 2016; Citak & Erten, 2021; Wrobel et al., 2022), in line with the idea of a causal connection. Indeed, given the parallel links seen in other diagnostic groupings who have been more thoroughly researched, it would be rather remarkable if early trauma and attachment disruptions did not influence the present-day struggles of this group. A lack of connection has been highlighted in the literature between these insights and clinical applications (Hett et al., 2022): a trauma- and attachment-informed conceptualisation of bipolar disorder is lacking. Addressing this has the potential to greatly deepen the understanding of this condition, as well as facilitating the clinical application of therapeutic techniques which may ameliorate some of the emotional and interpersonal struggles faced by clients, which otherwise may feed into maintaining symptomatology as well as real-world dysfunction. Recent research considering the application of Schema Therapy to this group has reported a wide range of early maladaptive schemas in participants with bipolar diagnoses, but research on modes has not yet been done (Ociskova et al., 2022). It is our proposal that the schema mode framework and the general concept of the multi-self have the potential to improve clinicians' understanding of the dynamic and changing presentations of people diagnosed with bipolar disorder, as well as providing a framework for collaborative sense-making around the impacts of early adversity, pervasive patterns of emotional and interpersonal responding, the impacts of conflicting motivations and impulses, and how negotiation between these might be approached.

Aims of the original research presented

There is a clinical rationale for exploring the applicability of a schema mode framework and Schema Therapy approach to groups of people with diagnoses of psychosis and bipolar disorder, given the prevalence of relevant issues such as attachment disturbances and emotional and interpersonal difficulties in these groups. In the original research presented in the first part of this book, we applied a qualitative methodology to addressing the following aims:

- To explore whether participants could make sense of the mode concepts and could give examples of how these states of self might have manifested in their own lives
- To analyse the content and subjectively described meaning of the experiences associated with these mode states in our groups
- To illustrate the mode activation experiences reported by the participants, with reference to descriptions in the existing literature
- To note if any patterns of association were evident between mode experiences and symptoms, which might be useful in developing theory and further research

How the research was carried out

Two separate but co-ordinated studies were carried out using the same method: one applying this to a group of participants diagnosed with psychosis, the other to a group with bipolar diagnoses. The first phase of the research was conducted by Whitehead and Engledew (Engledew, 2018; Whitehead, 2018). Semi-structured interviews were used to gather data, guided by reading the mode descriptions, and in the analysis we noted evidence of the modes but also any interesting patterns or unexpected features.

Thematic Analysis (TA; Braun & Clarke, 2006) was used because it was well matched to our research aims, allowing a flexible, transparent and systematic approach without sacrificing depth. TA was suited to our purpose, in that it lends itself to both types of analysis that we wished to carry out: the first being to assess the relevance of a specific mode framework for our participants, and the second seeking to explore in depth their subjective experiences and to generate novel ideas and theories. TA can be applied across a range of theoretical and epistemological positions: our research aimed to explore the participants' subjective experiences, but we were aware that we necessarily brought to the interviews and analysis ideas from our professional backgrounds.

Each of the two studies included seven participants, recruited mainly through Community Mental Health Teams from one borough within an inner-London NHS Trust. One of the participants in the psychosis study was recruited from an in-patient mental health ward within the same borough. The psychosis group included individuals aged 26–53 years, with five males and two females. All had been diagnosed with a non-affective psychotic disorder (six with paranoid schizophrenia, one with schizoaffective disorder). The bipolar group included individuals aged 31–58 years, with two males and five females, all with bipolar type-I diagnoses. Ethical approval for the studies had been granted by the local NHS Ethics panel, and all participants gave informed written consent to take part.

A semi-structured interview schedule was used, based on the schema mode descriptions presented by Young et al. (2003). This included standardised prompts and used written mode descriptions presented on cards, but also had scope to follow up specific responses to encourage in-depth descriptions of examples from participants' lives. Young et al.'s eight original dysfunctional schema modes were described on the prompt cards. The interview asked about participants' present-day experiences and did not seek explicitly to identify the origins of these in childhood or elsewhere. In line with our position of openness regarding the potential origins of these self-states, we have chosen in the two research chapters to simplify the dysfunctional parent and child mode names in line with other authors such as Lazarus and Rafaeli (2023): we will refer simply to punitive, demanding, vulnerable, angry and impulsive or undisciplined modes.

All interviews were audio recorded and transcribed. The first analysis was structured by the theory of the schema modes. The interview transcripts were coded into categories corresponding to each of the eight dysfunctional schema mode descriptions. This allowed us to see how many participants gave descriptions corresponding to each mode. Once the quotes corresponding to each mode were grouped together, we performed the second analysis, looking for emergent themes and structures of meaning in the participants' accounts. This involved searching for themes and sub-themes in the material, identifying similarities and relationships between these, making connections between subordinate and higher-order themes, and recursively reviewing the material to check that themes were coherent and representative of the interview data. Themes and sub-themes could then be named, considered in their context, connected with existing theory and literature, and presented in narrative form.

Structure of the book

The first half of this book will present original qualitative research exploring the relevance of the schema mode concepts for groups of individuals with diagnoses of psychosis (Chapter 2) and bipolar disorder (Chapter 3). We have sought to illustrate the subjective experiences of the study participants, linking them to each schema mode concept and to existing descriptions in the literature. Chapter 4 brings together these findings, considering how modes may contribute in different ways to our understandings of psychosis and bipolarity, drawing links with several theoretical models and considering the mode concept in depth. The second half of the book will turn toward clinical applications. Chapter 5 outlines an application of the Schema Therapy mode approach to working with people who have experienced psychosis and bipolarity, with an emphasis on assessment and formulation, followed by the selection of therapeutic techniques. In Chapter 6, Taylor and colleagues present a protocol, case examples and results of imagery-based work for psychosis-related trauma. In Chapter 7, Paulick shares a schema-informed imagery rescripting approach to working with voices in psychosis. Chapter 8 presents an in-depth illustration of Schema Therapy adapted for working with paranoia, with a focus on modes, and Chapter 9 finally illustrates Schema Therapy application for clients with bipolarity.

References

Aas, M., Henry, C., Andreassen, O. A., Bellivier, F., Melle, I., & Etain, B. (2016). The role of childhood trauma in bipolar disorders. *International Journal of Bipolar Disorders, 4*(1), 2.

Addington, J., & Addington, D. (2008). Social and cognitive functioning in psychosis. *Schizophrenia Research, 99*(1), 176–181.

Arseneault, L., Cannon, M., Fisher, H. L., Polanczyk, G., Moffitt, T. E., & Caspi, A. (2011). Childhood trauma and children's emerging psychotic symptoms: A genetically sensitive longitudinal cohort study. *American Journal of Psychiatry, 168*(1), 65–72.

Bakos, D. S., Gallo, A. E., & Wainer, R. (2015). Systematic review of the clinical effectiveness of Schema Therapy. *Contemporary Behavioral Health Care, 1*(1), 11–15.

Bamelis, L. L. M., Evers, S. M. A. A., Spinhoven, P., & Arntz, A. (2014). Results of a multicenter randomized controlled trial of the clinical effectiveness of Schema Therapy for personality disorders. *American Journal of Psychiatry, 171*(3), 305–322.

Bonoldi, I., Simeone, E., Rocchetti, M., Codjoe, L., Rossi, G., Gambi, F.,... Fusar-Poli, P. (2013). Prevalence of self-reported childhood abuse in psychosis: A meta-analysis of retrospective studies. *Psychiatry Research, 210*(1), 8–15.

Braun, V., & Clarke, V. (2006). Using thematic analysis in psychology. *Qualitative Research in Psychology, 3*(2), 77–101.

Citak, C., & Erten, E. (2021). Impact of childhood trauma and attachment on resilience in remitted patients with bipolar disorder. *Journal of Affective Disorders, 280*, 219–227.

Crowe, M., Inder, M., Swartz, H. A., Murray, G., & Porter, R. (2020). Social rhythm therapy: A potentially translatable psychosocial intervention for bipolar disorder. *Bipolar Disorders, 22*(2), 121–127.

Cutajar, M. C., Mullen, P. E., Ogloff, J. R. P., Thomas, S. D., Wells, D. L., & Spataro, J. (2010). Schizophrenia and other psychotic disorders in a cohort of sexually abused children. *Archives of General Psychiatry, 67*(11), 1114–1119.

Dualibe, A. L., & Osório, F. L. (2017). Bipolar disorder and early emotional trauma: A critical literature review on indicators of prevalence rates and clinical outcomes. *Harvard Review of Psychiatry, 25*(5), 198.

Engledew, Z. (2018). *An exploration of schema modes in bipolar disorder.* University of East London.

Freeman, D., Emsley, R., Diamond, R., Collett, N., Bold, E., Chadwick, E.,... Twivy, E. (2021). Comparison of a theoretically driven cognitive therapy (the Feeling Safe Programme) with befriending for the treatment of persistent persecutory delusions: A parallel, single-blind, randomised controlled trial. *The Lancet Psychiatry, 8*(8), 696–707.

Giesen-Bloo, J., van Dyck, R., Spinhoven, P., van Tilburg, W., Dirksen, C., van Asselt, T.,... Arntz, A. (2006). Outpatient psychotherapy for borderline personality disorder: Randomized trial of schema-focused therapy vs transference-focused psychotherapy. *Archives of General Psychiatry, 63*(6), 649–658.

Gould, R. A., Mueser, K. T., Bolton, E., Mays, V., & Goff, D. (2004). Cognitive therapy for psychosis in schizophrenia: An effect size analysis. *Focus, 48*(1), 335–101.

Gumley, A. I., Taylor, H. E. F., Schwannauer, M., & MacBeth, A. (2014). A systematic review of attachment and psychosis: Measurement, construct validity and outcomes. *Acta Psychiatrica Scandinavica, 129*(4), 257–274.

Hardy, A. (2017). Pathways from trauma to psychotic experiences: A theoretically informed model of posttraumatic stress in psychosis. *Frontiers in Psychology, 8*, 697.

Hardy, A., Emsley, R., Freeman, D., Bebbington, P., Garety, P. A., Kuipers, E. E.,... Fowler, D. (2016). Psychological mechanisms mediating effects between trauma and psychotic symptoms: The role of affect regulation, intrusive trauma memory, beliefs, and depression. *Schizophrenia Bulletin, 42*(suppl_1), S34–S43.

Harnic, D., Pompili, M., Innamorati, M., Erbuto, D., Lamis, D. A., Bria, P.,… Janiri, L. (2014). Affective temperament and attachment in adulthood in patients with bipolar disorder and cyclothymia. *Comprehensive Psychiatry*, *55*(4), 999–1006.

Heriot-Maitland, C., McCarthy-Jones, S., Longden, E., & Gilbert, P. (2019). Compassion focused approaches to working with distressing voices. *Frontiers in Psychology*, *10*, e130.

Hett, D., Etain, B., & Marwaha, S. (2022). Childhood trauma in bipolar disorder: New targets for future interventions. *BJPsych Open*, *8*(4), e130.

Humphrey, C., Berry, K., Degnan, A., & Bucci, S. (2022). Childhood interpersonal trauma and paranoia in psychosis: The role of disorganised attachment and negative schema. *Schizophrenia Research*, *241*, 142–148.

Kefeli, M. C., Turow, R. G., Yıldırım, A., & Boysan, M. (2018). Childhood maltreatment is associated with attachment insecurities, dissociation and alexithymia in bipolar disorder. *Psychiatry Research*, *260*, 391–399.

Körük, S., & Özabacı, N. (2018). Effectiveness of Schema Therapy on the treatment of depressive disorders: A meta-analysis. *Current Approaches in Psychiatry/Psikiyatride Guncel Yaklasimlar*, *10*(4), 460–470.

Lam, D. (1999). *Cognitive therapy for bipolar disorder: A therapist's guide to concepts, methods and practice*. Wiley.

Lam, D., Jones, S. H., & Hayward, P. (2010). *Cognitive therapy for bipolar disorder: A therapist's guide to concepts, methods and practice*. John Wiley & Sons.

Lazarus, G., & Rafaeli, E. (2023). Modes: Cohesive personality states and their interrelationships as organizing concepts in psychopathology. *Journal of Psychopathology and Clinical Science*, *132*(3), 238–248.

Lincoln, T. M., Rief, W., Westermann, S., Ziegler, M., Kesting, M.-L., Heibach, E., & Mehl, S. (2014). Who stays, who benefits? Predicting dropout and change in cognitive behaviour therapy for psychosis. *Psychiatry Research*, *216*(2), 198–205.

Livingstone, K., Harper, S., & Gillanders, D. (2009). An exploration of emotion regulation in psychosis. *Clinical Psychology & Psychotherapy*, *16*(5), 418–430.

Mansell, W., Morrison, A. P., Reid, G., Lowens, I., & Tai, S. (2007). The interpretation of, and responses to, changes in internal states: An integrative cognitive model of mood swings and bipolar disorders. *Behavioural and Cognitive Psychotherapy*, *35*(5), 515–539.

McKay, M. T., Cannon, M., Chambers, D., Conroy, R. M., Coughlan, H., Dodd, P.,… Clarke, M. C. (2021). Childhood trauma and adult mental disorder: A systematic review and meta-analysis of longitudinal cohort studies. *Acta Psychiatrica Scandinavica*, *143*(3), 189–205.

Morriss, R. K., van der Gucht, E., Lancaster, G., & Bentall, R. P. (2009). Adult attachment in bipolar 1 disorder. *Psychology and Psychotherapy: Theory, Research and Practice*, *82*(3), 267–277.

National Collaborating Centre for Mental Health (UK). (2014). *Psychosis and schizophrenia in adults: Treatment and management: Updated edition 2014*. National Institute for Health and Care Excellence (UK).

Ociskova, M., Prasko, J., Kantor, K., Hodny, F., Kasyanik, P., Holubova, M.,… Minarikova Belohradova, K. (2022). Schema Therapy for patients with bipolar disorder: Theoretical framework and application. *Neuropsychiatric Disease and Treatment*, *18*, 29–46.

Peeters, N., van Passel, B., & Krans, J. (2022). The effectiveness of schema Therapy for patients with anxiety disorders, OCD, or PTSD: A systematic review and research agenda. *British Journal of Clinical Psychology*, *61*(3), 579–597.

Peters, E., Hardy, A., Dudley, R., Varese, F., Greenwood, K., Steel, C.,... Morrison, A. (2022). Multisite randomised controlled trial of trauma-focused cognitive behaviour therapy for psychosis to reduce post-traumatic stress symptoms in people with co-morbid post-traumatic stress disorder and psychosis, compared to treatment as usual: Study protocol for the STAR (Study of Trauma And Recovery) trial. *Trials*, *23*(1), 429.

Renner, F., Arntz, A., Peeters, F. P. M. L., Lobbestael, J., & Huibers, M. J. H. (2016). Schema Therapy for chronic depression: Results of a multiple single case series. *Journal of Behavior Therapy and Experimental Psychiatry*, *51*, 66–73.

Stain, H. J., Brønnick, K., Hegelstad, W. T. V., Joa, I., Johannessen, J. O., Langeveld,... Larsen, T. K. (2014). Impact of interpersonal trauma on the social functioning of adults with first-episode psychosis. *Schizophrenia Bulletin*, *40*(6), 1491–1498.

Stanton, K. J., Denietolis, B., Goodwin, B. J., & Dvir, Y. (2020). Childhood trauma and psychosis: An updated review. *Child and Adolescent Psychiatric Clinics*, *29*(1), 115–129.

Steardo, L., Luciano, M., Sampogna, G., Zinno, F., Saviano, P., Staltari, F.,... Fiorillo, A. (2020). Efficacy of the interpersonal and social rhythm therapy (IPSRT) in patients with bipolar disorder: Results from a real-world, controlled trial. *Annals of General Psychiatry*, *19*(1), 15.

Taylor, C. D. J., & Harper, S. F. (2017). Early maladaptive schema, social functioning and distress in psychosis: A preliminary investigation. *Clinical Psychologist*, *21*(2), 135–142.

Van Winkel, R., Van Nierop, M., Myin-Germeys, I., & Van Os, J. (2013). Childhood trauma as a cause of psychosis: Linking genes, psychology, and biology. *The Canadian Journal of Psychiatry*, *58*(1), 44–51.

Varese, F., Smeets, F., Drukker, M., Lieverse, R., Lataster, T., Viechtbauer, W.,... Bentall, R. P. (2012). Childhood adversities increase the risk of psychosis: A meta-analysis of patient-control, prospective- and cross-sectional cohort studies. *Schizophrenia Bulletin*, *38*(4), 661–671.

Whitehead, H. (2018). *An exploration of schema modes in psychosis*. University of East London.

Wrobel, A. L., Russell, S. E., Jayasinghe, A., Lotfaliany, M., Turner, A., Dean, O. M.,... McInnis, M. G. (2022). Attachment insecurity partially mediates the relationship between childhood trauma and depression severity in bipolar disorder. *Acta Psychiatrica Scandinavica*, *145*(6), 591–603.

Wykes, T., Steel, C., Everitt, B., & Tarrier, N. (2008). Cognitive behavior therapy for schizophrenia: Effect sizes, clinical models, and methodological rigor. *Schizophrenia Bulletin*, *34*(3), 523–537.

Young, J. E., Klosko, J. S., & Weishaar, M. E. (2003). *Schema Therapy: A practitioner's guide*. Guilford Press.

Chapter 2

Exploring modes in psychosis

We present here findings regarding the mode experiences of our group with psychotic diagnoses, illustrating their subjective descriptions and highlighting patterns. The modes of punitiveness, vulnerability and extreme anger loomed large in the accounts of our participants, and all three of these were linked with aspects of psychosis. Simplified names are used here for these modes, whose sources are usually traced to childhood experiences, although diverse causes are possible. Given the proposed origins of modes, this picture suggests potential histories of trauma and unmet needs in early life, which indeed some of our participants described spontaneously. It is known that people experiencing psychosis very often carry significant histories of trauma, particularly of an interpersonal nature. Our participants' accounts may illustrate some connections between earlier adversities, ongoing patterns of responding and relating, and aspects of psychotic experiences. Two dysfunctional coping mode types were coded in most participants' accounts: compliant surrender and detached protector. Individuals connected activation of these coping modes with overwhelming emotion linked to other modes and symptoms, but more frequently described using these to cope with repeated and distressing experiences in the mental healthcare system and in a stigmatising society. Table 2.1 summarises the modes reflected in participants' responses, alongside the themes identified in their accounts.

Punitive mode

Perhaps the most striking finding in the participants' responses to the mode descriptions was the dominance of the punitive mode. This mode was described by Young et al. (2003) as attacking, criticising, and restricting the individual, often although not always reflecting an internalisation of a parental figure who had acted in this way. Arntz and Jacob (2012) further elaborated on the clinical description of the mode, highlighting its tone as being harsh and unforgiving, with signs and symptoms typically including 'self-loathing, self-criticism, self-denial, self-injury, suicidal fantasies and self-destructive behaviour' (Arntz & Jacob, 2012). These modes have been conceptualised as generally arising as a result of the punitive actions of a parent or other caregiver in early years, but

DOI: 10.4324/9781003350583-2

Table 2.1 Modes and themes in the group with psychosis

Mode	Themes
Punitive	Self-attack
	Mistakes as catastrophic
	Psychosis exacerbates sense of self as bad
Vulnerable	Separate from others
	The influence of voices and paranoia on feeling separate
Angry	Mistreatment by others
	Controllability
	Voices, paranoia and stigma as fuel
Compliant surrender	Protection of self and others
	Voices and paranoia influence compliance
Detached protector	Active avoidance of painful emotions
	Detachment from reality
	Changeable over time

can also relate more closely to experiences of bullying, victimisation and harassment by other authority figures or peers, or emerge from the impacts of other types of adverse environments. Clinically, we might expect to see a dominance of painful emotions including shame felt by individuals with this type of mode activation, which can lead to behavioural withdrawal and corresponding reductions in assertive social behaviours.

Six out of seven participants gave descriptions corresponding to activation of a punitive mode, and our analysis identified three themes in their accounts: 'Self-attack,' 'Mistakes as catastrophic' and 'Psychosis exacerbates sense of self as bad.' By contrast, responses regarding a demanding mode were so scarce as to generate insufficient data for analysis.

Self-attack

Some participants described very explicit self-hatred and violent self-attack, as conveyed by Tom's account of stabbing knives through pictures of himself, such was his feeling of self-hatred:

Tom: I used to stick knives through photos of myself because I didn't... I hated myself.

Other participants, such as Ali and Jane, described instead self-deprivation and guilt:

Jane: I don't harm myself, but I do feel guilty when I do things I enjoy.

Ali described active self-deprivation to the point of self-sabotage as he spoke about feeling undeserving of money and getting rid of it when finding it in his possession:

Ali: You find a way to go and waste it.
Ali: It's like a, guilt factor and, and that you don't deserve it.

The accounts shared a common thread of pervasive self-criticism in relation to one's behaviour towards others, even in the absence of corresponding evidence. Kadir explicitly reflected on this sense of guilt and self-blame without apparent rationale.

Kadir: I keep blaming myself but is it my fault, I don't know.
Kadir: I feel I deserve to be punished.

The sense of self criticism as being aversive was conveyed by Ali's expression of his desire for change – itself framed in a self-critical form:

Ali: I want to get over it, I don't want to be self-critical, I don't want to curse myself.

These participants' descriptions are concordant with Arntz and Jacob's (2012) description of a subtype of punitive mode with a focus on interpersonal behaviour and a sense of not having done enough for others. The authors traced one possible origin of such modes to childhoods where a primary caregiver was either ill in some way or isolated and unsupported, such that the child was parentified and felt responsible for the caregiver's wellbeing, scrutinising their own behaviour and berating themselves for imperfections as a result. This may not be the most typical version of the punitive mode, but one of a range of manifestations that could be relevant for our group. Kadir gave an example conveying this sense of generalised interpersonal guilt:

Kadir: I feel I could have done at least more for... my family... I feel like I could have done better really, you know.

He was not able to identify anything specific that he had neglected or omitted, any rational basis for this sense of not having done enough, but felt it powerfully nevertheless. Jane also described interpersonal guilt, reporting that this would extend even to her neighbours, arising in situations where she may be doing something quite innocuous, such as the washing up, but this would seem to be causing them disturbance. Although she knew she couldn't help it, she would still feel bad.

Jane: I'll be washing up and thinking, which I can't help, and then they're shouting and I'm thinking I'm causing them distress and I really can't stop it.

Mistakes as catastrophic

The second subtheme relating to the punitive mode concerned a sense of extreme judgement around making mistakes. Participants reported catastrophic interpretations, accompanied by intense and long lasting emotions, following on from even the most minor errors. Kadir gave multiple descriptions of these sorts of extreme judgements and negative emotions:

Kadir: If I make a mistake in anything I do, like even if I drop a cup or something when I'm washing up or something, and I break a cup of anything, you know it's like, I think the world is going to come to an end.

Kadir: Anything I cook, if I don't think it's come out nice, how I want it, then I really really feel down. It gets to me a lot.

The disabling functional impact of these judgements and feelings was highlighted by participants. Kadir in the above quote emphasised how the experience gets him down, while Mukhtar said that his anger at making a mistake 'ruins the whole day.' Jane said she worried so much about making a mistake that she avoided even everyday tasks, such as using herbs in cooking.

Psychosis exacerbates sense of self as bad

The third subtheme linked the experiences of voice hearing and paranoia with negativity towards the self, in several direct and indirect ways: the immediate impacts of the content of the symptoms, the disruption to preferred activities and tasks, and later self-scrutiny around behaviour while psychotic. Tom explicitly reflected on a struggle to distinguish his own self-criticism from a sense of being watched and scrutinised by others:

Tom: I'm so critical of myself. A lot of the time in my own head it's like well, am I just being so critical of myself or am I being watched, and it's a horrible feeling.

Tom linked his struggles with psychosis back to 'huge problems' with his father, who had been punitive, abusive and neglectful towards Tom throughout his early life. Most of Tom's experiences of psychosis were described as being organised around a sense of being harassed, berated and viciously attacked by his father, who also often seemed to have turned others, including hospital staff, against Tom, and organised some form of conspiracy to make him 'crack,' to perpetuate his incarceration in the mental health system and even to lead to his death.

Tom: I had one bout of psychosis where I thought my dad was using his computer to put thoughts into my head. And that started off with... again that I was useless, that I was no good... And it went from like just saying I was useless to, it got worse to the point that why I had to die, what time I had to die, it got really, really horrendous.

Tom made the links between his own traumatic childhood experiences of his father and the content of his later psychotic experiences very explicit, pointing the interviewer directly towards his sense of the connection, and reflecting openly on an episodic ambiguity between his own negative thoughts about himself and perceived scrutiny or harassment from other people. Jane, on the other hand, narrated a clearer felt distinction between content that she perceived as being generated by herself or others (experiencing her own self-critical thoughts as distinct from sensing criticism and persecution from others), but described a persuasive interaction between the two:

Jane: I do feel like, if all this bad stuff's happening, people reading my mind, they're out to hurt me, then, maybe I deserve it... but it doesn't stop me being any more scared.

Jane's account illustrated the potential for paranoia to build upon, but also exacerbate, a sense of self as being bad and deserving of punishment. This is reminiscent of Trower and Chadwick's (1995) description of a type of 'bad me' paranoia, whereby individuals tend to consider themselves blameworthy and deserving of punishment, and correspondingly see others as justifiably targeting them for those reasons. One way to understand variations and fluctuations in the presence and degrees of 'bad me' paranoia experienced by affected individuals could be in terms of the activation at certain times of a punitive mode, blaming and attacking the self.

Jane further described experiencing abusive intrusive thoughts towards others that were seemingly triggered by the psychotic experience of thought broadcast – sensing that others could hear what she was thinking, leading to intrusive derogatory thoughts that were not congruent with her own sense of her personal views:

Jane: And all of a sudden I think they're listening and I think the worst possible things you could want people to hear, like personal things or, just like, just, racist things. And that, which, I know I'm not racist, but.

Jane emphasised that she would not have been thinking insulting things about people prior to the onset of thought broadcast, but as soon as she felt her thoughts to be audible, the unacceptable ones would occur. Her concern was not that these overheard thoughts might hurt others, but that she would be seen as a bad person and attract harm. These experiences were described as very debilitating, leading Jane to escape and avoid valued activities, such as playing football, and spiralling to preoccupy most of her time at home, 'consuming everything.' We might expect that withdrawal from social activities and spending more time alone could unintentionally make things worse, by reducing access to rewarding external input or a sense of achievement, and allowing more time for rumination and worry. Jane did not spontaneously trace her worries about other people back to her own inner concerns or early history, but she nevertheless felt guilty and was persuaded by the content of the psychotic experiences into a feeling that she deserved bad things to happen to her.

Participants also drew an indirect connection between psychosis and punitive mode activation, via the process of scrutinising their own past behaviour in states of psychosis, and applying criticism to this, with accompanying feelings of guilt and shame. Tom gave an example relating to doubting his mum's identity when he was psychotic:

Tom: I was like my mum isn't really my mum and it's really hard, but now I've come out of it I do have a massive, so I just feel guilty because it's like, she's just been amazing, she's come down so much and that.

Tom also recounted having bouts of very violent intrusive thoughts, such as stabbing his mum or pushing another family member down the stairs, and 'it would always be people who were really good to me.' Tom emphasised that he would never have acted on these ego-dystonic thoughts, and indeed had never hurt anyone, but that the experience of those thoughts would trigger fraught internal dialogue and was 'absolutely horrible.'

Overall, our participants' accounts were striking in the extent to which punitive mode congruent experiences were reported, with all but one participant giving vivid descriptions of self-attack, self-deprivation, exaggerated guilt about behaviour towards others, or a sense of being a bad person. All six participants who reported experiencing this mode also linked its activation to aspects of psychosis. Direct links were drawn between the content of psychotic experiences, such as derogatory or attacking voices, and punitive mode activation, but indirect connections were also traced, including via guilt relating to one's behaviour in states of psychosis.

Vulnerable mode

Vulnerable modes are characterised by feeling intense unhappy or anxious affect, which can include sadness, desperation, isolation, helplessness, or a sense of being abandoned and unloved. Young et al. (2003) proposed that vulnerable modes can emerge from unmet needs in childhood, developing into a pervasive pattern and subsequently arising in the absence of any directly corresponding proportional circumstances. Vulnerable modes might present with any of a range of emotional tones, such as feeling lonely, abandoned, abused, humiliated, inferior or dependent, and these different manifestations might be linked with different forms of childhood adversity and caregiver behaviours (Arntz & Jacob, 2012). Clinically, we would expect that an individual with vulnerable mode activation might appear frightened, sad, helpless or overwhelmed, seeming to lack autonomy and resilience, and seeking help or reassurance, or perhaps conveying shame and a sense of inferiority and alienation, impacting social relations and adaptive behaviour.

All but one of our participants identified with vulnerable mode activation of one sort or another, and generally this was described as having been a longstanding pattern. Sheila expressed simply: 'I feel like sad or anxious for no reason sometimes,' while Kadir similarly reflected: 'I get frightened a lot... I don't know why.' Several participants spontaneously provided illustrative details of earlier childhood and family experiences that contextualised the emergence of these emotional states. Questions about childhood adversity were not explicitly asked in the interview; however, the information volunteered by participants in their accounts illustrated links that they saw between their past and present struggles. Two linked themes emerged from our analysis of the participants' accounts: 'Separate from others' and 'The influence of voices and paranoia on feeling separate.'

Separate from others

Participants such as Mukhtar and Kadir tended to describe their experiences of isolation and separateness from others as having been longstanding and recurring throughout their lives.

Mukhtar: I've always had a picture of being like um alone.
Kadir: Like my family, you know, like, as I say I've always been sort of like, drifted away from them all the time, I've never been sort of like that really close bond.

Kadir further reported that the sense of vulnerability would build to a point where he felt desperately afraid of a sudden violent attack that might come even in the middle of the night.

Kadir: I get scared, I get like, any minute now someone's gonna break through the door and like you know with a big chopper or something and kill me in the middle of the night when I'm sleeping or something.

Betrayal of trust, rejection and abandonment by friends and family were commonly linked in the participants' accounts with pervasive ongoing feelings of isolation and vulnerability, as in this striking image conveyed by Kadir:

Kadir: I feel I've been… pushed on this roadside and left for dead while you know, they've all gone off you know, gallivanting, off… I feel bad, I feel horrible.

As well as adverse experiences in close relationships, wider social factors including stigma and racism were also highlighted as linked to this mode, for example by Mukhtar:

Mukhtar: You can also say nobody loves you, you feel completely alone, weak and helpless. A lot of this has to do with stigma. Do you know?

Mukhtar: It was racism, also bullying I used to go through at school. I mean the school I went to. I don't know, that's just life you know, you just have to live with it and cope. But I mean yeah, that was the school, and like the people.

The influence of voices and paranoia on feeling separate

The influence of psychotic experiences such as voice hearing and paranoia on the sense of feeling separate from others was also discussed by several participants, and they drew these connections in three different ways. The content of voices and visions was described as directly fuelling a sense of vulnerability. In addition to this, psychotic symptoms were seen as disrupting individuals' connections with a shared social reality, which was said to feed into isolation and helplessness. Third, vulnerability was said to be exacerbated by the damaging impact of social stigma related to psychosis and the associated sense of abandonment by others. Kadir recounted vividly the disturbing impact of the violent content of voices and visions that he experienced:

Kadir: Um, sort of like: 'I want to kill you, I want to kill you and your missus tonight' and stuff like that. I sort of like hallucinate, about you know people at the door with choppers or something you know… Like knives, yeah whatever, swords, knives, machetes. And I can picture it, cause like in my head, I'm looking at it sort of thing and it's real but it ain't real. It's horrible, it's disturbing.

As well as such extreme content of hallucinations directly triggering feelings of vulnerability, participants also referred to a more generalised impact of engagement with 'unshared reality' (Clarke, 2021) on a sense of being alone and disconnected from the social world.

Mukhtar: I think it's because you're hearing the voices. Because when you hear the voices, even when you're hearing the voices it's what's causing this, that's what causes the alone. I think if I wasn't having the voices I wouldn't yeah, it's all triggered by the voices.

Mukhtar explained that his sense of separation from friends and family was linked with his experiences of voice hearing and his beliefs in supernatural powers. Highlighting the importance of other people's reactions, he recounted how stigmatised and abandoned he had felt when friends took him to undergo an exorcism, believing him to be 'possessed by a demon people.' He explained that he had started hearing voices after being beaten up, and had explained all of this to some close friends. The group shared a cultural belief in demonic possession, which was widespread in their community, and they had interpreted Mukhtar's voice hearing as an indicator of that affliction, with exorcism being the corresponding intervention. Mukhtar himself did not share this view, however: 'my beliefs are different.' He summarised, 'it really caused a like a, big like space between like, yeah, distance between them and me... I still have friends but um my closest friends um, they really, like, it turned really ugly with them.' This seems a stark illustration of how devastating and isolating the impact can be of others' responses to unshared beliefs. Ali conveyed a similar sense of disconnection from others in his relationship with psychosis with the following:

Ali: So-called friends who's not really friends. And so-called family who's not really family. But only friend I have is me myself and my illness.

This quote conveys a sense of almost being resigned to an unshared reality, in response to feeling separate from other people. Participants spoke repeatedly of being treated differently compared to siblings and others in the community, feeling misunderstood and sometimes completely ostracised from society since becoming unwell. Kadir summed up his experience of social stigma and alienation thus:

Kadir: It's like we've got the plague or something, and they're going to catch a disease off us or something.

Thus a pervasive sense of isolation and vulnerability seemed often to have stemmed from early years, preceding the onset of psychosis, but then been devastatingly exacerbated not only by the experience of psychosis itself but by the rejecting responses of others to the individuals affected.

Angry mode

Angry modes are characterised by feelings of intense frustration, anger, rage or fury, which are typically experienced as seeming out of control and out of proportion to the present-day triggering event. Young et al. (2003) conceptualised this type of mode as resulting from unmet needs in childhood, leading into pervasive patterns of emotional reactions that can be understood as being meaningfully associated with the frustrated attempts to get those needs met, but which become no longer appropriate in the circumstances of the individual's adult life. Arntz and Jacob (2012) described versions of this mode on a spectrum from extreme rage through to obstinate resistance. An enraged type of angry mode may produce explosions of aggression, shouting, screaming, hurting people or damaging objects. An obstinate version of the mode, in contrast, may present as passively resisting requests rather than expressing anger openly, but may come across to others as stubborn or uncooperative.

Our interview schedules did not contain any explicit questions about adverse childhood experiences, although some individuals did volunteer such information spontaneously. We thus did not address directly the question of whether participants' anger could be seen as arising from unmet core needs in childhood. Indeed, their accounts conveyed to us a clear sense that the participants were navigating a range of present-day circumstances at which experiencing a degree of anger would seem very reasonable, at least from some perspectives. We made the decision to include in the analysis relating to this mode concept all data relating to anger, leading to the caveat that some of the experiences described may be seen as possibly proportionate angry responses to present-day frustrations and violations. Six of our seven participants reported experiences related to the angry mode, with three themes identified in the accounts: 'Mistreatment by others,' 'Controllability,' and 'Voices, paranoia and stigma as fuel.'

Mistreatment by others

Five participants spoke of specific experiences of mistreatment by others: some historical and others more recent. Mukhtar and Kadir both described feeling angry as a result of being misunderstood by family members. Kadir explained regarding his sister: 'It makes me feel angry, when she says, "stop feeling sorry for [yourself]," you know, she talks about, it winds me up.' Sheila similarly spoke about a friend who she often gets angry with: 'there's stuff that she's said to me and done… So I'm always angry at her.' Nasir made a point of differentiating his anger at mistreatment by others from a different type of anger that might be related to paranoia:

Nasir: It's not always tied up with paranoia. There is um… I guess there is sort of like anger at the situation, being mistreated.

Tom gave a vivid account of outbursts of anger and rage being out of control, tracing these specifically back to childhood and connecting them with difficulties that he was going through at the time:

Tom: Well, when I was younger, like what I was saying before, I was so destructive and, literally this is when I was 8, 9, 10, I would literally, I remember I smashed doors, the glasses in there, plants, rip up books,

I was a real... because I didn't know how to deal with... what I was going through.

Mukhtar interestingly highlighted an additional pathway to anger via feeling alone and abandoned. When asked a clarifying question about whether he felt the vulnerable mode and the angry mode concurrently or whether one replaced another, he emphasised the latter emphatically:

Mukhtar: Um no, it's, that's what happens. Once you feel angry and the rage and everything, um you don't, none of that matters, yeah, a lot of those things, you don't care about them.

Mukhtar's report seemed to indicate that for him, a transition from feeling alone and isolated into anger and rage brought at least some relief from the more vulnerable and abandoned feelings.

Controllability

Participants reported varying degrees of controllability around anger and violent thoughts or impulses. Kadir gave several examples of situations where anger and aggressive impulses may arise and become quite noticeable, but in each case emphasised that he would never act on these.

Kadir: Someone's done a bad thing to me. Then obviously I'll get upset and I'll get violent thoughts about what I'd like to do [laughs]. I never take out, take out the er. You know, do it in proper, you know.

Jane, similarly, recounted several examples where she has felt really intensely angry, to the extent that 'I could have smashed my flat up,' but each time has been able to stop short of doing any physical damage to people or objects, although 'I shout and that when I'm arguing.' Mukhtar, on the other hand, emphasised that he had been unable to control anger at times, and that this had caused serious problems, leading even to hospitalisation.

Mukhtar: I've gone through a lot of anger and rage, and, I won't be able to control myself. Um. Furious and shout. This causes serious problems. So I mean I'm talking about, I've had relapses where I've had to go back to the hospital and had to go back on the medication.

The theme of controllability related to a fear of the consequences of acting on anger, and also to the specific topic of medication use. Tom reported that one prescribed neuroleptic had made him 'really aggressive,' whereas Nasir and Mukhtar both spoke of the opposite, with medication making them feel calmer. Mukhtar's reported struggle to control anger was linked with being off medication: 'So I was off the medication and it was these, the anger and rage and trying to control myself.' Later in the interview, he expressed: 'because I'm on the medicine... it's calmed me down.' Nasir spoke of sometimes even taking more medication than prescribed, in order to feel calmer: 'Sometimes I have to take extra doses of sulpiride. If it's sort of like very severe sort of thing.'

Three participants explicitly reported efforts to avoid anger activation, due to fears of the consequences of this. Nasir gave an account of how he had stopped exercising due to a fear that he might harm others. This had followed an experience where he had been exercising at home and seemed to hear comments made about him by passersby outside.

Nasir: I'd get into a rage. I want to punch stuff, I punched the wall. I punched the doors, I think I put a few holes in a few doors. I literally stopped exercising after that because I was afraid... I was afraid I'd sort of catch one of these people and do them in.

Alongside fears of doing damage to others when angry, the other main feared consequence described was of escalating coercion within the mental health system, and especially of being detained and having to go back to hospital. Mukhtar and Jane both expressed this type of fear, with Jane explaining 'it's the difference between home treatment and being sectioned [laughter], innit?'

Voices, paranoia and stigma as fuel

Each of the six participants reporting angry modes connected these with elements of psychosis, drawing links in both direct and indirect ways. The experience of hearing voices was described as directly triggering anger. Both paranoia and voice content were also said to trigger memories that could activate angry rumination about past events, and anger was also traced back to the experiences of stigma that the participants had been subjected to in relation to having psychosis. Kadir gave an example of anger being triggered by the content of hallucinatory experiences:

Kadir: If I was to sort of hallucinate and see things going on that I don't like. Like you know, with Mary or something involving Mary or family and friends and stuff, then it does make me angry.

Sheila went further in narrating her relationship with voices, summing it up as 'anger and rage, I do feel it with the voices. They wind me up.' She was able to describe some of the content of the voices: 'That I'm stupid. And there's this thing that I did when I was younger, and they call me a name.' Sheila explained that she would try to keep calm in the face of the abusive content, sometimes successfully, but sometimes would become overwhelmed with anger and drawn into protracted out-loud shouting arguments:

Sheila: It's horrible, yeah. Sometimes I can keep calm and just you know, let them cuss me, but other times I just lose it and then we start fighting and I start swearing out loud, at them and stuff.

As well as a direct triggering of anger by psychotic symptoms, participants traced two indirect pathways of effect between psychosis and anger. The first of these involved mediation by memories: voices or paranoia would activate memories of previous mistreatment by others, and these memories would in turn activate anger related to past events. Mukhtar gave an example of this happening, explaining how the voices that he heard would bring up memories of being treated badly and even elaborate on these, 'but in this case there's nothing really happening around you, and then they still are creating, based on memories.'

Mukhtar: Yeah they trigger, yeah they use those old memories, so your memories from the past and stuff you've gone through.

Mukhtar was able to give several examples of the sorts of memories that might be triggered, including experiences of bullying and harassment from his school years, as well as examples of behaving oddly, for example what he called 'hanging with crows' during episodes of psychosis, when he had thought that he could control the birds with his mind. He then went on to reflect that there are lots of potential memories to choose from: 'I mean I can think of so many memories and they can come up,' but among these, the voices would seem to pick out the worst, most appalling ones to activate and emphasise.

Mukhtar: Yeah they bring up… if I wanted to I could create, have my own memories, but if you leave it to the voices you know the memories they create, it's really appalling and it kind of relates to you. I mean that's basically what you can say about them. Their memories are really poor and appalling memories.

Nasir also identified difficult memories as contributing to the relationship between anger and paranoia, and emphasised that when such memories lead into mode activation, anger and paranoia can become reciprocally intensifying, in a vicious cycle.

Nasir: Because the paranoia will feed the anger and the anger will feed the paranoia.

The second indirect pathway suggested between psychosis and anger was mediated by social stigma. Stigma around mental health and psychosis was explicitly brought up by two participants as a contributing factor to anger activation. Mukhtar referred to societal misunderstandings of psychosis using the phrase

'People recognise me as a psychopath.' He linked the resulting experience of anger to 'mainly what I've become, meaning what has happened to me, like my illness, I've ended up with an illness.'

Ali later spoke further about the sense of his community as well as wider society stigmatising people who have struggled with their mental health, likening the impact of this to being physically pounced on and strangled:

Ali: Very rarely this society understand the mental health, the effects. Instead of helping them, the society, the community I'm from, they want to pounce on him and strangelise and… not physically but like…

Overall, the familiarity with extreme states of anger in the group was striking, with corresponding fears voiced about the consequences of these, and a range of control strategies employed. The participants identified certain present-day triggers of anger, but also spontaneously linked its manifestations with memories from the past and early adversities. As with punitive and vulnerable modes, six out of seven of our participants reported angry mode experiences. Responses relating to demanding and impulsive or undisciplined modes were so minimal as not to constitute sufficient data for analysis. Data analysed for each of the three dominant modes yielded themes, and among these for each was the relationship between psychotic experiences and the activation of the mode. Some participants explicitly described such relationships as reciprocal in both directions, and some also discussed mediating pathways of the relationship, such as via memories of past traumatic events or experiences of social stigma related to mental health.

Coping modes: compliant surrender

In the subsequent portion of this chapter, we will turn towards coping modes. Young et al. (2003) described maladaptive coping modes as also arising typically in childhood in order to navigate difficult or overwhelming situations; their function was proposed as being either to avoid further harm or to escape difficult emotions. These modes tend to have functioned, at times usefully, as a means to survive in harmful environments and/or to cope with the activation of other modes. The difficulties tend to arise, however, in the longer term, as the over-reliance on certain forms of coping takes a cumulative toll on the individual, on others, on their relationships and their ability to grow and develop adaptively as circumstances change. Two types of dysfunctional coping modes elicited significant accounts from our participants: the compliant surrender mode and the detached protector mode. Over-compensator mode data generated was insufficient for thematic analysis.

The compliant surrender mode has been described as passive, submissive and dependent (Young et al., 2003). Individuals in this mode may appear subservient, self-deprecating or reassurance-seeking: subjugating themselves to avoid conflict at all costs, in some cases even accepting abuse, or simply not taking steps to get their own ordinary needs met. Five of our participants recounted experiences that were categorised under the compliant surrender mode. The data yielded two themes: 'Protection of self and others' and 'Voices and paranoia influence compliance.'

Protection of self and others

This theme was traced in all five participants' accounts: they spoke of seeking to avoid in general negative consequences for themselves, as well as for others, with such consequences including emotional upset. Tom summarised what for him seemed to have been a pervasive longstanding pattern in relation to others:

Tom: So, yeah, with regards to conflict I do not like it at all so, um, I do try and avoid that as much as possible, because I just, I don't like it at all kind of thing.

Tom explicitly linked his patterns of compliance and surrendering to early childhood experiences, especially in relation to his father's blaming and abusive behaviour.

Tom: Yeah, I mean as I say that one again is just wanting to make sure that everyone else around me is happy, and I guess that again that links back to, like with my dad saying that I'd ruined everything, I think that might be why I want to try and please everyone and make sure um… no one's treating me badly.

Tom used a number of examples from earlier in his life, as well as more recent times, to illustrate his sense of always putting others' needs and preferences first, as well as submitting to unfair treatment rather than raising an issue. The following description related to a situation with his brother, in which the brother had made consecutive conflicting demands of Tom, criticising him first for seemingly helping his nephew too much and the next minute for not helping him enough.

Tom: Like the one before, I try to help people, so yeah I just try and go along with it, rather than say, actually hang on, this isn't fair,' I just took it kind of thing.

Nasir described a similar pattern of conflict avoidance in his own behaviour, and linked this explicitly to fears about consequences both for himself and for others.

Nasir: I do tend to avoid conflict with all people. I don't know, maybe it's fear, because I'm afraid?

Nasir: It could be a combination of fear and what I might do. A fear of what I might do to them or a fear of self, fear that I might get harmed.

In contrast to Tom's clear indication of conflict avoidance as a longstanding interpersonal strategy, Mukhtar emphasised that submissive compliance had become necessary specifically since his experiences of psychosis.

Mukhtar: So I avoid conflicts now a lot. Yeah, that's probably one of the things you can say. Yeah I don't get into a fight. Before I could get into fights, yeah but I couldn't I can't do that anymore, because of the voices.

Voices and paranoia influence compliance

Three participants linked the compliant surrender mode to their experiences of psychosis, and once more, both direct and indirect links were drawn between elements of psychosis and mode activation. Mukhtar in the quote above explicitly labelled voice hearing as causing him to avoid potentially aggressive conflict. Jane's earlier quoted comment 'it's the difference between home treatment and being sectioned [laughter], innit?' highlights concerns around the mental health system's responses and the potential for coercive treatment as prominent motivational factors for deciding to surrender. Mukhtar spontaneously raised the topic of medication compliance when asked about experiences in line with this mode, emphasising that he would take the tablets against his own preference, to please his family:

Mukhtar: Mainly, you know to, also to avoid conflict and stuff, yeah. Like you can say for taking the medication. Like I take the medication, so I don't want to take the medication… To avoid conflict.

There is a clear sense in these accounts of individuals resorting to a compliant surrender mode in the face of the seemingly overwhelming power of others' positions around the management of their mental health. Indeed, most of our participants had personally had the experience of being compelled with formal coercion under the powers of the Mental Health Act, having their freedoms restricted and sometimes chemical restraints administered against their will in order to subdue them and reduce the potential for risky behaviour in times of psychosis. The reality of such events may serve to remind us of the protective and adaptive functions of a compliant surrender mode when an individual is in fact faced with overwhelming power attached to others with whom one may come into conflict. As with any protective strategy, a behaviour essential to survival in adversity can become dysfunctional when relied upon excessively in other circumstances. Even outside of formal settings of mental healthcare or overwhelming power dynamics, participants conveyed a sense of feeling socially inferior and not entitled to assert their needs and preferences. Mukhtar referred to the fact that he was not the one paying for the household bills to explain his submissive approach to the family's television viewing:

Mukhtar: Yes, like TV, like they watch TV and I just go along with like what they're watching. Yeah, that's a good, that's an example you could say. So when they're watching TV, I don't say anything, I let them watch.

Interestingly, as well as elements of psychosis being linked with the expression of a compliant surrender mode, participants described other situations in which the opposite was true, and psychotic experiences served to interrupt the compliance pattern that they may have otherwise played out.

Jane: When I'm feeling paranoid I'm more likely to argue... when I'm paranoid that sort of tends to take over.

Similarly to Jane, Tom narrated episodes of psychosis as times when his usual tendencies towards compliance and serving others' needs would make way to an entirely different way of being, in which he would be more likely to resist the demands of others. He explained that this was organised around a sense of being unwanted and everyone being against him: 'that thing when I'm paranoid it's like they don't want me there anyway, so it's like, those thought processes would go out the window...' He shared an illustrative example of a time when he was in hospital and knew that his mother had travelled a long way to visit him and would only be able to see him if he came out of his room and through the ward into the visiting area:

Tom: So I said to the nurses I'm not coming out because obviously everyone's against me. So yeah, thinking about that yeah, I'd let my mum come down, no, when I was in that state I didn't put my mum's needs first, so, um.

Our findings overall suggest that most of our participants viewed themselves as tending to avoid conflict by subjugating their own needs in favour of the preferences and desires of others, either pervasively throughout their lives, or as a more recent response to the identity impact of being someone who has experienced psychosis. The relationship of the compliant surrender mode with elements of psychosis had the potential to be complex and multifaceted, with states of psychosis having at times the capacity to break through patterns of compliance, but also the potential to subsequently increase fears around negative consequences of not complying, increasing the imperative to surrender.

Coping modes: detached protector

The second of the two coping modes evoked by our participants' accounts was the detached protector: a state of disconnecting from other people, difficult emotions and other mental content by way of psychological distancing or detachment. This can include quite conscious and deliberate attempts to shut off emotions, but also more seemingly involuntary states of numbness, blankness, dissociation and depersonalisation. Young et al. (2003) described the detached protector mode as functioning 'like a protective armor or wall, with the more vulnerable modes hiding inside' (p. 275). They suggested that this mode can sometimes be the most difficult to change, having developed early on in life to survive traumatic environments, and eventually becoming automatic to the extent that individuals do not know how to get out of it. Behavioural patterns such as social withdrawal, compulsive distraction, substance abuse, bingeing and self-injury can be linked to activation of this mode, as can psychosomatic complaints.

Five of our seven participants reported experiences categorised in line with a detached protector mode. An overarching theme of 'Disconnection' was identified in the data, with three subthemes: 'Active avoidance of painful emotions,' 'Detachment from reality' and 'Changeable over time.' All five participants reported forms of active avoidance of painful emotions, and all five spoke about changeability over time, but four of them also described states of detachment and disconnection that felt subjectively quite involuntary.

Active avoidance of painful emotions

A range of active protective strategies against painful emotions was described by participants. Ali reported having to do something physical 'to sweat myself out so it goes out of my system,' while Jane shared that she had started drinking alcohol in an attempt to calm herself down. Mukhtar described using self-harm to block out voices and deal with emotions:

Mukhtar: Yeah, really hard, you have to hit yourself, you can either slap yourself or you can hit yourself... it would straighten the emotions out.

Nasir gave a very clear description of how following two incidents where he was sexually abused by older relatives, he started actively avoiding the memories of those incidents by blocking them out and focusing extremely hard on his school work:

Nasir: After I came back from [country], I came back to this country, I was about 11 years old when I came back, I went to school and I basically just put myself into schoolwork and stuff, and focused on, and I tried to ignore reality, and just sort of blocked out, blocked out, tried to force the memory away sort of thing, by trying to keep busy. Um [...] so in that way I tried to push myself to succeed, tried to look after the family and stuff like that.

Later, Nasir also described going to work more to try to forget the past, as well as using pornography to empty his mind and to block out flashbacks of childhood abuse.

Detachment from reality

As the interview continued, Nasir described how his active efforts at detachment had started to give way to involuntary dissociations from reality:

Nasir: I remember in school, there was an occasion, a few occasions when I started having blackouts, tingly feelings down the arms and down the face, and I had a couple of blackouts... I'm not sure exactly why it was, um... I assume because of the stress.

The other three participants described detachment from reality occurring in the present day. Mukhtar explained, 'I don't feel any emotions... it's more like dead... there's nothing going on.' Ali described how feelings of being alone, weak and helpless would transform into a completely different state of being 'frozen... nothing is registering.' He summarised his sense of disconnection with the following:

Ali: So when I'm not connected then it's not really, I'm not taking part. Then even my skin is there... but it's out of reach.

Jane similarly described going through 'phases where I'm just like in a bubble or something,' subsequently highlighting a sense of passivity and helplessness that characterises this experience: 'it's like everything's going on around me. There's nothing I can do.' She explained the multifaceted nature of the experience, both buffering the severity of emotional pain but also creating a sense of being unsafe in the disconnection from her surroundings and from ongoing events.

Jane: It feels like it doesn't hurt as much. It doesn't, things don't bother me, but... I don't feel safe when it's happening, just like I might miss something.

Jane's summary seems to capture some of the simultaneous functionality and dysfunctionality of the detached protector mode: at the same time lessening pain, but potentially preventing contact with important aspects of unfolding reality.

Changeable over time

All five participants spoke of the detached protector mode changing over time, with most drawing some form of either direct or indirect connection to experiences of psychosis. Four participants expressed a view that voice hearing or paranoia would increase the likelihood or intensity of detached protector mode activation. Ali would isolate and cut himself off in response to hearing voices, Mukhtar's self-harm strategy would be used at times when voice hearing brought on overwhelming emotion, and Jane's 'bubble' experiences would also be brought on by paranoia. Tom gave a vivid account of 'shutting down' when trying to cope with feeling paranoid

Tom: I suppose in that sense, I tend to shut down, so when I'm in that mode, I wouldn't be doing any art work, I wouldn't be doing work or anything, because, the way I reacted to that one, I literally hid my head under my desk and just curled up.

Tom's account highlights the dysfunctional impact that this type of mode activation can have. Much as it is understandable that an individual in intense pain would do everything possible to close the experience off and gain distance from it, this comes at a heavy cost. Outside of these episodes of suffering and coping, Tom would be engaged in an active life, including productive and impactful work campaigning to fight stigma around mental health using photography and the creative arts. At times of maladaptive mode activation, however, he described being completely debilitated, hiding from the world, and at times becoming such a high risk to himself that he required urgent inpatient hospital treatment.

In summary of coping modes, most of our participants gave accounts corresponding to compliant surrender and detached protector modes. Overcompensator mode concepts generated such scarce data so as not to be sufficient for analysis. Participants' accounts of the compliant surrender and detached protector modes did link these to situations of coping with activation of punitive, vulnerable and angry modes, as conceptualised by Young et al. (2003). Connections were also made by all participants, however, to coping with elements of psychotic experiences, ongoing environmental adversities and with the stigmatised experience of living with a diagnosis of psychotic illness. The compliant surrender mode was perhaps linked most frequently with coercive experiences in the mental healthcare system, where giving in to the very real power of hospital regimes can sometimes be the only option. The detached protector mode concept yielded striking descriptions of how a response that started in conscious and deliberate avoidance of painful emotion could, over time, give way to an experience of detachment and dissociation that has come to feel quite involuntary. The potential for interactions between detached protector coping and the phenomenology of psychotic experiences invites further attention.

Summary and reflections

Our participants gave accounts of their experiences that corresponded to five schema mode concepts: the punitive, vulnerable and angry modes, and two coping modes: the compliant surrender and detached protector. Each of the first three modes was reported by six out of seven participants; each of the two coping modes was reported by five out of seven participants. The mode concepts of being demanding, impulsive or undisciplined and overcompensating yielded such minimal data that it was insufficient for thematic analysis.

While illustrating what the activation of these schema modes might be like for individuals experiencing psychosis, we are not claiming to be able to generalise our findings to a broader population of people with the same diagnoses. The patterns of experience that we see from in-depth interviews of a small number of individuals may not be replicated in other groups. In reflecting on our exploratory findings, we hope that interesting and informative ideas can arise from the patterns and connections discussed, which could lead to further research and theory development.

Three key observations stood out to us as meriting comment among the patterns seen in the data. The first was the striking prevalence of punitive, vulnerable and angry mode activation in our participants' accounts. This may indicate significant histories of early adversity and trauma, which indeed is often the case for people who experience psychosis. The second key observation of interest was that the punitive, vulnerable and angry modes seemed most closely connected with psychotic symptoms such as paranoia and voice hearing, whereas dysfunctional coping modes were also linked with symptoms but more often connected to experiences of navigating mental healthcare systems, environmental adversities and the social stigma associated with psychosis. Clinically, this may indicate the relevance of considering clients' social circumstances and interpersonal interactions when seeking to address coping mode activation. Finally, we considered noteworthy the detailed accounts given of how a detached protector mode can shift from what is at first, at least in some cases, a deliberate avoidant coping response, into a tendency to experience dissociation and shutdown involuntarily. This echoes Young et al.'s (2003) original description of how this type of mode can become automatic, posing a substantial therapeutic task for learning how to reduce reliance on it.

References

Arntz, A., & Jacob, G. (2012). *Schema Therapy in practice: An introductory guide to the schema mode approach.* John Wiley & Sons.

Clarke, I. (2021). *Meeting mental breakdown mindfully: How to help the comprehend, cope and connect way.* Routledge.

Trower, P., & Chadwick, P. (1995). Pathways to defense of the self: A theory of two types of paranoia. *Clinical Psychology: Science and Practice, 2*(3), 263–278.

Young, J. E., Klosko, J. S., & Weishaar, M. E. (2003). *Schema Therapy: A practitioner's guide.* Guilford Press.

Chapter 3

Exploring modes in bipolarity

By contrast with the participants with psychosis, the group with bipolar diagnoses reported a significant dominance of demanding modes and linked the activation of these with progression into manic mood phases. Angry mode activation was also connected with, and intensified during, manic mood states for this group. Punitive modes too were reported by most of our participants, but by contrast with the demanding modes, punitive modes were linked with depressed mood states rather than manic ones. Vulnerable mode activation was, interestingly, linked with experiences of both manic and low mood states by these participants, suggesting a painful sense of isolation and separateness from others that accompanies not only depression, but also the elevated mood states in mania. We will draw here on the detailed subjective accounts of the study participants to illustrate how the interplay of mode activations might relate to escalating and alternating mood states as these unfold over time. As with the group experiencing psychosis, the two coping modes described by the bipolar group were the compliant surrender and detached protector, with no overcompensating modes being discernible from the individuals' responses. Table 3.1 summarises the modes coded in our participants' accounts, alongside the themes identified in their descriptions.

Demanding mode

Demanding modes are conceptualised as states of continually pushing and pressuring the self to meet excessively high standards (Young et al., 2003). Extreme standards might be applied in different life domains, such as in professional and academic achievements or in one's behaviour in relationships with others. A striving for faultless and perfect performance may typically be accompanied by a great deal of distress attached to the potential for not meeting these standards. In contrast to the punitive mode, the demanding mode usually does not involve ferocious self-hate, but can be linked with over-work and a relentless striving for achievement and perfection, even at the expense of health and other life domains.

DOI: 10.4324/9781003350583-3

Table 3.1 Modes and themes in the group with bipolarity

Mode	Themes
Demanding	Self as demanding
	Battling with demandingness
	Perceived influence of mania
Punitive	Blame over past regrets
	Self-attack
	Perceived relationship to low mood
Vulnerable	Feeling alone
	The dangerousness of depending on others
	Isolation exacerbated when manic
	Acting on vulnerable feelings
Angry	Anger caused by mistreatment from others
	They think I'm being aggressive when I'm not
	Controllability of responses to anger
	Anger mixed with other emotions
	Anger in mania
Compliant surrender	Self as submissive
	Resisting subjugation
Detached protector	Disconnection from thinking and feeling
	Detached coping as fuelling negative emotions

Five of our participants reported attitudes and states corresponding to this mode and described related behaviours. All made links with their mood states, and some spontaneously traced the origins of these states to childhood experiences with caregivers. Three themes were identified in participants' accounts corresponding to the demanding mode: 'Self as demanding,' 'Battling with demandingness' and 'Perceived influence of mania.'

Self as demanding

Several participants described themselves as perfectionists, including Zahra, who explained that even when she was cooking, each vegetable would need to be cut in a specific way into pieces of identical size:

Zahra: I am perfectionist and whatever I do, I want it to be done really well.

Lucy gave a vivid account of her demanding mode using an example of doing some physical exercise, spontaneously reporting how she would push herself to overdo it: 'No, carry on. Keep going, keep going... No. You're staying and you're gonna do it.' She emphasised that she would end up causing herself pain through acting on these demands, compelled by the knowledge that she would feel bad about herself if she did not comply.

Lucy: I push myself to the extreme where I will hurt myself and I wouldn't feel… Say if I only stayed for half an hour. I would feel bad about myself. I wouldn't feel that I achieved anything. But when I was manic, that went to another level. I would push myself. I would get on a treadmill and I'd get to 10k, even though I hit the wall, I would carry on. It's like I've got this in me that I could just push myself to an extreme.

The self-imposed negative consequences of falling short of extreme standards were also emphasised by Eymen, who reported that he would feel like 'a quitter' if a task wasn't finished perfectly. He highlighted the internal drive of his high standards, in the absence of any extreme external demands:

Eymen: I do try to do things meticulously well and it's not because of any pressure to achieve, it's just because I can be a bit pedantic. Even if something is impossible to do… It would take me four times longer but I would still have to do it.

Amy linked her tendency to put pressure on herself with an upbringing among a family of high achievers with relentless standards. She described her sense of the family's responses when she struggled academically: 'they just assumed that it was because I wasn't good enough.' A similarly harsh critical attitude was then reflected in Amy's own thoughts at times of struggle:

Amy: And I'm just 'argh,' you know, just like 'why don't I just get on with it? Work a bit faster.' And I just start thinking 'I'm just always going to be a bum.'

Battling with demandingness

Participants reported struggling to control demanding impulses and attitudes, despite acknowledging their potentially harmful impacts. Sharon described herself as 'a dog with a bone' when focused on the demand to complete tasks, while Eymen conveyed the sense of pressure to keep striving despite the potential to make things worse using the following analogy:

Eymen: It's ummm, it's like being snowed under and you know that you're under, but you have to keep digging to get out.

Zehra explicitly expressed wishing that she wasn't so demanding towards herself, knowing that there were negative consequences for her health: 'I am trying not to do like before because it is affecting my health mentally and I have back problems.' She conveyed her ongoing struggle with trying to soften her exacting standards in the following:

Zahra: I wish I didn't do that. I know that it's not going to help, being perfectionist, and I'm trying not to do. I'm trying my best. Sometimes
every day I am trying not to do it, sometimes I do it. But it's less than
before I can say.

Perceived influence of mania

All five participants who reported demanding modes linked the activation of
these to experiences of mania in one way or another. Zehra and Lucy both
recounted pressuring themselves to achieve highly in their university courses,
to the extent that their mental health deteriorated. Zehra emphasized how
much stress and pressure she had felt not to make mistakes on her course, while
Lucy gave a vivid account of taking study to the extreme, still trying to revise
even when she was already in bed for the night:

Lucy: So I was going to bed, you know, learning. I couldn't stop it. It was on
and on, it was constant. And I was so... I put myself in such a state, I
ended up becoming unwell. Because I really wanted to pass well.

Most of the participants linked demanding mode activation with subsequent
ascent into states of mania. Connections in the reciprocal direction, of manic
experiences feeding back into subsequent demandingness, were also suggested.
Michael explained illustratively how the very anticipation of a future manic
phase made him work yet harder to get work finished before such a time that
he might become unable to do so. He described the sense of pressure around
completing as many tasks as possible before becoming unwell again:

Michael: ...you think: 'I might only have this amount of time.' So in a limited amount of time I've got to do this amount of task before
mania... before another episode comes. So it's the... it's the thought
of an episode that drives you to maybe not be as relaxed as others
may be.

Lucy, in contrast, suggested that she would be more demanding of herself
when 'getting manic,' while Eymen linked demandingness to a phase of 'not
completely manic but on the manic side. Elevated.' Sharon described a similar
connection between heightened mood and pressuring herself to achieve:

Sharon: I think that my [manic] mood state influences the mode. By making
me more tenacious and obsessive. Really focused at this point to try
to get the job done and, yeah, to achieve. Because I really am putting myself under pressure.

This combination of connections drawn in both directions is consistent with a proposal that demandingness and mania might have the potential to reciprocally influence each other over time, and that perhaps this could form a vicious cycle that perpetuates dysregulated mood fluctuations. While our participants conveyed insight into how unhelpful demandingness could be for their health and wellbeing, they struggled nevertheless to resist being drawn into this recurrent pattern.

Punitive mode

The punitive mode relates to experiences of self-criticism with more extreme, disliking, self-hating or self-attacking content, compared to the demanding mode (Young et al., 2003). Self-blaming and self-attacking thoughts in this mode might be acted out through explicit self-punishment, deprivation and even violent abuse. The same five participants – Sharon, Zehra, Amy, Lucy and Eymen – who identified experiences linked to the demanding mode also related experiences corresponding to the punitive mode, suggesting the co-occurrence of both types of critic mode in the same individuals in our sample. All of these participants linked punitive mode activation with experiences of low mood and depression, as opposed to the demanding mode, which was linked with mania. Three themes were identified in the accounts of these individuals relating to the punitive mode: 'Blame over past regrets,' 'Self-attack' and 'Perceived relationship to low mood.'

Blame over past regrets

Four of the five participants described blaming themselves for past actions, and they conveyed a ruminative or even obsessive quality to this process of self-criticism around regrets and perceived mistakes. Amy went so far as to blame herself for the entire experience of bipolar disorder: 'I deserve it. Because I bullied my little sister.' Eymen described analysing himself 'in despair' and feeling 'like I've wasted my life, and by doing that, I've not given my family all the things that they deserve.' Sharon similarly described 'guilt' and dislike towards herself, linked to a sense of having treated others badly. Zehra's description of her painful regrets and punishment of herself was more generalised, not so specific to interpersonal guilt, but attaching to all sorts of choices and decisions that she wished she could have made differently, accompanied by a criticism amounting to self-hatred:

Zehra: It's all about the things that I have done in the past. I regret them and I'm wishing not to have done them. And at that moment, I hate myself basically.

Sharon highlighted an awareness that obsessive rumination and regrets can never allow us to change the past, emphasising how helpless and painful these mental processes can feel:

Sharon: Oh, just obsessing over things that you can't change and maybe des-
          perately trying to imagine what your life might have been like if you
          had made the right choices.

Self-attack

Self-attack in forms including condemnation, belittling, self-destructive and self-punishing behaviour was reported by four of the participants. The content of self-attacking thoughts commonly related to a sense of inferiority: not being good enough to achieve things in life, being deficient in some way or lacking intelligence. Sharon said 'I must be stupid,' while Amy reported thinking 'there must be something wrong with me,' and feeling 'like a bum and a drain on society.' Lucy summarised her self-critical thoughts and the painful impact of these with the following:

Lucy: I just feel, that I'm stupid, I'm no good you know, or I'm never going
        to do anything with my life. I'm never going to achieve anything. Yeah,
        it's just horrible.

Eymen situated his sense of worthlessness explicitly in relation to certain standards of achievement that he saw in society, which he saw as perpetuating his sense of inferiority despite having much to appreciate in life, such as his family.

Eymen: I just feel, you know, if you know how it feels to feel worthless? I
         don't feel like I've achieved much in my life... I've got lovely kids
         and a great family. But you're not weighed by those things in this
         society. Your worth isn't measured by those things.

Participants linked the activation of punitive states of mind with actions that either actively or covertly caused themselves harm or undermined their health and wellbeing. Amy listed a range of ways that she would punish and neglect herself in the following:

Amy: Taking drugs to punish myself. Smoking to punish myself... And then
       I don't eat that well and I start getting takeaways maybe or just not
       eating at all... So self-neglect really. Which is another form of punish-
       ment, isn't it?

Eymen described seeing a self-sabotaging pattern that felt more covert: 'I think there's a part of me that likes to, not consciously, but unconsciously to sabotage what I am doing.' He further explained a sense of there being a reciprocal interaction between thinking badly of himself and punishing himself:

Eymen: I feel disappointed in myself. And umm, I am the person that is punishing myself. I'm not being punished by anyone else.

The awareness of this type of vicious cycle of negativity and punishment towards the self was also expressed by Amy in her description of self-sabotage, highlighting the impact on her sense of self:

Amy: I feel like I self-sabotage a lot. I cut my nose off to spite my face and then I have recriminations and just feel even shittier about myself. So it's a never ending cycle.

Lucy's description of her experiences of self-criticism similarly conveyed the sense of looping, spiralling negativity:

Lucy: It just goes into spirals. It just goes worse and worse and worse and worse. And it's like I'm in hell. Just laying there in hell. It's awful.

Perceived relationship to low mood

Four out of the five participants reporting experiences of a punitive mode linked these explicitly to episodes of low mood and depression. Influences in both directions were suggested, conveying once more the sense of a vicious cycle. Most participants reported that self-criticism and punitiveness would be more likely to emerge when mood is low, as in Eymen's reflection: 'Well at the moment, I think because I'm a bit low, it's just despairing with myself.' The complimentary effect in the opposite direction was also highlighted, of punitive mode activation exacerbating low mood, as in Sharon's account:

Sharon: That kind of follows on to other, you know, everything else and not following my ambitions or not following through with love affairs and that kind of thing. And feeling a lot of regret basically. And then that becomes quite depressing.

In summary, all five of the same participants who described having a demanding mode also reported punitive mode activations. Most of these individuals described blaming themselves for past events, condemning, belittling, and attacking themselves, either in overt ways or with covert acts of self-sabotage. All but one of these participants explicitly suggested links between punitive mode activations and depressed mood states. Connections in both directions were drawn, suggesting the possibility of a mutually reinforcing feedback loop between low mood and punitiveness, each exacerbating the other. Such an impression of spiralling, looping self-perpetuating negativity was indeed evident in participants' subjective accounts of these experiences, suggesting a painful sense of helplessness and hopelessness when caught in this type of vicious cycle.

Vulnerable mode

All seven of our participants described experiences matching aspects of the vulnerable mode, which relates to feeling completely alone, isolated, frightened and helpless (Young et al., 2003). Arntz and Jacob (2012) described a range of subtypes of vulnerable modes, with somewhat diverse emotional tones, such as loneliness, abandonment, humiliation, inferiority or dependence, but all linked with a sense of fragility and weakness, and commonly accompanied by a desperate desire to be taken care of.

We tried to differentiate between the activation of a vulnerable mode in our group and the more situationally orientated anxiety or discomfort that might be experienced in specific corresponding contexts. The difference may not always be clear in this type of interview data, and indeed we see these experiences as existing on a continuum. Four themes were identified in our participants' accounts of vulnerable modes: 'Feeling alone,' 'The dangerousness of depending on others,' 'Isolation exacerbated when manic' and 'Acting on vulnerable feelings.' Interestingly, participants linked vulnerable mode activation to both types of mood episodes: depressive and manic.

Feeling alone

Feeling alone was variously described either in relation to a lack or insufficiency of actual connections with other people, or in terms of a pervasive sense of loneliness that persisted even in company and despite knowing that others are connected and do care. Eymen's account was of a concrete sense of social isolation and disconnectedness:

Eymen: I do feel alone. Like I have no friends. I say that I'm going out. But the truth is, I've got nowhere to go and no one to see.

Lucy, on the other hand, emphasised knowing that she is loved, and having access to the company of those who love her, but even when surrounded by those people, feeling a deep loneliness:

Lucy: I can always entertain that feeling of feeling alone. But I feel lonely in myself, even if I've got everyone who I love and adore with me. I still feel lonely sometimes.

Lucy reported having this type of mode activation frequently, with potential internal as well as external triggers, 'every time I sort of have like, a moment you know?' She connected her experiences of this type of vulnerable mode activation with times of low mood and depression:

Lucy: It's more so when I'm feeling really low, when I'm feeling really down. And when I'm on my own I suppose. When all my thoughts are all negative and I can't control them. Just feeling in despair. That's quite a lonely feeling as well. Cos no one can… you can't come in and shake my brain out. You know? It's there. That can feel quite lonely.

Other participants drew links between feeling more alone and their experience of bipolar disorder in general, as in Amy's statement: 'Well abandonment when I was a child and then when I'm an adult, so called friends dumping me because of bipolar and stuff.' Eymen explained that his loneliness was exacerbated by a sense that he could not express himself openly with those close to him, for fear that they might misinterpret or catastrophise his struggles in line with assumptions about mental illness or with his previous episodes:

Eymen: The only people I have are at home and even then, I feel like I can't really talk to them because I'll just worry them. They'll think there's something wrong.

Lucy reported scrutinising and blaming herself for abandonment by others at times of feeling alone and vulnerable, suggesting a potential interaction in these moments between a critical mode and a vulnerable one:

Lucy: I'm upset that, you know, people just, everyone's just gone. But maybe I've pushed them away. I don't know.

The dangerousness of depending on others

This theme reflected participants' experiences of being rejected or mistreated by people. Four participants reported feeling abandoned by others, and links were recurrently made to their struggles with mental health and bipolar disorder, as in Amy's quote above regarding being 'dumped.' Zehra similarly described being left unsupported by friends, in particular while being depressed – an experience that she still felt upset and preoccupied with to this day.

Zehra: When I was ill, when I was in depression… They all went away and didn't ask for a couple of years. They didn't come and call or nothing.

Amy illustrated the sense of dangerousness around depending on others using a painful experience of being rejected and criticised by her family members when feeling unwell and seeking support, highlighting the emotional impact:

Amy: And I try to explain to him [grandfather] that I'm unwell and he's just like 'you always say that' [shouting]... so I try to explain it to them that I'm a bit vulnerable and it's like 'it's all about you' [shouting] and I get upset and things like that [sobbing].

Both Amy and Lucy described a sense of vulnerability in feeling too attached to others or too emotionally reliant on them, leading either to staying in unhappy relationships or being overwhelmed with fear around potential losses. Lucy summarised her worries in the following:

Lucy: It's terrible fears of... mostly death, you know, like 'oh, I'm going to lose my family, what am I going to do?'

As well as the potential to be abandoned or rejected, some participants expressed anticipating that others might abuse or take advantage of them, in Michael's words 'see it as an opportunity to take something.' Amy described her sense of others' potential hostility:

Amy: Some people are really nasty and they pretend they're really nice. And then they show their true colours. Those are the ones to be aware of.

Isolation exacerbated when manic

Strikingly, experiences of feeling alone and separate were linked not only to low mood episodes, but also those of elevated mood. Five participants reported that they felt more alone or separate from others when in a manic mood state. They described shifts in a sense of self that made it difficult to connect with others, and vice versa. Both physical and psychological isolation were described. Lucy gave an account of struggling with helplessness while alone and unable to sleep in manic states:

Lucy: Some nights I don't sleep at all [when manic] and I get so anxious and on edge all the time. I feel that no one can help me and I'm stuck with this brain. You know. It's there. I can't get it out.

Sharon said that nobody seemed on her wavelength at times of mania, leaving her feeling 'very isolated in my own world,' while Basima described herself at these times as feeling 'completely different' and sensing herself being 'pushed away' by others because of this. Basima gave a compelling account of her vulnerability at times of mania, even though she might want to connect with others socially:

Basima: You just need protection [when manic]. Because you're vulnerable, you're extra vulnerable, there's chance of you being taken advantage of as well. You feel like you can't express your emotions, so they just take advantage of that.

Amy gave a specific report of her experiences of milder states of elevated mood, using the term hypomania. She explained the sorts of things that she might do when hypomanic using an example of making unusual telephone calls to her grandparents:

Amy: Because I called them in the middle of the night to try and get them to go to bed because they fall asleep in front of the TV, and I was a bit hypomanic, and he hasn't talked to me for a few months. And I feel a bit helpless and anxious and abandoned on that front.

It was clear from Amy's descriptions how isolated and frightened she felt at such times of elevated mood and in relation to others' responses. She conveyed an insightful summary of how, even while seeming to see the positive in everything, the sense of vulnerability persisted:

Amy: But when I'm hypomanic I see the best in everything... And I put myself in situations where I'm in harm's way, like thinking... Not thinking, but treating strangers like friends so that's where I'm in a vulnerable situation.

Acting on vulnerable feelings

The second superordinate theme, of 'Acting on vulnerable feelings,' was identified in four of the participants' responses. Some compulsions to act were directed to try to bring people closer when feeling alone, while others acted to push them away or retaliate for feeling rejected. We might be starting to see here some mode mixtures or transitions towards other modes connected with the vulnerable mode, including potentially the angry mode or the detached protector, which might become activated to try to get needs met in a different way or to cope with painful feelings of abandonment. Zehra expressed regret at pleading with her daughter to come home when she was lonely, reflecting 'I couldn't stop myself.' Lucy reported feeling vulnerable when others were unresponsive on the telephone, and considering doing the same in return:

Lucy: A little bit of pain. You know, then you've just got to think to yourself: 'Ah well. Maybe I'll just do that to them when they call me' [laughs]. It's just mad.

Basima recounted a recent interaction in which she had asked her husband to take her out to dinner, and he had turned her down. She described herself as feeling 'lonely and a bit abandoned,' and snapping back: 'Fine. Don't take me out. I'll take myself out.' On further enquiry about her response, Basima was able to explain how she had retreated from the painful rejection to feel a bit safer in a stance of independence and self-sufficiency, or at least a show of these:

Basima: I think it's the fact that I have the 'I don't care' attitude. I don't care what you say, It's not going to put me down. I'll do whatever makes me happy and umm, I don't need you to make me happy. Yeah.

The two impulses: on the one hand, desperately seeking to connect with someone, and on the other, wishing to turn away from the one who seemed rejecting, were united in Amy's account of her actions in the middle of the night when her boyfriend had kept her waiting and not called:

Amy: I then got dressed. Out of my pyjamas, my comfy pyjamas, and I didn't need anything. I got dressed to go out and wander the streets... and I made friends with this guy in a hotel. He does graveyard shifts, so I just go and chat to him for a while. But it's still putting myself in harm's way... Because I wanted to connect with someone.

To summarise, all of our participants could identify with aspects of the vulnerable mode, and most reported feeling painfully alone or isolated at times. Participants repeatedly drew connections, perhaps somewhat surprisingly, between the experience of feeling alone and manic mood states, as well as episodes of depression. A common sense of threat and vulnerability was conveyed around dependency on others, and a range of impulsive responses to feeling abandoned included some desperately seeking connection, as well as those turning away or retaliating at perceived rejection.

Angry mode

All of our participants reported experiencing anger, and all connected this to situations of conflict with other people. Three out of the seven gave clear accounts of having regular experiences in which anger seemed extreme relative to the situation, and which fit the description of an angry mode (Young et al., 2003). These individuals' interviews contained many examples of anger throughout, and not just when discussing the angry mode. Angry modes have been conceptualised as emerging in response to unmet core needs in childhood, but, in contrast to vulnerable modes, these are characterised by intense frustration, anger and even rage, with the potential for aggressive outbursts. Arntz and Jacob (2012) proposed several subtypes of angry modes, ranging from an obstinate type associated with passive resistance, through to the enraged mode, in which the individual may scream and lash out, aiming even to destroy the perceived aggressor.

We sought to differentiate, to the extent possible from our data, between reasonable and proportionate expressions of anger at mistreatment by others on the one hand and angry mode activation on the other. We envisage these as lying on a continuum, and wish to acknowledge the subjectivity and cultural relativity of a judgement regarding what types of angry responses are seen as being proportional. Clinically, an individual's own sense of angry affect being out of control, and potentially of feeling like a child in the midst of the experience, would be indicators of angry mode activation rather than a type of healthy adult expression of anger. Five themes were identified among our participants' responses corresponding to angry mode activation: 'Anger caused by mistreatment from others,' 'They think I'm being aggressive when I'm not,' 'Controllability of responses to anger,' 'Anger mixed with other emotions' and 'Anger in mania.'

Anger caused by mistreatment from others

Three participants cited being treated badly by others as being a cause of their anger. Sharon gave a vivid account of such a reactive feeling, whose expression could be explosive. She described herself as having 'a short fuse,' and summarised the unhelpful impact of this, highlighting that outbursts can happen at work, where this would not typically be seen as appropriate:

Sharon: I do become angry and shout, and that can cause problems for me. I have done it at work as well.

She further explained how belittling it felt to be treated in certain ways at work, conveying a very understandable sense of frustration and annoyance, but again emphasised the dysfunctional impact of the uncontrolled expression of her angry responses:

Sharon: That also drives me insane, you know? That I've been in the job 30 various roles and I've been treated as if I'm a junior with two years' experience… Well, sometimes I'll verbalise my frustration in a way that is not very diplomatic perhaps. Because, people, people don't respond well to that anger that they can physically see coming off me. And they're probably frightened, that I might hit them [laughs]. I don't know.

Basima similarly identified that an angry mode would be triggered for her by 'unfair treatment, or someone being judgemental,' and that this type of situation could make her 'snap.' Amy summarised a similar combination of feeling justified in anger, but seeing how frightening her outbursts could be for others by saying 'Well, I get angry and I scare people with my anger, but I don't touch anyone. They do it to me.' She gave an example of her intense anger response being triggered by critical comments from her sister:

Amy: My sister tries to say that I depress everyone. And that makes me fucking angry because I get the blame even for my depression, and then it's like 'Well, you can snap out of it.' So it's their ignorance.

They think I'm being aggressive when I'm not

Five participants described occasions when others thought they were being aggressive, but they did not themselves agree or perceive things that way. Michael reported being so confused by being told he was 'verbally aggressive' that he had to 'consult with one or two colleagues about what the verbally aggressive one meant.' Eymen described having similar experiences of confusion, illustrating these with the following example:

Eymen: I've had, you know people in the council or the housing office telling me that I'm being aggressive. And I just get confused you know? Because I've just maybe, spoken a bit loudly, and they think I'm being aggressive. I'm really, not aggressive.

There is great potential for cultural differences to influence how expressions of anger are perceived, although we cannot know for sure from our data to what extend these were operating in the specific examples described. There can also be a significant impact of strong emotional states on individuals' capacity to mentalise, or imagine the mental states of others, during highly charged interactions. Basima gave an explicit account of how her appraisals might shift with feedback and with angry affect subsiding, leaving her wondering if she had responded in an unhelpful way:

Basima: She [Mum] was like 'what did you do that for?' and then she's like 'I don't really want to speak to you anymore.' So I just kind of came to the realisation that I didn't probably do the right thing.

Controllability of responses to anger

The subtheme concerning controllability of responses to anger was identified in most of the participants' responses, with a broad range of accounts regarding how much choice individuals felt they had in how they might respond. Sharon expressed confidence in her ability to control her anger when this was necessary, and further suggested that she might allow herself less diplomatic expressions when feeling safer in her relationship with her employer:

Sharon: I mean, I could control it. The thing is, I've been in lots of corporate jobs, you know, where I have controlled it, and I would usually walk away, erm, go out for cigarettes and go to the toilet; take deep breaths and just bottle it you know? But maybe because it's in the public sector and I've got a permanent job for the first time ever, I feel more at liberty to speak my mind [laughs].

In contrast, Eymen described struggling to express anger in any strategic way, and instead admitted to having violent outbursts, specifically towards his teenage son. He connected his uneasiness around the expression of anger with not identifying as a violent person:

Eymen: You just get so angry that everything is boiling up, but you just, you can't even express it. So, I don't really get angry. I'm not a violent person.

In discussion of examples where circumstances may have triggered anger, he then described a recent situation in which he had found cigarettes inside his teenage son's pocket. Without mention of identifying or addressing the emotion of anger directly, he described lashing out straight away:

Eymen: I just felt my whole face get really hot and I just grabbed him...

Anger mixed with other emotions

The fourth theme, 'Anger mixed with other emotions,' was identified in four participants' responses, all of whom reported constellations of other emotions, such as disappointment, sadness, guilt, and vulnerability, preceding, accompanying or following the activation of the angry mode. Amy described an interaction in which she had split up with her boyfriend via an email after she felt that he had not called her, and she explained the feeling of vulnerability that had preceded the impulse to reject him in retaliation:

Amy: I cemented the fact I can't be doing with this. You've got to be a man of your word, or just don't say it [raising voice]. Because he knows I'm feeling vulnerable right now.

The potential function of anger can be seen here in shifting the person from a state of feeling vulnerable and dependent into gaining control through retaliation or by demanding to be treated with more care. Along similar lines. Sharon conveyed an awareness that her angry responses in difficult situations might serve a protective function, in place of feeling more vulnerable emotions such as sadness:

Sharon: Because you know, maybe I'm not very good at dealing with depression and feeling sorry for myself, and I'm more likely to get angry about things than feel the grief or the sadness or, you know.

Basima's account addressed not so much the emotional antecedents but rather the consequences of angry outbursts, which for her upon subsiding would typically be transformed into guilt at the impact on others:

Basima: The feelings [of anger] all went away, and it was replaced with guilt... Afterwards it kicked into me, the realisation. And then I thought, 'What did I do?'

Anger in mania

Five participants made explicit links between states of mania or hypomania and expressions of anger, with an overarching sense that emotional responses may be harder to control when in an elevated mood. Michael summarised his sense of this alteration in mania with the statement 'it's that things get hyper-sensitive.' Sharon expanded on a similar experience:

Sharon: When I'm getting hypomanic, I can quite often be very short tempered and intolerable of people, and also I feel like a knot in my stomach a lot of the time... Then, then I get really short. It's just like being really overtired, you know?

Lucy and Eymen both reported uncontrollable expressions of anger and rage when hospitalised in a manic state. Lucy expressed a lack of understanding as to why she may have been violent, although she knew that this had happened in the context of feeling vulnerable, being pinned down and injected with medications against her will:

Lucy: Because when I was last admitted into hospital and it's never happened before, ummm I got really violent. I don't know why. I think because I was off my gong. You know, I hit a nurse or something.

Eymen similarly reported being sent 'into a fury' by being told that he could not see his children while he was in hospital, and he further explained that his response had led him to be placed in seclusion for some time. He described his state as 'impulsive' and incapable of seeing the bigger picture and reasoning through the situation.

Eymen: I wasn't able to work out that it was just a temporary thing and that ultimately the staff were just being unreasonable and unkind and that it would be something that I would be able to resolve with patience.

Experiences of anger were present throughout the accounts of all of our participants diagnosed with bipolarity, and three of them described regular occurrences in which they felt out of control and responded in ways that seemed disproportionate to the context, suggesting angry mode activation. We have sought to distinguish between proportionate angry responses to others' unwanted actions from an intense anger or rage corresponding to the angry mode; however, typically, the angry modes were indeed triggered by perceived mistreatment from others, albeit that the magnitude or form of expression of the anger could be seen as outstripping what might be functional or helpful in the situation at hand. Participants reported negative impacts on their relationships with loved ones and colleagues resulting from uncontrolled expressions of anger. Other emotions, such as sadness and guilt, were linked in individuals' accounts of episodes of anger, and most drew connections between manic or hypomanic states and dysregulated anger expressions.

Coping modes: compliant surrender

All of our participants reported experiences corresponding to the compliant surrender mode. This is one of the coping modes, conceptualised as a state of pervasively prioritising others' needs before one's own, acting passively, submissively, or subserviently, typically driven by a fear of conflict or rejection. Participants overwhelmingly expressed negative attitudes towards this mode of being, reporting a desire not to resort to this approach. Two themes were identified in their responses: 'Self as submissive' and 'Resisting subjugation.'

Self as submissive

Six participants gave accounts of acting submissively in interactions with others. Diverse manifestations of this submissiveness were described, a common theme being a sense that they put up with or tolerated poor treatment from others, such as being verbally abused, hurtfully criticised, or ignored. Lucy and Amy both described being treated badly by the same people over and over again, and Amy seemed to blame herself for allowing this to continue:

Amy: Yeah. Because I've forgiven people who were nasty to me and everything. I've forgiven them too many times, and it's like, no wonder that I've got crap friends.

Lucy described putting up with being regularly ignored by her boyfriend, for days at a time, feeling 'vulnerable,' 'But I was so into him that I'd put up with it. And it kept...' she trailed off short of finishing that sentence, going on to describe other people seeming to ignore her in a similar way. Lucy explained how she would keep her difficult feelings to herself:

Lucy: I'm thinking 'I called hours ago, how comes you didn't answer?' But you don't let anyone know what you're actually feeling. No, no.

We can see how keeping feelings of vulnerability to herself and acting as though she had no problems with being ignored might have contributed to allowing Lucy's boyfriend to carry on the same pattern of behaviour unchecked. Zehra and Eymen also reported keeping difficult feelings to themselves in order to avoid conflict or protect others from worry. Zehra gave an example of accepting hurtful criticism from her daughter without saying anything in response, while Eymen reported concealing his struggles and pretending that everything was fine in order to shield his family from concern:

Eymen: Well, I have to pretend things are OK when I'm with my family. So that they don't worry.

Resisting subjugation

All of our participants' responses suggested some attempts at resisting subjugation. Negative consequences for the self of remaining in a submissive position in relation to power dynamics were acknowledged, and typically individuals positioned themselves as evolving, from more frequently adopting a compliant surrender position in the past, to reducing this and taking care of their own needs more as time passed. Sharon seemed to feel resentful towards her ex-girlfriend, despite the fact that she had been 'instrumental in stopping me going completely off the rails,' linking the resentment explicitly to a subjugated role. Her description coveys the feeling of stuckness around being in an unequal power balance, having needed to depend on someone for help in the past and now feeling held in a subordinate position:

Sharon: But she kind of uses that in a way, you know, a power balance. That she then can call... do what she wants and that... And I've been in that relationship with her for many years.

Eymen specifically named resentment as his emotion related to having taken on increasing amounts of voluntary work for his community group, leaving him feeling like he was being taken advantage of and perhaps even mocked:

Eymen: I just felt resentful... it just felt that they were laughing. Like I was everyone's mule. Carrying the weight of this 'thing,' you know?

Resistance to subjugation was also expressed in participants' statements regarding the need for change in these patterns of interaction. There was a recurrent sense of not feeling properly respected or appreciated by others, as in the examples from Sharon and Eymen above. Amy reported feeling 'ridiculed' by her relatives. She described actively trying to shed this role and alter the dynamic in relation to her family:

Amy: I'm trying to get out of this role that I'm in, where I'm mistreated and subordinated and stuff like that.

Zehra similarly reported having held a role in her family in which she would seemingly make more effort, prepare food, look after others and be responsible for maintaining contact – a role which she no longer wanted, seeking a more even balance of mutual care:

Zehra: They don't call, they don't come [cousins]. I have to get in touch all the time. First of all I have to do. But I don't want to be first anymore. I want to do that equally.

Three participants raised issues with their own health and wellbeing as motivators to change and to start attending to their own needs more. Eymen described changing his orientation as a result of feeling unhappy after prioritising others as much as he had done in the past:

Eymen: Well, I had to just start thinking of my own mental health. You know? And, I wasn't happy as well. It was making me really unhappy.

Better use of clear boundaries and saying no to people were identified repeatedly as helpful strategies for resisting subjugation more in relationships and taking more care of one's own needs. Basima specifically reflected on how having talking therapy had helped her greatly via improvements in assertiveness with others:

Basima: It's really helped, like being able to say no to people and being able to stand up and be assertive in a good way.

In summary, all of our participants reported experiences consistent with a compliant surrender coping mode, with most having silenced their own feelings and needs in relationships for fear of conflict or rejection. Negative consequences around this coping mode were spontaneously discussed by a majority of participants, and efforts of various kinds to resist or counteract subjugation were described by all. This coping mode was overwhelmingly seen as dysfunctional or unhelpful by the individuals concerned, and most saw themselves as reducing their dependence on it as time went on.

Coping modes: detached protector

The detached protector coping mode is conceptualised as a buffering response against painful experiences, including those linked with schemas, which uses emotional and behavioural distancing strategies to reduce or avoid distress. Individuals with this type of mode activation may avoid external experiences such as interactions with others, or internal ones such as certain memories or challenging emotions. Six of our participants related experiences corresponding to detached protector modes, and for the most part these were described as being quite conscious and deliberate, although negative consequences were also highlighted. Two themes were identified in the responses:

'Disconnection from thinking and feeling' and 'Detached coping as fuelling negative emotions.'

Disconnection from thinking and feeling

Participants reported seeking disconnection from uncomfortable thoughts and feelings, both through active avoidance of triggers and by use of self-soothing strategies. Three of our participants explained that they would withdraw and avoid emotional triggers due to feeling that they were overly sensitive to becoming distressed. Zehra reported withdrawing and staying at home away from others who might cause distress:

> Zehra: I close myself at home. I am not going out. And, if I distress myself, I start flinching and uh, some body movements happen unwantedly to get away from them.

Sharon, on the other hand, avoided thinking about herself and her problems, stating 'that can make me depressed, and that's not a state that I want to be in.' This sense of dangerousness around engaging with one's own internal experiences, and subsequent avoidance of thoughts and feelings, might contribute to an increasingly pervasive character of aloof detachment from emotions. Sharon conveyed a sense that she identified with this type of disconnectedness, as she spoke about not dealing with sadness, almost dismissing it by saying that she would not handle it 'in a very self-indulgent way.' Michael similarly described an impression that his identity had become formed around emotional detachment. He gave the following compelling account of some feedback he had received from a friend about the impression that he brought across to others:

> Michael: ...one of my friends used to say [laughs] that I reminded him of a Greek mythical immortal that had no feelings and no [laughs]... yeah. It's the way I've presented myself to people. So yeah, somewhere along the line from my personal socialisation development, I found coping strategies, mechanisms, to not really get pain or hurt emotionally...

Strategies for self-soothing or distraction were reported by all participants, used to cope with difficult experiences such as self-critical thoughts or feeling lonely. Lucy described using alcohol to numb feelings of inadequacy when spending time with her friends. Eymen reported that he would stay in bed and try to stay asleep for as long as he could to hide from difficult emotions:

> Eymen: That's my way of hiding at the moment. And it works. Because you go to bed and you shut your eyes and nothing exists any more. You just dream and usually dreaming is more pleasant than real life, you know?

Other less extreme strategies mentioned included watching lots of TV and over-working. Two participants identified over-eating as a self-soothing strategy, as in Basima's account:

Basima: Sometimes if I feel bored or if I feel lonely I can feel like I need to eat something. And then I just kind of use that emotion to snack on things.

Detached coping as fuelling negative emotions

Four participants reported feeling dissatisfied with coping strategies of avoidance and distraction. Amy described the impact on her of over-reliance on this type of coping as making her the 'world's worst procrastinator,' adding that this then made her 'even more depressed.' Sharon gave an example of deliberately leaving a self-compassion book that she had been reading on the train after it had triggered some self-critical thoughts, resulting in subsequent regret and even more self-criticism:

Sharon: And then I regretted it because I did want to read more you know?... I just felt quite angry and annoyed with myself.

A similar sense of a vicious cycle, with avoidance inadvertently leading to even more of what one was trying to avoid in the first place, can be felt in Lucy's account of her struggles with low mood and social withdrawal:

Lucy: I keep making excuses not to go out because it's just so much headache. And then I feel low because I'm thinking, 'Well, I'm not socialising, I'm not doing anything.' It's like a vicious cycle, how I'm feeling now.

Participants' accounts indicated insight into the negative unintended consequences of avoidant and detached coping, and there were indications that they were more explicitly aware of this than the group with psychosis in our previous chapter. While the participants' negative appraisals of these strategies might suggest a desire to find a better way to care for themselves, the insight also seemed to lead to self-criticism, potentially indicating activation of a demanding or punitive mode in response to noticing detached protector coping. Given the links already drawn between the critic mode activations and recurrence of episodes of depression and mania, these forms of negative appraisal around existing coping strategies could be seen as having the potential to feed another vicious cycle leading back into more episodes and more felt need for maladaptive forms of coping. The clinical approach to supporting individuals to appraise the dysfunctional impacts of their current coping efforts while managing unhelpful manifestations of self-criticism will be addressed in our subsequent chapters concerning therapeutic adaptation and application of a Schema Therapy-based approach.

Summary and reflections

Both demanding and punitive mode activations were vividly evident in most participants' descriptions of their experiences, with links made between the demanding mode and mania and between the punitive mode and depression. Vulnerable mode descriptions were also given by the majority of participants, and, perhaps unexpectedly, this mode was connected not only with episodes of depression, but of mania too. Angry mode activation, on the other hand, yielded associations with mania specifically. Our participants related their experiences to two types of coping modes: the compliant surrender and the detached protector. Descriptions of the latter conveyed more of a sense of deliberate strategic use, while the compliant surrender mode seemed more linked to feeling stuck in subordinate roles in relationships with other people. Both coping mode types were overwhelmingly described as having a range of negative consequences, however, and participants reported self-critical think-ing around their use, as well as efforts to change. The insight into the coping modes' drawbacks had the potential to activate a punitive or demanding mode, which could then lead to more distress, and a greater need for further coping, and so on.

References

Arntz, A., & Jacob, G. (2012). *Schema Therapy in practice: An introductory guide to the schema mode approach.* John Wiley & Sons.

Young, J. E., Klosko, J. S., & Weishaar, M. E. (2003). *Schema Therapy: A practitioner's guide.* Guilford Press.

Chapter 4

Developing the concept of modes in psychosis and bipolarity

Introduction

In this chapter we will argue that modes may contribute to the conceptualis-ation of psychosis and bipolarity and to therapy practice in four ways: first, modes can themselves influence and contribute to distress; second, there is evi-dence in our case illustrations suggesting interactions between modes and symptoms; third, modes may provide meaning or content for the symptoms of delusions and hallucinations; finally, modes and their schemas, particularly if these are extreme, are already a form of disconnection from the unified system of the person and may contribute to the fragmentation found in psychosis and bipolarity. We traced the potential connections of the schema mode framework to significant historical and contemporary theories of psychosis and bipolarity, particularly noting the importance of dissociation. In further discussing frag-mentation and disconnection, we link our ideas to a background theory of cer-tainty and everyday knowledge which suggests that aspects of delusions, extreme ideas, and voices can be understood as generated in the context of the loss of a person's former grasp of the world. A final section looks at how modes may fit on a continuum of states of the self and consider other key features of modes and schemas.

Overview of findings regarding modes in psychosis and bipolarity

The findings presented in Chapters 2 and 3 indicated that participants with diagnoses of psychosis and bipolar disorders could easily make sense of the concept of modes, and that questions about these self-states prompted rich descriptions of the individuals' own experiences. Examples from our partici-pants' lives often echoed Young et al.'s original (2003) schema mode descrip-tions, supporting the relevance for our groups of this framework.

Among the group with psychosis, it was striking that almost all of the participants reported experiences of punitive and vulnerable modes. In con-trast, most of the bipolar group reported a demanding part, and linked its

DOI: 10.4324/9781003350583-4

activation with ascent into manic phases, while descent into depression was connected to punitive and vulnerable modes. All of the bipolar participants and all but one of the psychosis group described an angry mode, and this was linked with mania and with psychotic symptoms, respectively. A striking finding in the bipolar group was that mania was linked not only with demandingness and anger but also with vulnerability. Both groups in different ways reported using the mode of compliance in order to fit in with their past and present social circumstances. Most individuals in each group also reported a detached protector part, and the accounts of those with psychosis seemed to track an evolution of this coping mode from something quite strategic and deliberate into a more automatic and involuntary form of disconnection.

Four contributions of modes to clinical conceptualisation

Modes and distress

A key point concerning modes is that these often contribute directly to forms of distress: the person can feel bombarded and overwhelmed by demanding thoughts, belittled and condemned by the highly critical or even self-hating comments of the punitive part, while various child modes such as those conveying extreme fear, anger or shame directly manifest vulnerability and suffering. Coping modes such as compliance and detachment attempt to avoid distress; however, they also block the person from developing close relationships and pursuing long term goals to overcome their current problems. Modes and schemas give a rich description of emotional and interpersonal struggles, one that we believe is comprehensible and acceptable to clients, and thereby facilitates in-depth collaborative therapeutic work, as will be illustrated in later chapters.

Symptom and mode interactions

A key finding of our research was that participants described multiple interactions between their specific mode states and psychotic or bipolar symptoms. The activation of modes was said to lead to an increase in certain symptoms, such as demandingness feeding into manic escalation of mood; however, in addition, symptoms were also described as potentially increasing the experience of a mode or modes, such as the state of mania activating modes of anger and vulnerability. These complex patterns, unfolding over time, of symptoms and recurrent self-states have perhaps not been well captured in other research; we believe that exploration of this in clinical work could make a useful contribution both to therapeutic practice and evolving theory.

The contribution of modes to meaning in psychotic symptoms

Some common symptom patterns of psychosis are striking in the extent to which they correspond to specific combinations of modes from Young et al.'s (2003) framework. A frequent presentation involves delusions of persecution by malicious entities or organisations who are seen as plotting to monitor, torment or even kill the person, who correspondingly feels extreme fear and vulnerability. We believe it is possible that this persecuted worldview directly reflects or expresses a vulnerable child mode, which might be distorted by the state of psychosis such that the sense of being under attack is taken literally and specific aggressors identified to account for it. The perceived persecutors can be seen as a psychotic transformation of a punitive mode, in line with Tom's quote from Chapter 2: 'A lot of the time in my own head it's like well, am I just being so critical of myself or am I being watched, and it's a horrible feeling.' Typically our participants with psychosis reported both vulnerable and punitive modes. In addition to modes there are, of course, other sources of meaning that influence psychotic content such as a person's unique life circumstances and history, specific motivations, and attempts by the person to narrate and use metaphor (Rhodes, 2022).

Rhodes (2022) described a range of states of self based on an open exploration of the experiences reported by participants with psychosis: the resulting categories were compatible with the modes listed in Young et al. (2003). Vulnerability was again very prominent: participants reported that they were inferior or irredeemably damaged in some way, echoing descriptions of the vulnerable child state. Some, in contrast, reported not feeling persecuted by other persons or things, but that they themselves were becoming a terrible entity that could scare others: this could be likened either to an enraged child mode or an overcompensating mode of bully and attack, used to cope with underlying fear. Although rare, it is striking that sometimes individuals report actually believing that they have become a child during psychosis: two examples were described in Rhodes (2022); an example is also described by Bleuler (1950). While complete psychotic transformations might be quite rare, it is much more common for an individual to take on a new vulnerable identity, for example, being a religious disciple persecuted by others. Noting a parallel between psychotic persecutory concerns in contrast to a sort of dread the person often feels in everyday situations, and which may be linked to earlier adversities, suggests therapeutic approaches which will be illustrated in later chapters.

There are many types and meanings of delusions (Rhodes et al., 2005), with several categories mapping onto certain modes. Alongside the persecutory type already described, another common category is grandiose delusions, involving beliefs about having special powers or a special mission. These can be seen as closely linked with the mode of self-aggrandisement, which is considered to overcompensate for various negative schemas. Another less frequent type is the erotomanic delusion, which involves believing oneself to be loved by a special person, usually famous. It seems possible that this reflects a basic desire for love, but furthermore, for protection conveyed by the target's high social status, as might be sought by a vulnerable child mode.

Verbal hallucinations, and the meanings they express, are another common psychotic symptom that seems to map well onto modes: the most typical content of voices tends to be criticism, putdowns, insults, or on the other hand, demands that the person should do things differently. The meaning of these parallels the sorts of things one might expect from punitive and demanding modes. We would suggest that many voices can be conceptualised as psychotically transformed versions of modes: that is, an expression of the mode but experienced as externally generated, independent and existing outside the person.

Some clients may not seem to manifest or report demanding or critical modes of the self, and yet still might hear critical or demanding voices. In such cases it is worth exploring who the voices might be reminiscent of and any experiences with other people that they might echo, as some forms of verbal hallucination can be linked with inaccessible or partially processed memories, and sometimes might even have a flashback-like quality. Some voice content can actually be comforting and supportive: here the hallucinations might be seen as transformed desires for care and protection from a caring adult, again held by the vulnerable child part of self.

Modes may provide not only meanings about the self in psychosis, but also be a source of meaning concerning identities and roles attached to symptoms. A voice may not only make negative comments, but actually seem to represent a past abuser or present-day hostile agent; the voice takes on a 'character' in how it speaks. Delusional systems assign roles of attacker, critic, protector, victim and so on to those surrounding the individual. The ideas we present here might relate to the features that Shiel et al. (2022) have described as the experience of 'illusory social agents' in psychosis. The mode framework might help us to better understand the origins of these identity features of symptomatology in underlying aspects of self, potentially advancing formulations pointing towards the most therapeutic courses of action.

Modes and meanings in bipolar states

States of mania or hypomania are central to bipolarity: elevated mood can bring with it a feeling of power and being special, ranging from everyday themes such as being charming or successful through to more extreme ideas which may cross a line over to delusions. The more unrealistic these ideas become, the more they seem to parallel the mode of self-aggrandisement, which is conceptualised as overcompensating for an underlying sense of defectiveness. Manic and hypomanic mood states are complex and involve diverse features: Farr et al. (2023), for example, noted that participants reported feeling exceptional but also sometimes extremely angry or sometimes vulnerable and alone. We suggest that modes experienced by people with bipolarity might be expressed at times in exaggerated ways due to being coloured or amplified by an extreme mood state. In intense phases of mania or depression, the probability is increased of modes being manifested in highly distorted ways, and sometimes with a delusional level of conviction.

When participants with bipolarity are depressed, they commonly report feeling vulnerable, defective and worthless, and subject themselves to extreme negative criticisms; depression in bipolarity, and in fact other sorts of depression, might well be seen as involving the unleashing of extreme experiences of the vulnerable child and punitive parent modes. The experience of such modes can persist even when the person is neither manic nor depressed, but in the depressed phase they are greatly dominant and exaggerated; furthermore, any sense of a caring, realistic, rational adult mode of self seems to be absent at such times.

Modes and fragmentation of the self in psychosis and bipolarity

A fourth contribution of the concept of modes is how it illuminates the challenge for those with extreme and fluctuating difficulties in maintaining a unified sense of self over time. The movement between different contrasting states in itself creates inconsistencies for a person in managing their social relationships and predicting how they will react in different situations. The fragmentation over time can also prevent the person from experiencing consistent healthy adult mode activation, shifting instead between conflicting states such as being vulnerable and being demanding, and not learning how to be reasonable and caring towards themselves. Therapies organised around a multi-self concept typically include as a central aim the bringing into awareness of the person's different self-states and developing capacity to see an overview, like the conductor of an orchestra, considering the needs of the different parts. This position is what Schwartz (1995) referred to as 'internal leadership,' and is also very much akin to Gilbert's (2009) 'compassionate self.'

Bipolar patients have to struggle with many sources of disruption and unpredictability; on one level, they have to deal with the extremities of mood fluctuations; our findings in Chapter 3, however, also pointed to the fact that they experience diverse modes, which we suggest occur not only during depression or mania, but often in everyday situations, constituting recurrent problems for the person. The challenges of maintaining a unified self may be particularly difficult for those with bipolarity as shown in interviews conducted with the same participants over time (Farr, 2021); we believe this to be an important therapeutic target, as explored in later chapters.

A core aim of Schema Therapy is to help develop a practical, realistic and caring healthy adult mode, which is aware of the different aspects of self and can look after those parts that feel desperate or inferior, listen to parts that are angry without being overwhelmed, and be aware of detachment, learning potential means to bypass this state. More positive relationships among the parts of self, as well as a greater confidence in their navigation and regulation, are developed as avenues towards a more coherent and valued identity, as well as the reduction of distress. These observations we believe apply whether mode states are the product of trauma and subsequent disassociation or may have other origins.

Modes and theories of psychosis and bipolarity

Janet, Bleuler and the history of parts of self in psychosis

There is an extensive history of theories conceptualising how psychosis might relate to a fragmentation of the self: Moskowitz's et al. (2019a) share several illuminating perspectives on these, with links to contemporary models. Pierre Janet, beginning in the nineteenth century (for example, Janet, 1886), highlighted the importance of trauma and the splitting of the self, which he termed dissociation, in the development of psychopathology. His work has been reinvigorated by modern traumatologists, including van der Hart et al. (2006), and those in the sensorimotor tradition such as Fisher (2017) and Ogden (2019). Janet's writing may not have been centrally concerned with understanding psychosis but had a great influence on Eugen Bleuler, who coined the term 'schizophrenia,' meaning 'a splitting of the mind' (1950, originally 1911), and in whose text we find an extensive development of the idea of fragmentation of the self as fundamental to psychosis. Indeed, recent re-appraisals of Bleuler's writing have highlighted and emphasised the centrality of the concept of psychological splitting and dissociation to his theory (Moskowitz & Heim, 2011). Bleuler proposed that in schizophrenia, groups of mental processes that usually function together can become uncoupled or disconnected. He borrowed the term 'complex' from Carl Jung, using it to indicate different states of the person, and arguing for splits between these self-states in schizophrenia. Bleuler proposed that this might help in understanding better the seeming contradictions between delusional content and the person's other beliefs and behaviour:

> the splitting of the personality is never more strikingly expressed than in the relation of the delusions to the remainder of the psyche. Parts of that total complex which we call the ego, the "self," always remains alien to the delusions. This constellation accounts for the fact that the non-affected part of the ego may disbelieve and even criticise the delusions; on the other hand, the incorrigibility and senselessness of the delusions are precisely due to the fact that many associations contradictory to the delusional are simply not brought into any logical connection with it.
>
> (1950, p. 127)

Bleuler argued that the loosening of associations, and other pervasive patterns such as ambivalent emotions, are core to schizophrenia, while specific symptoms such as voices or delusions are secondary. He may have attributed the causality of psychosis mainly to alterations in the biological and neurological functioning of the person, but he did also note that it was possible that similar changes might be induced by trauma. Research has subsequently supported a proposal that these can be one and the same, without a need to necessarily differentiate between traumatic and biological causes. Irrespective of ideas about fundamental causation, the idea of fragmentation of self remains central to those theories of psychopathology which draw upon dissociation, and more recently such positions have been argued for psychosis by van der Hart et al. (2006) and Moskowitz et al. (2019a). This conceptualisation is, we believe, compatible with the application of a schema mode framework, and potentially with other multi-self approaches including internal family systems therapy (Schwartz, 1995) and voice dialogue (Stone and Stone, 1989).

Modes and maintenance of psychosis and bipolarity

The schema mode framework complements existing cognitive-behavioural theories, and we propose that it has the potential to meaningfully elaborate and deepen such models' explanatory power for experiences of psychosis and bipolarity. It is notable that core beliefs, commonly featured in CBT models, have significant conceptual overlap with early maladaptive schemas. The mode concept, in turn, has particular relevance to changing presentations and experiences over time, which pertains to how symptoms and distress are maintained. The links made by our participants in Chapters 2 and 3 between mode activations and symptom exacerbations may not generalise to all others with the same diagnoses but indicate that such connections are possible.

A key component of cognitive–behavioural formulations are the maintenance cycles, by which difficulties are carried on over time. These have been conceptualised in diverse ways, but tend to involve an understandable coping strategy having unintended consequences: some common maintenance factors in CBTp formulations include avoidance, withdrawal, worry and rumination, scanning for danger and seeking safety in various ways (for example, Freeman, 2016). The strategy makes sense as a means to avoid immediate difficulties or to try to clarify uncertainty but ends up strengthening threat beliefs; the therapeutic intervention seeks to share this insight and to support the individual to try to alter their responses, though this can be very difficult. We note that many of these sorts of typical maintenance processes resemble the activities of modes, including coping modes. We speculate that a schema mode framework could improve our understanding of these diverse coping responses, illuminating how they developed and where the need for them might come from, potentially indicating additional therapeutic avenues. A developmental perspective might in itself help those clients who take interest in a longitudinal formulation to trace the origins of their troubling present-day experiences in historical events that were not their fault, facilitating greater self-compassion as well as potential motivation for targeted therapy tasks. A further speculation regarding hallucinations is that these could be understood as representing thoughts or experiences of dissociated modes or parts of the self, which it might be possible to engage with therapeutically, to build insight into and potentially to integrate. Such a conception is in line with theories emphasising the role of dissociation in the genesis of at least some types of psychosis (van der Hart et al., 2006; Moskowitz et al., 2019a).

We would suggest that the schema mode framework can similarly complement established cognitive behavioural theories of bipolar disorder, helping to bring meaning to the changeability of clients' presentations, as well as their ongoing struggles to regulate mood. Mansell et al.'s (2007) model, for example, helpfully includes the constructs of ascent and descent cycles as maintaining processes: patterns of thought, feeling, physiology and behaviour that convey the individual either upwards into (hypo)mania or downwards into depression. These are very important to understand and address. But why do individuals respond to some triggers with ascent patterns and to others with the opposite? One striking pattern in our bipolar participants' accounts from Chapter 3 was the respective linking of demanding modes with mania and of punitive modes with depression. Our exploratory data of course merits caution in its interpretation, but it seems possible that bringing a mode understanding to formulating an individual's mood ascent and descent cycles could improve insight into the driving factors behind these recurrent patterns, what sorts of circumstances might activate a demanding or punitive mode for example, as well as how they developed and what might be necessary to lessen their force. It is possible that individuals with bipolarity might relate especially well to a multi-selves mode framework, given their experiences of very diverse self-states.

Phenomenological perspectives on modes and our grasp of the world

We present here the theory of 'background' (Searle, 1992), which is a theory of meaning but also concerning a person's grasp of foundational certainties and practices relating to the everyday world. We will argue that states involving the dominant activation of schema modes, as well as those of extreme moods, and states of psychosis involving symptoms such as delusions, may involve types of disconnection from not only explicit beliefs and practical knowledge of the person but crucially from everyday background certainties. One subsection will focus on hallucinations as potentially involving disconnection from background knowledge, and as relating to fears and expectations connected to mode states. The last subsection looks at how bipolarity may involve a disconnection of modes concerning not only delusions or voices, but also extreme mood states.

The concepts of certainty and background

Wittgenstein (1969) remarked in his writings on certainty that as we dig deeper in challenging everyday assumptions, in the end we find a level of belief that we cannot prove, cannot offer further evidence or reasons for; it is as if we have come to a sort of 'bedrock,' of which we just say: 'I believe this is so and cannot say any more.' We can try to articulate such certainties in the form of verbal statements or rules, although these are imperfect representations, and much more is shown by our ways of reacting and behaving in the world, and in our pragmatic dispositions. Searle (1992), drawing on Wittgenstein, suggested that we can think of all that we take for granted as being enabled by a 'background' of dispositions to both generate ideas but crucially to also act in the world in specific ways: the background is foundational knowledge that allows a person to function in their everyday environment.

Rhodes and Gipps (2008) argued that the background allows or facilitates not only certainty, but a sense of what is real and not real, what is literal in contrast to what is metaphorical, and what can be trusted. Trust is clearly fundamental for our relationships with other people, but also applies to systems, governments, natural and built environments and other features of the world, as well as one's own perceptions. Trusting is a practice that is difficult to explain or articulate; likewise, we might be able to run, dance, and greet friends, but could not describe how this is carried out in words. The topic of trust is central to our understanding of those who have survived abuse and trauma, where the loss of trust, or not having developed it in the first place, is a strong feature in their testimonies (Rhodes, 2022). Ratcliffe (2017) developed several arguments concerning trust and its involvement in depression and psychosis. It is interesting to note that the issue of trust applies both to attitudes of care and affection but also a practical sense or know-how of what or who is trustworthy. A lack of trust can become a barrier to further learning when this is needed, such as in therapy (Fonagy, Luyten, and Allison, 2015).

An implication of the background concept in application to psychopathology is that when people hold what are taken to be delusions, and which Blankenburg (2001) and Stanghellini (2004) described as violating a shared 'common sense' by their community, we might understand the person as not simply making errors of logic, theory generation, scientific reasoning, perception and inference making, but rather expressing an alteration in something more foundational and pre-verbal concerning their relationship to the everyday world, its perceptions and potential actions.

Modes and disconnection from foundational certainties

Bringing together the concept of background and the theory of schema modes, we would propose that the healthy adult mode is that version of the person that does have full access to everyday certainties and foundational knowledge, allowing a skilful engagement with the world. A person's functioning with a relevant background is not a matter of being all or nothing, but rather connection with it is on a continuum, and different modes of the person will have differential access. The adult mode will have the most coherent and deep connection, while other modes will have only partial contact: the more a person experiences activation of dysfunctional modes, is absorbed or 'blended' with such modes, the more they are disconnected from the person's pragmatic certainties. Someone absorbed in a vulnerable child mode, for example, might be engaged with memories and reactions from childhood that do not reflect the pragmatic knowledge of an adult, such as how others tend to respond to their help seeking. Someone in a punitive mode likewise seems to lack access to important pragmatic social knowledge resulting in the person not being able to assess the inappropriateness of distorted and out of proportion self-attack; these ways of thinking and experiencing are usually highly focused, extreme and ignore wider contexts. When in a punitive mode, the person can experience self-attack and not seem to care if this in fact leads to self-destruction.

An individual's connection to the background and grasp of a shared reality can seem to vary across different areas of life: often there may be a contrast between aspects of social functioning and, on the other hand, issues of logic, practical skills and technical expertise. It is not rare to see clients who have highly technical jobs which they perform well, yet when it comes to social issues, such as who to trust, or in particular, how to take on a caring and sensible attitude towards themselves, they somehow seem lost, childlike, and sometimes destructive. Connecting this observation with the mode framework, we might suppose that a healthy adult part is able to maintain leadership and rely on explicit everyday knowledge, assumptions and so forth but also on background knowledge and all these within certain familiar contexts, perhaps without great emotional significance; however, in other situations, perhaps less predictable and more emotionally provocative ones, a more dysfunctional mode or modes may become dominant, and their associated disconnect ways of thinking and reacting.

The idea of a disconnection from everyday certainties and the wider background may help illuminate how individuals who are dissociated are also prone to believing extreme ideas, as well as having extreme experiences. Dissociation itself is a form of disconnection of parts or features of the self (van der Hart et al., 2006); we suggest that the more extreme manifestations of dissociation, involving a fragmentation of the personality, will also entail a disconnection from the background to varying degrees. If the disconnection is only temporary and moderate, this may allow unrealistic and exaggerated ideas to be given credence, though perhaps not to the extent of delusions. When a person is in a strongly dissociated mode, and their connection to the background very fragile, they may countenance increasingly extreme ideas.

Delusions and background

Delusions not only present unusual and sometimes extraordinary ideas but also carry a range of implications about the world which a person would normally take to be obviously impossible. When the previously well person becomes convinced that government organisations are transmitting thoughts into their mind using an implanted device somewhere in the brain, this claim can be seen as violating many things that we, and the person themselves previously, would have taken for granted. There is no evidence of any surgical operation, nor of the device itself, in any kind of scan or test, but the lack of evidence does not seem to impact the individual's conviction. No technology or method is known for the transmission of thoughts, and no reason can easily be identified for why the government would invest time and efforts in submitting an innocent citizen to such elaborate and cruel activity. The delusional belief goes beyond a fleeting catastrophic worry, but persists for extended periods and causes significant distress and functional impairment; however, when the person recovers from psychosis, they tend to reject those previously very compelling ideas, finding their own previous convictions baffling.

Delusional claims, to various degrees, seem to reject or ignore everyday and interpersonal certainties (Rhodes and Gipps, 2008); the very wide range of topics can include knowing that others and oneself exist and are alive, that solid walls cannot be walked through, that one's thoughts are silent and private, and that a human needs to eat food and breathe air. In addition, there is a range of assumptions and taken for granted ways of acting concerning others, such that most people we meet can be trusted to some degree, that they are what they appear to be such as bus drivers or doctors and are not government agents in disguise. When such everyday certainties are violated in a delusional worldview, the person can be seen as disconnected from their foundation of pragmatic knowledge and from their own former grasp of their world.

Hallucinations, modes and the background

We present here an analysis of hallucinations drawing on the concepts of modes, dissociation and disconnected background. We suggest that hallucinations, like delusions, also involve a separation from background certainties; furthermore, the disconnection from background is a constituent aspect of the dissociation involved with extreme mode states. We outline two possible examples of what may be thought of as patterns or pathways of hallucination onset. Our description here centres on voice hearing; we would hypothesise similar pathways for hallucinations in other modalities.

Onset and development with accelerating conviction

A person may on occasion experience extreme ideas and emotions that are associated with mode states such as the vulnerable child, with its deep sense of mistrust, or punitive parent. In states of fear, the person may engage in trying to work out what is going on, what is the nature of the threat that they feel, and all this might contribute to an anticipation of danger. The person could go on to imagine what a persecutor is saying or doing, and how they may be plotting harm. This can involve vivid mental imagery of terrible things that might happen, and sometimes experiences of unusual bodily sensations or distorted perceptions. What is experienced, thought, imagined and felt are potential inputs to the creation of a hallucination. Furthermore, anxious anticipation and mistrust, as Ratcliffe (2017) argues, particularly in the context of social isolation and a history of trauma, may play a key role in distorting ongoing experiences and impairing a person's ability to differentiate, for example, between what is remembered as opposed to perceived.

For those individuals with secure connections to background certainties, the continuation of distorted thinking is less likely; there may be moments of shock in which a person might succumb to threatening perceptions and thoughts, but credence in the feared entities fades as the person returns to a calm state. In contrast, the individual who experiences these fears with a fragile connection to the background, and who does not become calm, will not find it easy to discount such ideas or images: they might in fact become increasingly certain that these things are real and 'out there' in the world. Over time, as the person continues to focus on threats and danger, there may be new episodes of accelerating disturbed anticipation prompting further threatening mental content and background disconnection, followed by an increasing sense of the real and external nature of what is experienced, which in turn leads to yet more expectations, dread and background instability. Over time, a relationship with the voice often develops, and beliefs may become established about its identity and attributes, which can be understood to link with and to potentially emerge from longstanding interpersonal schemas.

Onset and development with immediate conviction

For some individuals, a voice is experienced immediately as real and external to the person, with no uncertainty. The individual continues to hear the voice, and often there is further elaboration of its character and purposes. The voice's existence and identity is not questioned because the individual experiences it without a connection to background certainties and a shared sense of reality. If a person already has preoccupying fears or delusional ideas, then a voice is likely to fit these conceptions; for example, if the person already believes themselves to be persecuted by a neighbour, then a voice of such a neighbour may be heard. The theory that delusions might make a major contribution to the occurrence of hallucinations was put forward by Janet, and supported by the observations of subsequent theorists (see Moskowitz et al. 2019b).

Maintenance

Whatever the pathway to hallucinations, maintenance involves a continued disconnection from background certainties, and often repeated episodes of being in a vulnerable child mode or other modes states, of experiencing extreme emotions, of terrible anticipation and dread based on the power and immediacy of what is perceived and felt; all of these contribute to a further loosening of the person's grip on everyday certainties, reducing access to shared reality and the healthy adult self. Without grounding in the shared world, the person can only hold with certainty that which is immediate, emotional, vivid, and often terrifying.

Linking the ideas of Bleuler to background theory

The background theory as it relates to psychosis on the one hand, and Bleuler's theory of splitting or disconnection of functions on the other, while coming from different traditions, can be seen as pointing in a similar direction: we see them as compatible and complementary. A disconnection from foundational certainties may well manifest in disjointed psychological processes, a separation of functions or connections. Where we differ from Bleuler is that we strongly believe that trauma is a major route into psychosis, though we also accept there may be a biological route; whatever the original initiating cause or change might be for psychosis, subsequently there will be manifestations in the psychological, experiential, and neurological levels of the person, and explanations relating to these different levels are relevant in parallel.

Bipolarity, modes and background

We wish to argue that extreme bipolar mood states can also involve a disconnection from foundational certainties. The accounts of participants in Chapter 3 indicated the involvement of several different mode states in mania, including demandingness and anger, and for depression, modes including punitiveness and vulnerability. Shifts into extreme mood states can thus be seen as a temporary fragmentation of the self, with the parts being disconnected in varying ways from background pragmatic knowledge. Mania may present differently depending on severity: in a milder elevated state of mood, the person might have unusual or impractical ideas, but is not deluded. A more extreme state can involve psychotic symptoms, for example persecutory or grandiose delusions. As with other forms of psychosis, when the person is well, such ideas are not accepted at all; the difference in credulity between being euthymic and manic could be linked with the strength of connection to the foundational background and everyday certainties.

When depressed, the individual may experience fears and doubts linked with the vulnerable child mode, but also suffers ferocious attacks from punitive modes. For some individuals with extreme depression, this too can be accompanied by psychotic symptoms, although this is quite rare; holding exaggerated negative ideas, however, is common, for example being convinced of future failure and abandonment despite consistent positive feedback from others. In depression, the person discounts positive appraisals and encouragement, quite unable to believe them. While not delusional, especially these fears are only predictions, their expectations seem unrealistic to others and indeed to themselves when in a better mood: we might see the depressed individual's judgement as also being affected by disconnection from former practical wisdom.

Theoretical considerations regarding modes and schemas

A continuum of states of self

Modes can be understood within the context of diverse therapies and theories of states of self, as well as everyday descriptions of variations in the states of a person. There are several widespread phrases for describing the ways in which a person might experience themselves to vary, such as 'a part of me thinks...' or 'a side of me is...' or 'I wasn't myself.' Rhodes (2022) proposed a general definition for diverse states of self as follows:

> a state of the self is a pattern of emotions, thoughts, behaviours, and attitudes which manifests itself as interconnected: furthermore, it is an open pattern, such that it repeats itself over time and yet might also change some of its constituents.
>
> (p. 91)

Modes as conceptualised by Young and colleagues are rather distinct, recurrent patterns, and do not relate to all possible changes in one's mental state; the mode framework may be a better fit to some people's experiences of their self-states than to others. Conceptualising the multiplicity of self-states on a continuum, or rather continuums of difficulty and complexity, we can illustrate three examples of what a person's constellations of states of self might look like:

1. The person generally functions well, while varying in state over time; for example, on occasions being playful, but at other times extremely serious. They may display a wide range of moods and emotions, from contentment to extreme distress. It is, however, usually the case that the person feels themselves to be more or less the same in different contexts, and that there is in fact a large degree of overlap in attitudes, thoughts, feelings, and ways of acting, which stay consistent from context to context.
2. Some individuals experience problematic states at least in some contexts, and these might involve powerful emotions or extreme attitudes, behaviours and motivations. Such states may not exactly fit the mode concept and may not have clear links to specific schemas. The causation of such states is taken to be open and could include traumas, difficult situations and experiences, extreme beliefs, or other diverse mental processes.

3. A clear manifestation of modes as described by Young et al. (2003) includes distinct states that involve the activation of schemas and associated behaviours and reactions, such as avoidance or overcompensation. In more extreme forms, these involve forms of dissociation and disconnection between aspects of the personality. Again, causation is an open question, but the more dissociated the parts, the more we would expect the involvement of trauma and adversity at early stages in the person's development.

In clinical work, a therapist be working with multiple levels or types of self-state simultaneously and would not assume that all variations of the person fit under the umbrella of a mode. Modes, too, vary in extremity and to the extent by which they can be skilfully overseen by a healthy adult part. A key aspect of the original description of modes given by Young et al. (2003) was that they were conceived as existing along a number of dimensions, with seven in particular being mentioned: from dissociated to integrated; unacknowledged to acknowledged; maladaptive to adaptive; extreme to mild; rigid to flexible; from pure to blended. This multidimensional framework conveys the openness and flexibility of the mode concept as originally set out, perhaps reflecting the fact that it was derived from clinical work and proved useful in that context.

Some elaborations of the schema mode framework have proposed many more mode types than the ten given in Young et al.'s original (2003) text; Arntz et al., (2021), for example, generated an extensive list by applying three possible coping styles to each of the early maladaptive schemas. To a certain extent, the choice of category system can be a matter of preference; therapists tend to agree that in clinical application the actual described and personally named self-states of the client should be worked with, the categories being only a guideline. Rowan's (2010) review of diverse ways in which parts of the self have been conceptualised concluded that it may not be possible to come up with one definitive system. Clinicians may differ in their preferences for fewer or more categories to hold in mind, but different classifications may also be useful for certain clinical presentations. Young's original set of modes had been developed for clients with long-term interpersonal difficulties and those diagnosed with personality disorders; it may be the case that an alternate, probably overlapping set of modes may be useful for working with different types of psychopathology: this is yet to be investigated extensively. Rhodes (2022) presented qualitative research illustrating possible types of state of self in a group of people with psychosis, producing a set of categories which were similar but not identical to Young et al.'s original (2003) classification. The ongoing refinement of a mode framework applied to different groups may also benefit from drawing further on other models that have conceptualised diverse states of self in their own ways: these include the internal family systems model of Schwartz (1995), compassion focused therapy (Gilbert, 2009) and the sensorimotor tradition (Fisher, 2017).

Behaviours in relation to schemas and modes

For some clients Schema Therapy may target one or more of an individual's specific schemas due to their prominence, while for other clients the main focus might be on working with a set of modes. Either way, part of the conceptualisation involves exploring associated behaviours and sometimes their origins. Any schema or mode can be linked with different sorts of actions, which function in diverse ways. Such behaviour patterns can develop at any age, and some may have been acquired at the very time of the formation of schemas. Behaviours linked with a vulnerable child mode, for example, can comprise a mixture including adult and adolescent responses alongside reactions, some pre-verbal, and associated with very early developmental stages.

Understanding the formation of early behaviours may be informative both for case conceptualisation and intervention planning. Behaviours expressed in the earliest years are relevant to attachment styles (Bowlby, 1969), and may be often linked with implicit and explicit memories formed alongside schema: these can be thought of as a sort of network of early associated memories, and may indicate useful targets for imagery work. It has also been noted in the therapies and theories drawing on the ideas of Janet, such as Fisher (2017) and Ogden (2019), that during trauma a person might have felt the need to carry out protective actions such as escaping or fighting, but these were impossible at the time. The person might retain the frustrated urge to try to perform such protective behaviours as a consequence of the trauma, and a fruitful therapeutic strategy could include the active expression of such actions.

Reflections on constituents of modes

We wish to make a few further observations and speculations on the nature of modes and schemas. Modes can be seen as ways of behaving, thinking, feeling, being motivated, and all in a person-specific relationship to schemas. There are therefore many aspects of modes, and we will briefly comment on some of these features: we hope that some of these ideas might prove useful to therapists in clinical work, as well as informing new questions for further research and theoretical development.

Each type of mode tends to have a different pattern in its relationship to early maladaptive schemas. Some modes, in particular the vulnerable child mode, will involve the activation of several schemas (such as abandonment or abuse) and linked concordant behaviours. In contrast, a mode such as the detached protector seems to function as an attempt to deactivate schemas in general. Some modes might well be conceived as including a combination of activation and deactivation; for example, a mode of compliance might seem to operate to deactivate certain schemas such as being abandoned, while directly activating others such as approval seeking and self-sacrifice. A self-aggrandising mode might convey an attempt to deactivate vulnerable schemas such as defectiveness, while activating schemas of entitlement.

Different modes may demonstrate diverse and complex ways of thinking. The healthy adult mode is seen as reflecting a broad, flexible and overarching perspective, while in contrast a child mode tends to be simplistic and focused on immediate threats, to the exclusion of other considerations. Furthermore, the nature of schemas themselves, as Bartlett (1995/1932) argued, is such that they act as filters and tend to simplify and distort new information to fit the established schema pattern. It is interesting to note how schemas inform the person of the nature of the self and world, that is, they seem to show or express what is true or 'obvious' for the person, however negative. A person who is immersed in the state of vulnerable child may therefore be certain of abandonment or defectiveness, and at the same time have lost access to pragmatic certainties and knowledge of the world held by the adult self, as discussed earlier, the very perspective that could counterbalance the fears of the vulnerable part.

Different modes relate to patterns of emotion in different ways. Some modes seem to be strongly linked with a particular emotion, such as the angry child primarily feeling anger, while the vulnerable child might be dominated by fear. Some modes may involve a mixture of emotions over time. The schema mode framework is compatible with polyvagal theory (Porges, 2009), which can be informative in mapping the different emotion states and their various bodily manifestations, potentially illuminating the identification of modes. Polyvagal theory, besides reactions such as anger and fear, describes states of 'shut down' an experience of being 'immobilised' or 'collapsed' (Dana, 2018); it is interesting to compare these with modes such as being detached, noting possible similarities and but also differences.

Different modes may also connect to motivations in various ways. The types of motivations involved are in some ways unique for each person, but in general one can expect that the vulnerable child is seeking security or protection, while a detached mode wishes to avoid forms of distress. The demanding mode may be pursuing goals of being perfect or correct, and therefore is seeking safety from criticism. The compliant mode seeks connection to others and wants to be liked. It is difficult to speculate concerning the possible motives of the punitive parent, which often seems so destructive, but may relate, for example, to a need to gain some sense of power or control.

Another important feature of modes, as discussed earlier, is that each person will tend to have a unique set of collection of modes, a sort of repertoire of personality states, and these might form dynamic patterns. Schwartz (1995) speculates that, just like a family, the different parts of the person will interact in characteristic ways with each other. In a similar way, one sees in in carrying out Schema Therapy how there is often a powerful interaction between a vulnerable child and demanding or critical part of self.

Finally, when a person is immersed in a particular mode they not only react in extreme ways but might also perceive others in specific ways that are related to the mode's function or role, that is, the person expediences a sort of perceived other person mode: for example, an individual in a vulnerable child mode might expect others to be punitive or demanding, and they might interpret in extreme ways or too readily see these aspects in others' behaviour. Over time certain patterns of interaction might develop drawing on modes of self and perceived other person modes, objective or otherwise. Multiple theories have explored these types of relationships between self-states and perceptions of others, and mode theory is a contribution in exploring these areas of interpersonal relations.

Concluding comments

We hope to have shown in this chapter that the concept of modes may contribute to our clinical understanding and theories of psychosis and bipolarity in a variety of ways. In addition we believe the ideas presented in this chapter, as well as the ideas and findings presented in Chapters 2 and 3, and the subsequent therapy focused chapters, all point to the ways in which schemas and modes can provide new insights for therapeutic work with psychosis and bipolarity; the rest of the book will explore how this might in fact be realised.

References

Arntz, A., Rijkeboer, M., Chan, E., Fassbinder, E., Karaosmanoglu, A., Lee, C. W., & Panzeri, M. (2021). Towards a reformulated theory underlying Schema Therapy: Position paper of an international workgroup. *Cognitive Therapy and Research, 45*, 1–14.

Bartlett, F. C. (1995/1932). *Remembering: A study in experimental and social psychology.* Cambridge University Press.

Blankenburg, W. (2001). First steps toward a psychopathology of 'common sense.' (1969). Translated by A. Mishara. *Philosophy, Psychiatry, and Psychology, 8*, 303–315.

Bleuler, E. (1950/1911). *Dementia praecox, or the group of schizophrenias.* International Universities Press.

Bowlby, J. (1969). *Attachment and loss. Vol 1: Attachment.* Hogarth Press.

Dana, D. (2018). *The polyvagal theory in therapy: Engaging the rhythm of regulation (Norton series on interpersonal neurobiology.)* Norton.

Farr, J. (2021). *Understanding the experience of mood change and early intervention for people diagnosed with bipolar disorder.* ProQuest Dissertations Publishing.

Farr, J. Rhodes, J. E., Baruch, E., & Smith, J. A. (2023). First episode psychotic mania and its aftermath: The experience of people diagnosed with bipolar disorder. *Psychosis*, 1–11.

Fisher, J. (2017). *Healing the fragmented selves of trauma survivors.* Routledge.

Fonagy, P., Luyten, P., & Allison, E. (2015). Epistemic petrification and the restoration of epistemic trust: A new conceptualization of borderline personality disorder and its psychosocial treatment. *Journal of Personality Disorders, 29*(5), 575–609.

Freeman D. (2016). Persecutory delusions: A cognitive perspective on understanding and treatment. *The Lancet Psychiatry, 3*(7), 685–692.

Gilbert, P. (2009). Introducing compassion-focused therapy. *Advances in Psychiatric Treatment, 15*(3), 199–208.

Janet, P. (1886). Les actes inconscients et le dédoublement de la personnalité pendant le somnambulisme provoqué. *Revue Philosophique de la France et de L'etranger, 22,* 577–592.

Mansell, W., Morrison, A. P., Reid, G., Lowens, I., & Tai, S. (2007). The interpretation of, and responses to, changes in internal states: An integrative cognitive model of mood swings and bipolar disorders. *Behavioural and Cognitive Psychotherapy, 35*(5), 515–539.

Moskowitz, A., & Heim, G. (2011). Eugen Bleuler's Dementia Praecox or the Group of Schizophrenias (1911): A centenary appreciation and reconsideration. *Schizophrenia Bulletin, 37*(3), 471–479.

Moskowitz, A., Heim, G, Saillot, I, & Beavan, V. (2019b). Pierre Janet on hallucinations, paranoia, and schizophrenia. In G. Craparo, F. Ortu, & O. van der Hart (eds), *Rediscovering Pierre Janet: Trauma, dissociation, and a new context for psychoanalysis.* Routledge.

Moskowitz, A., Schafer, I., & Dorahy, M. J. (2019a). *Psychosis, trauma and dissociation: Emerging perspectives on severe psychopathology* (2nd ed.). John Wiley & Sons.

Ogden, P. (2019). Acts of triumph: An interpretation of Pierre Janet and the role of the body in trauma treatment. In G. Craparo, F. Ortu, & O. van der Hart (eds), *Rediscovering Pierre Janet: Trauma, dissociation, and a new context for psychoanalysis.* Routledge.

Porges, S. W. (2009). The polyvagal theory: New insights into adaptive reactions of the autonomic nervous system. *Cleveland Clinic Journal of Medicine, 76*(Suppl 2), S86.

Ratcliffe, M. (2017). *Real hallucinations: Psychiatric illness, intentionality, and the interpersonal world.* MIT Press.

Rhodes, J. (2022). *Psychosis and the traumatised self.* Routledge.

Rhodes, J., & Gipps, R. (2008). Delusions, certainty, and the background. *Philosophy, Psychiatry, and Psychology, 15*(4), 295–310.

Rhodes, J., Jakes, S., & Robinson, J. (2005). A qualitative analysis of delusional content. *Journal of Mental Health, 14*(4), 383–398.

Rowan, J. (2010). *Personification.* Routledge.

Schwartz, R. C. (1995). *Internal family systems therapy.* Guilford.

Searle, J. R. (1992). *The rediscovery of the mind.* MIT Press.

Shiel, L., Demjén, Z., & Bell, V. (2022). Illusory social agents within and beyond voices: A computational linguistics analysis of the experience of psychosis. *British Journal of Clinical Psychology, 61*(2), 349–363.

Stanghellini, G. (2004). *Disembodied spirits and deanimated bodies: The psychopathology of common sense.* Oxford University Press.

Stone, H., & Stone, S. (1989). *Embracing our selves: The voice dialogue manual.* New World Library.

van der Hart, O., Niejenhuis, E., & Steele, K. (2006). *The haunted self: Structural dissociation and the treatment of chronic traumatisation.* Norton.

Wittgenstein, L. (1969). *On certainty.* Blackwell.

Young, E., Klosko, J. S., & Weishaar, M. E. (2003). *Schema Therapy: A practitioner's guide.* Guilford Press.

Chapter 5

Adapting Schema Therapy for psychosis and bipolarity

In this chapter we briefly outline some key features and approaches used in Schema Therapy, and we consider how these might be appropriate and useful in working with clients experiencing psychosis and bipolarity. We review existing publications exploring the use of some of these techniques and strategies with these groups, as well as considering some other therapies with overlapping conceptualisations and techniques, in particular, those which work with multiple states of the self. We outline some basic methods of assessing modes for therapeutic work in the context of psychosis and bipolarity. Finally, a series of precautions and guidelines are suggested for adapting Schema Therapy for clients with presentations including psychotic symptoms.

The aims of Schema Therapy

Schema Therapy was developed originally for working with clients who had long-term emotional and interpersonal difficulties that were not resolving with standard Cognitive Behavioural Therapy (CBT). Such individuals may have experienced recurrent or chronic depression or have attracted diagnoses of personality disorders. In response to intervention techniques, they might have seemed rigid, avoidant, detached or uncooperative. It had been noted that such clients could, for example, logically understand cognitive challenges to negative beliefs, and even agree with them, yet still not find that this had any tangible impact on the ways that they were feeling or responding in real-life situations. Young and colleagues hypothesised that these individuals' long-standing problems were linked with early maladaptive schemas and hypothesised that such reactions can develop from unmet needs in childhood or adolescence, then persist into adult years, representing the attempt to get those needs met, but operating in ways that may be maladaptive and perpetuate forms of distress.

Another observation was that many clients had extreme and diverse emotional and interpersonal states that might manifest in different situations, these being conceptualised as modes of the self as described in earlier chapters.

DOI: 10.4324/9781003350583-5

As Schema Therapy evolved in practice, the concept of modes became particularly important, especially for those clients who had a large number of early maladaptive schemas; often, in fact, too many to address separately (Arntz & Jacob, 2013). The modes were seen to reflect and emerge from schemas, but also involved what are called schema 'operations' such as attempts to avoid the effect of painful schemas by moving into a state of detachment. Schema Therapy aims to explore and then change the manifestations of schemas, modes, coping styles, social relations and other aspects of the person's functioning, with a strong emphasis on the therapeutic relationship as a vehicle for change.

Why use Schema Therapy for psychosis and bipolar disorder?

This book makes the case that Schema Therapy may add great value to clinical work with people who have experienced psychosis or bipolar conditions. The findings presented in Chapters 2 and 3 indicated that mode concepts made sense to participants. Furthermore, their self-reports consistently suggested that mode activations might not only represent important experiences in themselves but could also interact with psychotic and bipolar symptoms. This insight, we believe, is already a strong reason for exploring the potential contribution of the schema mode framework to working with psychosis and bipolarity. In addition, considerable evidence has amassed attesting to the prevalence amongst people with these diagnoses of the very issues and difficulties targeted by this specialised therapy. Chapter 1 presented a summary of these, and below we will revisit several key points.

Significant attachment disruptions and histories of early trauma have been repeatedly found in groups with diagnoses of psychosis (Gumley et al., 2014; Stanton et al., 2020) and bipolar disorder (Dualibe & Osório, 2017; Harnic et al., 2014; Morriss et al., 2009). Reviews of research examining potential pathways mediating the effect of attachment disruptions on later psychotic symptoms have identified several specific psychological processes as candidates, including emotional dysregulation, negative beliefs about the self and others, and cognitive fusion, defined as accepting and taking certain thoughts as the literal truth (Sood et al., 2021). Similarly, connections leading from trauma to subsequent psychosis have been made via disruptions of emotion regulation, episodic memory, and personal semantic memory, which principally concerns deeply held beliefs about the self and others (Hardy, 2017). Consistently, emotional difficulties and fundamental meanings about self and others are found to be core processes. Given these sorts of findings, it would seem important that therapy for people experiencing psychosis involves work with emotions and interpersonal relationships, that is, those very areas for which Schema Therapy is particularly well suited.

An additional core idea more fully discussed in Chapter 4 is that the long-term impacts of trauma can lead to structural dissociation of the personality, meaning a separation of the self into parts (van der Hart et al., 2006). This has indeed been argued to apply to those with trauma histories and psychosis (Moscovitz et al., 2019), and we see no reason that it would not apply to those with bipolarity. While modes in Schema Therapy are not assumed always to be the product of trauma, the schema mode framework is certainly compatible with the conceptualisation of structural dissociation. Such a model therefore appears relevant in application to working with the long term effects of trauma in various clinical groups.

For bipolar disorder, the evidence of pathways connecting early trauma and attachment to later symptomatology is still somewhat sparse and it has been noted that a trauma and attachment-informed conceptualisation is lacking (Hett et al., 2022). Still, findings that early trauma severity and attachment disruptions in participants with bipolar diagnoses are correlated with worse symptoms and dysfunction (Aas et al., 2016; Wrobel et al., 2022) support a similar argument for addressing interpersonal and emotional functioning in this group. The rest of the present chapter will give greater focus to working clinically with people experiencing psychosis, while applications to bipolarity are more fully addressed in Chapter 9.

Given how common histories of trauma and abuse are in people experiencing psychosis, the question has arisen of how to work with the long term effects of such early difficulties. Rhodes (2022) suggested that direct reliving of trauma memories, as may be used in the treatment of post-traumatic stress disorder, might not be appropriate for those with psychosis, given how distressing such work can be. Schema Therapy offers several ways of working with trauma which could be thought of as indirect, including techniques deriving from the work of Arntz and Weertman (1999). In imagery protocols of this type, for example, the focus is not on reliving a traumatic memory but intervening in the imagery before or after the worst parts take place, protecting and nurturing the vulnerable younger self. Drawing on these sorts of methods might well, we believe, make a significant contribution to helping with the effects of early and complex trauma. The case studies presented in this book include those with clearly reported histories of severe interpersonal trauma but also others who do not reported such events. The occurrence of psychosis or extreme mood episodes can in themselves have a traumatic impact, as can the experience of treatment in the mental health system.

It will be important to consider the complexities of psychosis and bipolar conditions, and potential reasons for being cautious in the application of a new approach. Such precautions are addressed later in this chapter. The rest of the book presents early explorations of both full and partial Schema Therapy as applied to those experiencing psychosis and bipolarity. We hope that further research and larger scale evaluations will shed further light on what the most helpful aspects of this approach might be, as well as which aspects of clients' struggles might benefit the most from it.

Key features of Schema Therapy

Schema Therapy, in working with schemas and modes, can draw on any technique used in CBT, but places a special emphasis on experiential approaches, including imagery and chair work, as well as on the therapeutic relationship, and elaborating a developmental perspective. A full list of the many approaches and practices used is beyond the scope of this chapter, but we present here a brief selection of key features. There are some further details given in the following chapters of this book, while comprehensive presentations of Schema Therapy can be found in key texts such as Young et al. (2003), Arntz and Jacob (2013), and Heath and Startup (2020).

Conceptualisation and linking the present to the past

Schema Therapy typically makes use of a case conceptualisation developed over several sessions, with a particular focus on exploring core beliefs, schemas, modes and relationships, arising from detailed discussion of the client's life history. The formulation addresses the current functioning of the person, while placing this in a developmental context. Present concerns and difficulties are linked with potential origins in events during earlier life, often childhood or adolescence. For example, the therapist and client might explore how the content and tone of an inner critical voice resemble the voice of an adult who criticised the client as a child. Having realised how a pattern of self-attack started in childhood, resulting from events that were not their fault, can empower the adult to question this type of self-talk and potentially move on to changing how they treat themselves in the present and future.

Therapeutic aims

Many aims are possible, depending on the client's goals, relevant problems, and contextual factors, such as the number of sessions that can be completed. A common set of aims in Schema Therapy, however, can be summarised as follows: to stop or ease the impact of parts which are critical or demanding, to bypass detachment and thereby allow more access to emotions and potential new experiences, to find constructive ways of expressing anger, to develop or strengthen a caring adult self and to help the client to give care, acceptance and warmth to their vulnerable parts of self.

Stages of therapy

Therapy typically proceeds in phases from beginning through to end, working in turn on somewhat different targets, sometimes with different techniques.

Young et al. (2003) suggested an initial stage of bonding and emotion regulation, followed by specific work focused on schema and mode change, then a phase encouraging increased client autonomy. This overall arc echoes that of other therapies, including trauma-focused protocols that recommend a first phase of stabilisation before other types of work are initiated.

Imagery

Imagery is used in a wide range of ways to address many issues. A considerable amount of work may be focused on using imagery to explore past difficulties, and then to move on to a phase where care and compassion is given to the image of the young self in distress. Imagery work can also focus on present difficulties and on imagining how the person might wish to be in the future. Specific protocols of imagery work have been developed for working with memories of early trauma (Arntz & Weertman, 1999).

Chair work

Chair work, like imagery, can have a multitude of uses (Pugh, 2019). A key application in Schema Therapy is to open dialogues with various modes, and in general between parts of the self. A client, for example, might sit in one chair and from that position express self-criticism. The person may then be encouraged to move to another chair and to consider how a different part of the self might respond: it could then be noted that the criticism expressed was too harsh and unhelpful. This creates opportunities for perspective-taking from multiple positions, the potential occurrence of new ideas about how to move forwards, and active practice in different kinds of self-dialogue. Chair work can be used for exploring dilemmas, in which different parts of the self might be aligned with differing priorities, and negotiating around conflicts in which multiple modes may relate to mutually incompatible courses of action.

Therapeutic relationship, limited reparenting and empathic confrontation

The quality of the therapeutic relationship is held as central to facilitating progress in Schema Therapy. In service of this, the therapist emphasises a warm and caring attitude in their stance towards the client, rather than one of detachment or a focus on purely technical application of interventions. In the early stages, building a secure attachment through the professional relationship, termed 'limited reparenting,' is a key aim, with the therapist seeking to do what they can to address the client's unmet emotional needs, to the extent that is appropriate in this context. Building a relationship involving compassion and trust can also make possible the effective use of 'empathic confrontation,' in which modes and patterns that have become maladaptive or dysfunctional can be approached with understanding and appreciation, while at the same time setting limits and being firm with boundaries where needed.

The use of Schema Therapy for psychosis to date

Rhodes (2022) described using a modified form of Schema Therapy for psychosis, illustrating elements from work with a number of different individuals, as well as presenting an in-depth case study. In the latter, the client's voices, self-harm and depression were conceptualised using modes. The therapy focused on attempting to give care and compassion to an image of the young self, in addition to building up a sense that she could survive and ignore repeated attacks by a persecuting voice, which appeared to stand for, or somehow represent, a perception of her abusive father. The therapy was extended over a two-year period, spanning active phases and breaks, and on re-assessment the outcomes indicated a substantial reduction in the frequency of the voice hearing experience, a recovery from deep depression and a greater involvement in various community activities. The essence of the work was the development of a new relationship between the adult self and her former child self, becoming allied in resistance against the tyranny of the terrible voice and, further, becoming able to feel safe in spite of its threats.

There are a small number of published studies evaluating specific therapeutic techniques using imagery in the context of psychosis, and these have tended to draw on the approach of Arntz and Weertman (1999). Paulik, Steel and Arntz (2019) used imagery rescripting in a case-series of 12 participants with diagnoses of psychosis and histories of abuse. The results demonstrated a reduction in the voices, distress, frequency and intrusions of trauma. The work of Paulick and colleagues is presented in Chapter 7 of this book. Taylor et al. (2020) reported on short-term therapy with five participants who experienced distressing imagery in the context of psychosis with persecutory delusions; their approach combined imagery rescripting and the cognitive behavioural approach of Hackman (2011). There was a focus on the person's negative schematic beliefs and negative imagery. The results suggested significant reductions in negative schemas, delusions, imagery distress, and changes in measures of schemas and schema modes. Work by Taylor and colleagues is presented in Chapter 6.

Therapies for psychosis with similarities to Schema Therapy

In Chapter 4, we described some of the therapies that in different ways work with parts of the self and which were not initially formulated for working with psychosis; the history of these sorts of therapy is well summarised by Rowan (2010). Among those in recent times working with parts of the self and trauma are van der Hart et al. (2006) and Fisher (2017), who draw on the original work of Janet (1886). We also noted in Chapter 4 that several therapists working explicitly with parts of the self have explored applications of their approaches to psychosis: van der Hart in particular emphasising work with trauma and psychosis. Protocols have been published focused on hearing voices, such as Corstens et al. (2012) and Longden et al. (2021): a central aim of such approaches being to explore the development and evolution of the voices' manifestations in the client's life. A narrative of the development of the voices is informed by a careful analysis of the difficulties and stresses the person experienced around the time of their onset. A key intervention is then the voice dialogue approach, as developed by Stone and Stone (1989), in effect encouraging communication between parts of the self. Lysaker and Lysaker (2001) similarly formulated therapy for psychosis employing the concept of the dialogic self (Herman & Dimaggio, 2004), which suggests that a person is composed of many voices or 'I-positions' between which dialogue can occur; for example, one might speak from a perspective of confidence but subsequently say something else from a position of feeling vulnerable. A central aim of this therapy was to enrich the complexity of dialogue between the different positions.

The use of parts of self is also found in Compassion Focussed Therapy for psychosis (Heriot-Maitland et al., 2019): here a key task is to build up and strengthen a compassionate version of the self, from which position care and compassion can then be given to other parts that may struggle or react in triggering situations. Compassion Focussed Therapy does not use a set taxonomy of types of parts or modes, as in Schema Therapy, but the compassionate self concept shares a lot with the healthy adult mode, and there has been a suggestion that the two approaches could benefit from each other (Thrift & Irons, 2020). Sood et al. (2021) who focused particularly on the contribution of attachment have also begun to explore therapy whereby a sense of 'felt security' could be developed using imagery in which care is given to the vulnerable self.

While the above therapies do not employ a full mode conceptualisation, and differ in other aspects from Schema Therapy, we believe that they contribute convergent support to the utility of the multi-self concept and related techniques in working with psychosis. We will next move on to direct practices and techniques taken from Schema Therapy that we believe may have clinical utility.

Describing and accessing states of self

The mode states of a person can be explored and described using a wide range of questions and approaches. Accessing these is helped by the fact that it is quite common in everyday language to talk of oneself as having different states: a client might for example say 'part of me is not sure about this,' 'I didn't feel like my normal self,' or 'I was in two minds about the situation,' and the therapist can build further exploration upon such spontaneous talk. Other methods for accessing and conceptualising multi-self-states are as follows.

Questions about present and recent examples

The simplest way to explore modes is to note any strong feelings and reactions that have occurred recently; for example, with regard to hearing a voice or navigating an anxiety-provoking journey, or in dealing with other people. We might ask, 'Do aspects of the way you react concern you?' 'Are you ever surprised or puzzled by how you react in different situations?' and 'How would you list the different states you experience?' As appropriate, questions might explore the person's thoughts, feelings, bodily sensations, attitudes and social interactions. One can then ask, 'Is this a way of reacting that you have often experienced?' The client can be asked about how they tend to feel in some specific types of situations that are associated with strong or conflicting emotions. Some specific questions might be along the following lines:

Do you criticize yourself? In what way?
Do you make a lot of demands on yourself?
How do you speak or say things to yourself? What do you say?
Do you ever feel cut off or with little feeling or emotion?
What is it like when you are most distressed, upset, lonely, despairing? What feelings do you have at such times?
Do you ever experience anger or rage? What kind of situations does this happen in and what are you like at such times?
How do you behave and react in conflict with others?
Do you feel you are very different at different times? If so, in what ways are you different at different times?
What is it like when you feel got at or attacked by others?

For some clients, chair work can be helpful in these explorations: for example, the client could be asked to sit in a specific chair and express how a critical part of self might expresses its thoughts, with different chairs to be used for different parts. The therapist can also use the standard descriptions of modes given in the literature, asking whether the client recognizes any of these as occurring in themselves. Further exploration can involve asking the client to keep a structured record or diary of their shifting states, with questions on feelings, reactions and bodily sensations.

Direct exploration as occurring in sessions

The way that a client reacts and interacts with the therapist can greatly inform an assessment of mode states. It is helpful to note any changes occurring within the course of a session, such as the client becoming very quiet or withdrawn, which may indicate moving into a detached state, or becoming tearful, potentially indicating activation of a vulnerable mode. Given a good therapeutic relationship, one can ask how the person feels in that moment, how this might differ from a few moments before and how the shift might relate to topics being discussed. A client of course may demonstrate any of the mode states while talking to the therapist, including anger, fear or detachment. Reactions may manifest noticeably in the person's body, such as a tremor or shifting posture. Briedis and Startup (2020) give many examples of how one can incorporate a focus on the body in Schema Therapy, including how mode activations might be expressed in different physiological changes and movements.

Exploring person specific imagery

A technique sharing features with Internal Family Systems (Schwartz, 1995) as well as Compassion Focused Therapy, involves encouraging the client to generate their own unique mental images of their different self-states, with attributes detailed such as how they look, the tone of voice in which they speak. These could be based on a version of the client's own self-image, such as a younger self, or on another character entirely, or a non-human entity that might symbolise a mode. It can be informative to ask the client how they feel towards a newly generated image such as towards a demanding or punitive mode figure. The answer may reveal another mode related to the one most recently discussed: for example, if the client felt fear towards a punitive mode, the therapist may suggest envisaging what the fearful part may look like, sound like, and so forth, with an agreement to return to the punitive mode later on. There is therefore a great emphasis on what one part thinks or feels towards another; these reactions of the person towards aspects of themselves can be quite easy to miss unless there are explicit questions.

The client's attitude towards a vulnerable part is important to ask about, as this pertains to the central task of Schema Therapy in healing that mode: the person might feel a distance or a lack of warmth, or indeed disgust or irritation with a vulnerable part, and these may indicate important tasks to prioritise in therapy. Developing an open attitude such as curiosity or compassion towards a vulnerable part will be necessary along the way to fostering more functional relationships among diverse parts of the self.

Use of questionnaires

The questionnaires developed by Young and colleagues for modes and schemas can greatly inform clinical work. Sometimes a client's responses may confirm the presence of a mode which is fairly obvious from their case history or presentation, but at other times aspects may be highlighted that the person may not have spontaneously discussed. Some modes are less conspicuous and accessible for clients than others, perhaps because they have not attracted conscious reflection or due to seeming more socially unacceptable in the person's culture. Following up questionnaire responses, we seek to generate mode labels that make sense to the client to describe their individual and distinct experiences. The mode inventories can be useful in suggesting certain predominant themes in the person's life, but elaboration of versions unique to the person is always illuminating.

Assessing early life experiences

One approach suggested by Young et al. (2003) for the early stages assessment was to ask the client to imagine an upsetting situation with their primary caregivers, and then to explore if any schemas or modes emerge. We would not recommend the early use of this strategy with all clients experiencing psychosis, due to the potential high levels of distress that might be generated; it might be clinically appropriate for those whose presentation is very stable, and who are relatively well equipped to regulate emotion. Clients with bipolar diagnoses who are in a stable phase of relatively balanced mood are generally found to be able to tolerate and engage with this assessment technique, as in classic Schema Therapy.

Overview and conceptualisation

In applying and modifying Schema Therapy with psychotic and bipolar clients there are many potential sources of information, and these can be brought together in a shared conceptualisation. Specific and simple conceptualisations can be developed collaboratively with clients and modified as appropriate over time. Some clients might appreciate a complex developmental formulation, but for others it may be more useful to share something very immediate, such as noticing that the person becomes very fearful of others in certain types of social situations, which can be linked to the feelings of a vulnerable part. We would advise care to be taken where a client holds fixed delusions: the mode conceptualisation should not be offered as an alternative to an existing belief system but a complimentary way of understanding one's emotional and interpersonal responses to unfolding events, whatever those may be. Further details on case conceptualisation will be covered in later chapters.

Some preliminary guidelines for adapting Schema Therapy for psychosis

Given the reports already published applying aspects of Schema Therapy with psychosis and bipolarity, as well as the relevant supporting theories reviewed, a full or partial application of this therapeutic approach merits further exploration in these groups. We think this might have relevance both for those clients who report histories of abuse and trauma, but likewise for those who do not report such explicit mistreatment. The following chapters will illustrate various uses of Schema Therapy for psychosis, particularly paranoia and voices, and finally for bipolarity.

In this book we are not advocating the full use of Schema Therapy as originally practised for all those with psychosis regardless of symptom severity or phase of recovery. The approach is unlikely be accessible for those clients who are in crisis or extremely preoccupied with positive symptoms. Experiencing positive symptoms of psychosis, however, is not in itself, we believe, a barrier to therapy, as long as the individual wishes to pursue therapy, is clear on the issue of giving consent for therapy, is motivated to attend, can sustain a focus, carry out homework tasks and is willing to talk about personal difficulties. In order to appropriately adapt Schema Therapy for clients with psychosis and bipolar conditions, and to maximise its usefulness, we would advise some precautions and guidelines as follows.

The first key guideline we would advise for application to psychosis is that there should be, in general, a focus on immediate experience. The present experiential world of the client and any associated distress are central. We would generally caution against sharing elaborate hypotheses that go beyond conspicuous evidence or which make complex historical inferences: achieving a shared understanding of the here-and-now is a priority. If a client wishes to talk about a voice, discussion can focus around its present manifestations and how those affect the person; one should not rush to any hypotheses about the origin or causation of the voice, such as abuse or trauma or anything else. A focus on trauma might in fact not be relevant or suitable at any stage for some clients. Of course, as therapy unfolds the dialogue will change, and the client may become more interested in, and open to, multiple alternative explanations, and even ones focusing on early years. Such topics, however, should only be explored when the person is clearly ready, has means of achieving calm and stability, and is motivated.

Links made to the past, at any stage of therapy, should be offered cautiously and presented only as tentative ideas, something to consider and indeed to reject if they do not feel useful. When participants were asked about links between present psychotic symptoms and past abuse in the research reported in Rhodes (2022), none identified such links for themselves, although quite often they did link abuse with other issues such as anxiety and social difficulties. These findings suggested that it might in fact be quite rare for clients to see any possible links between early mistreatment and, for example, a current experience of voice hearing. To insist on any causal explanation counter to the client's own view risks disempowering them or damaging the therapeutic relationship. It might also in some cases be seen as blaming important others, such as early caregivers, which might not be tolerable for some clients, even where there has been obvious abuse. For these reasons we do not think it useful with most clients experiencing psychosis to present a full conceptualisation very early in the work making strong developmental or causal claims;

discussion of such ideas might become appropriate at a later stage. It is best, we believe, that any formulation should start in areas where there can be clear agreement and collaboration, which is often in the present, and only introduce further connections when the therapeutic relationship is established, and the client is in a more empowered position to reflect on and participate in these types of meaning-making.

If therapy does in fact need to address trauma, and the client is motivated to do this, then we would recommend the use of more indirect methods such as the type of imagery rescripting described earlier, rather than approaches focused on reliving traumatic memories, as the latter are more likely to be retraumatising. Furthermore, in complex trauma clients may find it very difficult to get any clear and exact memories to work on, which necessitates the use of indirect techniques.

Some clients express ambivalence about their convictions in voices or delusions at assessment or during therapy; however, at other times, particularly when in distress, the same client can swing into extreme conviction. It is therefore generally a helpful stance to remain open and not to assume how the attitudes of the client might unfold over time. We might further propose that any individual can hold quite seemingly contradictory beliefs simultaneously, and it might well be the case that different beliefs are held by different parts of the self.

If therapy is a type of journey, then it is one on which clients are often not at all sure whether it is a good idea to embark or proceed: it is not clear for them whether the other can be trusted, and it might be that the places discovered will be frightening if not destructive. It is potentially dangerous, like any expedition into undiscovered territory; as the person proceeds, each step needs to be safe and steady, and they need to feel that there is a way to pull back if situations become confusing or threatening.

Overview

A great deal of research and theory now suggests that a range of emotional, cognitive and interpersonal factors make major contributions to the experiences of psychosis and bipolarity, including emotion dysregulation, extreme beliefs about the self and others, and dissociation. These issues are key targets in Schema Therapy, which was developed specifically for those who have experienced attachment difficulties and interpersonal trauma. While a full developmentally focused therapy may not be appropriate for all clients, or at all times, specific conceptualisations and strategies addressing multiple states of self may be very useful even for those who would not find a complete Schema Therapy intervention accessible or acceptable. Clients in stable states and who are well resourced psychologically may in fact be able to engage in the full therapy. While using a developmental framework, Schema Therapy retains a focus on addressing present and unfolding patterns of experience, which we also find to be an advantage when working with complexity. Proceeding with caution, we hope that therapists can continue to explore these potential applications and developments.

The following four chapters are dedicated to exploring clinical applications, extending earlier work adapting Schema Therapy for working with individuals experiencing psychosis and bipolar conditions. Chapters 6 and 7 report on protocols of imagery rescripting, which can be a stand-alone therapeutic approach within the family of cognitive behavioural therapies but is also central to Schema Therapy, particularly where notions of mode states may be used to understand and address vulnerable and critical parts. Chapters 8 and 9 build on the approach of Rhodes (2022), using a schema mode framework for working with paranoia in psychosis and then with bipolarity.

References

Aas, M., Henry, C., Andreassen, O. A., Bellivier, F., Melle, I., & Etain, B. (2016). The role of childhood trauma in bipolar disorders. *International Journal of Bipolar Disorders*, 4(1), 2.

Arntz, A. & Jacob, G. (2013). *Schema Therapy in practice*. Wiley-Blackwell.

Arntz, A., & Weertman, A. (1999). Treatment of childhood memories: Theory and practice. *Behaviour Research and Therapy*, 37(8), 715–740.

Briedis, J., & Startup, H. (2020). Somatic perspective in Schema Therapy: The role of the body in the awareness and transformation of modes and schemas. In G. Heath, & H. Startup (eds), *Creative methods in Schema Therapy*. Routledge.

Corstens, D., Longden, E., & May, R. (2012). Talking with voices: Exploring what is expressed by the voices people hear. *Psychosis*, 4, 95–101.

Dualibe, A. L., & Osório, F. L. (2017). Bipolar disorder and early emotional trauma: A critical literature review on indicators of prevalence rates and clinical outcomes. *Harvard Review of Psychiatry*, 25(5), 198.

Fisher, J. (2017). *Healing the fragmented selves of trauma survivors*. Routledge.

Gumley, A. I., Taylor, H. E. F., Schwannauer, M., & MacBeth, A. (2014). A systematic review of attachment and psychosis: Measurement, construct validity and outcomes. *Acta Psychiatrica Scandinavica*, 129(4), 257–274.

Hackman, A. (2011). Imagery rescripting in posttraumatic stress disorder. *Cognitive and Behavioral Practice*, 18, 424–432.

Hardy, A. (2017). Pathways from trauma to psychotic experiences: A theoretically informed model of posttraumatic stress in psychosis. *Frontiers in Psychology*, 8, 697–717.

Harnic, D., Pompili, M., Innamorati, M., Erbuto, D., Lamis, D. A., Bria, P.,... & Janiri, L. (2014). Affective temperament and attachment in adulthood in patients with Bipolar Disorder and Cyclothymia. *Comprehensive Psychiatry*, 55(4), 999–1006.

Heath, G., & Startup, H. (eds). (2020). *Creative methods in Schema Therapy: Advances and innovation in clinical practice*. Routledge.

Heriot-Maitland, C., McCarthy-Jones, S., Longden, E., & Gilbert, P. (2019). Compassion focused approaches to working with distressing voices. *Frontiers in Psychology*, 10, 152.

Herman, J. M., & Dimaggio, G. (eds). (2004). *The dialogical self in psychotherapy*. Routledge.

Hett, D., Etain, B., & Marwaha, S. (2022). Childhood trauma in bipolar disorder: new targets for future interventions. *BJPsych Open, 8*(4), e130.

Janet, P. (1886). Les actes inconscients et le dédoublement de la personnalité pendant le somnambulisme provoqué. *Revue Philosophique de la France et de L'etranger, 22*, 577–592.

Longden, E., Corstens, D., Morrison, A. P., Larkin, A., Murphy, E., Holden, N.,... & Bowe, S. (2021). A treatment protocol to guide the delivery of dialogical engagement with auditory hallucinations: Experience from the talking with voices pilot trial. *Psychology and Psychotherapy: Theory, Research and Practice, 94*(3), 558–572.

Lysaker, P. H., & Lysaker, J. T. (2001). Psychosis and the disintegration of dialogical self-structure: Problems posed by schizophrenia for the maintenance of dialogue. *British Journal of Medical Psychology, 74*, 23–33.

Morriss, R. K., van der Gucht, E., Lancaster, G., & Bentall, R. P. (2009). Adult attachment in bipolar 1 disorder. *Psychology and Psychotherapy: Theory, Research and Practice, 82*(3), 267–277.

Moskowitz, A., Schafer, I., & Dorahy, M. J. (2019). *Psychosis, trauma and dissociation: Emerging perspectives on severe psychopathology* (2nd ed.). John Wiley & Sons.

Paulik, G, Steel, C, & Arntz, A. (2019). Imagery rescripting for the treatment of trauma in voice hearers: A case series. *Behavioural and Cognitive Psychotherapy 47*, 709–725.

Pugh, M. (2019). *Cognitive behavioural chairwork: Distinctive features*. Routledge.

Rhodes, J. (2022). *Psychosis and the traumatised self*. Routledge.

Rowan, J. (2010). *Personification*. Routledge.

Schwartz, R. C. (1995). *Internal family systems therapy*. Guilford.

Sood, M., Carnelley, K. B., & Newman-Taylor, K. (2021). How does attachment imagery for paranoia work? Cognitive fusion and beliefs about self and others mediate the impact on paranoia and anxiety. *Psychology and Psychotherapy: Theory, Research, and Practice, 94*(4), 973–993.

Stanton, K. J., Denietolis, B., Goodwin, B. J., & Dvir, Y. (2020). Childhood trauma and psychosis: An updated review. *Child and Adolescent Psychiatric Clinics, 29*(1), 115–129.

Stone, H., & Stone, S. (1989). *Embracing our selves: The voice dialogue manual*. New World Library.

Taylor C, Bee P, Kelly J, Emsley R, Haddock G. (2020). *iMAgery focused psychological therapy for persecutory delusions in PSychosis (iMAPS): A multiple baseline experimental case series. *Behavioural & Cognitive Psychotherarpy, 48*, 530–543.

Thrift, O., & Irons, C. (2020). Developing a compassionate mind to strengthen the healthy adult. In Heath, G. & Startup, H. (eds), *Creative methods in Schema Therapy*. Routledge.

van der Hart, O., Niejenhuis, E., & Steele, K. (2006). *The haunted self: Structural dissociation and the treatment of chronic traumatisation*. Norton.

Wrobel, A. L., Russell, S. E., Jayasinghe, A., Lotfaliany, M., Turner, A., Dean,... & McInnis, M. G. (2022). Attachment insecurity partially mediates the relationship between childhood trauma and depression severity in bipolar disorder. *Acta Psychiatrica Scandinavica, 145*(6), 591–603.

Young, E., Klosko, J. S., & Weishaar, M. E. (2003). *Schema Therapy: A practitioner's guide*. Guilford Press.

Chapter 6

Attachment, schemas and imagery focused therapy for psychosis (iMAPS)

By Nicola Airey, Katherine Berry[†] and
Christopher D. J. Taylor[‡]

In the last 40 years, the role of mental imagery in mental health conditions has been explored (Ji et al., 2019), including as a therapeutic strategy (see Hackmann and Holmes (2004) for a review). The use of therapeutic imagery with psychosis populations is a less researched but growing area. Within this chapter, we attempt to synthesise the most recent therapeutic imagery research for psychosis, which can target a range of symptoms. We also describe an imagery approach which integrates attachment theory, working with intrusive mental images and negative schemas to target trauma associated with experiencing psychosis. Interpersonal features such as early attachment relationships are important to consider, so that traumatising patterns are not repeated in therapy, and people can be helped to develop secure attachment relationships with their therapists. For psychosis populations, this is particularly important, given the high prevalence of traumatic or adverse childhood experiences (Varese et al., 2012), insecure attachment patterns (Carr et al., 2018) and trauma from aspects of treatment (Berry et al., 2013; Buswell et al., 2021) experienced by this group.

* Nicola Airey is a Clinical Psychologist who qualified from the University of Manchester in 2023. She currently works at Navigo Health and Social Care CiC in Complex Mental Health Rehabilitation.
† Katherine Berry is a Professor in Clinical Psychology at the University of Manchester and Co-director of the Complex Trauma and Resilience Research Unit (C-TRU) at Greater Manchester Mental Health NHS Foundation Trust. She has carried out extensive research into the psychological and social causes of severe mental health problems and the development and evaluation of psychological therapies.
‡ Christopher D. J. Taylor (ClinPsyD, PhD, AFBPsS) is a Consultant Clinical Psychologist with Pennine Care NHS Foundation Trust and Honorary Lecturer in Clinical Psychology at The University of Manchester. He has conducted a number of studies on core beliefs, schema and imagery in psychosis. In 2021, he was a recipient of the British Psychological Society's May Davidson Award for contributions to Clinical Psychology.

DOI: 10.4324/9781003350583-6

Imagery in psychosis

Imagery has been utilised in therapeutic forms across history and cultures for 20,000 years (Edwards, 2011). Mental imagery is defined as images within the mind's eye, but this is not limited to a visual representation; rather it can integrate any of the five sensory modalities (i.e. sight, sound, smell, taste, touch; Kosslyn et al., 2001). While the relationship between imagery and psychosis has been of interest since the 1930s (Cohen, 1938), research had predominantly focused on the role of imagery in the development, maintenance and causal mechanisms of psychosis. Two cross-sectional studies found that almost three quarters of participants experienced involuntary, intrusive imagery in relation to their psychotic symptoms (hallucinations, delusions), which tended to be linked to affective responses and core beliefs (Morrison et al., 2002; Schulze et al., 2013).

Further to this, a failure to recognise or identify intrusive images as being related to previous traumatic experiences has been postulated as a factor in why some people develop psychosis rather than Post-Traumatic Stress Disorder (PTSD) in response to traumatic life events (Morrison et al., 2003). Moreover, the interpretation of such intrusions is key; the perception that the intrusions are culturally unacceptable contributes to psychosis, with distress associated with threat or powerlessness in the face of these experiences (Morrison, 2001). It is well established that childhood adversity and trauma drastically increase the likelihood of psychosis (Varese et al., 2012), with trauma exposure also linked to psychosis symptom development (Schäfer & Fisher, 2011), greater symptom severity (Bailey et al., 2018) and the risk of relapse (Martland et al., 2020). Moreover, individuals developing psychosis are then exposed to further trauma, in the form of the psychosis itself or treatment experiences, which often include involuntary admissions, forced medication, seclusion and restraint (Berry et al., 2013). This can lead to 'psychosis-related PTSD,' the prevalence of which is estimated at between 11 per cent and 67 per cent (Berry et al., 2013; Buswell et al., 2021). Thus, individuals with psychosis may experience imagery as components of past trauma, their psychosis or psychosis-related trauma, leading us to seek to target imagery directly as part of the therapeutic repertoire for this population.

Therapeutic imagery

The available research around the use of mental imagery in therapeutic settings is predominantly in the form of case studies and case series. The first studies in this area utilised cognitive-behavioural approaches, with an emphasis on mental imagery during the course of therapy (Morrison, 2004; Serruya & Grant, 2009); by targeting imagery associated with delusions, reductions were seen in associated distress and the conviction in these beliefs. In the last decade, research has explored standalone imagery techniques, with many case series focusing on imagery rescripting. By utilising this technique, participants have been able to change intrusive images or memories related to different aspects of their psychosis. Distress reduction, amongst other positive outcomes, through imagery rescripting has been found for voice-hearing content (Paulik et al., 2019), nightmares (Sheaves et al., 2015) and present-focused self-referential meaning from trauma memories (Clarke et al., 2022). Notable changes have even been illustrated in as little as one imagery rescripting session (Ison et al., 2014).

Traditional trauma therapies typically include imagery components to support or enhance reprocessing of trauma memories. There is evidence for the use of prolonged exposure, Eye Movement Desensitisation and Reprocessing (EMDR) and Cognitive Behavioural Therapy (CBT) to treat PTSD in psychosis samples (e.g. Steel et al., 2017; van den Berg et al., 2015; Varese et al., 2023), with further trials ongoing. In addition to the case series evidence mentioned above relating to imagery rescripting, there is also evidence for the use of imaginal exposure and reprocessing with a trauma-focus in psychosis populations. Keen et al. (2017) integrated trauma-focused CBT, CBT for psychosis and imaginal strategies (reliving and rescripting) into a nine-month intervention. Within the nine participants, reliable improvements were seen in several outcome measures: 63 per cent PTSD symptoms, 25 per cent voices, 50 per cent delusions, 50 per cent depression, 36 per cent anxiety and 40 per cent wellbeing. Moreover, Brand et al. (2021) targeted trauma-related auditory hallucinations using imaginal exposure and saw a large reduction in auditory hallucination severity at one-month follow-up.

There is a growing body of evidence that suggests that 'positive' imagery, as opposed to imagery focused on changing negative experiences (symptoms, memories, intrusive images), has a useful role in psychosis. Positive imagery is an established and central technique in some therapy protocols, including EMDR (Shapiro, 2001), Schema Therapy (Young et al., 2003) and Compassion Focused Therapy (Gilbert, 2009), whereby imagery is utilised to strengthen positive feelings or instil feelings of safety in order to help people tolerate some of the more emotionally challenging aspects of therapy. There is evidence that positive imagery can have useful effects in psychosis populations also; for example, Smith et al. (2022) examined the effects of a positive guided imagery task used with 44 people with first episode psychosis; positive guided imagery, compared to neutral imagery, increased participants' ability to engage in positive future-directed thinking.

Moreover, both positive and negative-focused imagery techniques have been combined into an imagery-focused protocol for psychosis: iMAgery therapy for PSychosis (iMAPS). Taylor et al. (2019) describe the full treatment protocol, but, in brief, iMAPS comprises six sessions of imagery-based therapy. The first session involves defining imagery and exploring the client's experience of this (content, quality, controllability, frequency, threat, distress), assessing their history, core and schematic beliefs, psychotic experiences and coping behaviours, to inform a subsequent formulation. Session two is dedicated to continuing assessment and drawing the information into a collaborative formulation, with an identified imagery 'target' for future intervention sessions. This can be the intrusive mental images themselves, schematic core beliefs or negative memories associated with the schemas and images. Within the second session, imagery strategies are introduced using the 'safe place' exercise, whereby individuals develop imagery of a place of comfort and safety that can be used as a grounding or mental-respite strategy during therapy. It also acts as a gentle introduction to imagery work, with non-threatening content so a client can become familiar with practising these techniques. This can be helpful before using imagery techniques to tackle early negative experiences that have led to the development of negative schematic beliefs or working with distressing intrusive images. Sessions three, four and five use image change techniques to target difficult imagery and develop positive imagery, informed by the formulation. The iMAPS protocol finishes with a final summary session to review the problem imagery and consolidate learning (e.g. psychoeducation, new coping strategies, and changed imagery). Taylor, Bee, et al. (2020) and Cairns et al. (2023) demonstrated the feasibility of the iMAPS protocol as an in-person and tele-health intervention, which was bolstered by significant improvements in negative schematic beliefs, delusions and imagery distress. A third case series has recently adapted the iMAPS formulation model and therapy approach with an attachment focus by integrating considerations for interpersonal safety and intra-personal safety through guided imagery. The intervention saw good recruitment and retention, with an overall improvement in 'felt security' (i.e. a sense of safety and security in the moment) during the intervention phase, compared with baseline. This model and two case studies will be discussed later in the chapter.

There is a growing evidence base for the use of therapeutic imagery to target several psychological mechanisms that can maintain symptoms and distress in psychosis populations, such as images and schemas. Although this evidence is predominantly in case series form at this stage, findings support the feasibility and acceptability of imagery-focused interventions, delivered either in standalone format or integrated as part of a more complex therapeutic protocol.

The role for attachment in imagery therapy

Attachment theory states that humans are predisposed as infants to form bonds with caregivers in order to manage distress and enhance feelings of safety, allowing the child to explore and learn (Bowlby, 1969). When exposed to consistent, reliable and responsive caregivers, secure attachments are more likely to occur, supporting the development of adaptive coping and emotion regulation skills (Bowlby, 1988). Insecure attachments are more likely to develop when infants perceive their caregivers to be inconsistent, rejecting, reactive or frightening and as such, difficulties in regulating emotions and developing secure interpersonal relations are more likely to arise (Ainsworth,

1979; Main & Solomon, 1986). The consideration of attachment arguably has a role in all types of therapy: in formulating and processing relational experiences, considering countertransference, separation, boundaries, and in the termination of therapy (Berry & Danquah, 2016).

Therapy is ultimately the forming of a (time-limited) relationship within which support is provided with the aim of prompting meaningful change. Importantly, the qualities of 'good' therapeutic alliances are similar to those of secure attachments formed with earlier caregivers (Feeney & Van Vleet, 2010). Ideally a 'secure base' is formed within which corrective emotional experiences can occur, with the therapeutic alliance thus providing a platform for exploration of potentially anxiety-provoking experiences (Berry & Danquah, 2016). This process is particularly relevant for psychosis populations, who display disproportionately high levels of insecure attachment patterns: 76 per cent in psychosis samples compared to 38 per cent in non-clinical samples (Carr et al., 2018). Insecure attachment has been implicated in several areas of psychosis, including the development and maintenance of hallucinations, delusions and negative symptoms (see Berry et al. (2019) for a comprehensive overview). Hence, it is reasonable to suggest that if insecure attachment increases the risk of psychosis, then enhancing attachment security could play a role in improving distressing symptomology and recovery prospects.

The facilitation of a sense of 'felt security' is a means of priming feelings of interpersonal safety through therapeutic techniques, including using guided positive imagery. An example could be baking with a loved one in childhood or a fond family memory on a favourite holiday, where the individual felt psychologically safe, secure and relaxed. Drawing upon such imagery can elicit similar feelings in the present and have other positive effects including improvements in affect and reductions in paranoia (Pitfield et al., 2020; Sood et al., 2021). Newman-Taylor (2020) demonstrated that felt security could offer a means to facilitate safe and effective trauma processing without exacerbating arousal in a woman with psychosis. While this evidence is positive, enhancing security may not be straightforward in people with insecure attachment styles; in cases with high levels of anxious attachment, negative effects of secure attachment imagery may be seen (Hutton et al., 2017). This aligns with the concept of fear of compassion (Mikulincer & Shaver, 2010): insecurely attached individuals may have felt neglect and abandonment in earlier caregiving relationships, and fear that negative experiences will follow displays of compassion. Nevertheless, utilising attachment imagery may be a useful tool to facilitate more challenging trauma-related or emotionally burdensome aspects of therapy, as was at the heart of Schema Therapy (Young et al., 2003).

Schemas in psychosis

Schemas incorporate our beliefs about ourselves, others and the world around us, thus providing a framework for us to make sense of our life experiences. If core emotional and relational needs are not met, then early maladaptive schemas (EMS; Young, 1990) begin to develop; these being a persistent pattern of emotion, thought or other experiences. Several studies have examined early maladaptive schemas in individuals with psychosis, using cross-sectional and qualitative approaches. Bortolon et al. (2013) found 48 people with psychosis had higher scores than non-clinical control participants on six early maladaptive schemas (emotional deprivation, social isolation, defectiveness/shame, enmeshment, failure and subjugation). This association held when controlling for low mood/depression. The study also identified that early maladaptive schemas were associated with positive symptoms of psychosis. One specific schema, mistrust/abuse, was a significant predictor of positive symptoms. The EMS highlighted in these two studies differ slightly, depending on whether the 75-item Young Schema Questionnaire (YSQ) Short Form (measuring 15 EMS) or the 90-tem YSQ-Short Form questionnaire (measuring the revised 18 EMS; Young & Brown, 2003) was used.

Taylor and Harper (2017) recruited 20 people with psychosis and found that 8 EMSs were significantly associated with distress (abandonment, mistrust/abuse, social alienation, failure, dependency, vulnerability to harm, enmeshment and subjugation of needs). They also identified that two schemas, dependency and enmeshment, were significantly associated with poorer social functioning, also suggesting a key role for schemas in maintaining psychological difficulties in people with psychosis.

In a further study, Sundag et al. (2016) suggested that participants with psychosis and depression scored higher than healthy control participants (more intense EMS and a greater number of these EMS). The overall number and intensity of EMS were associated with positive symptoms but not negative symptoms, suggesting that targeting EMS in therapy could facilitate change in positive symptoms of psychosis. The EMS which differentiated participants with psychosis from those with depression was enmeshment/self. Sundag et al. (2016) proposed that this schema specifically could be a vulnerability factor for developing psychosis. In a subsequent study, Sundag et al. (2018) examined schemas in relation to paranoid responses to social stressors, using a social stress induction task. The participants with persecutory delusions responded with a greater increase in paranoia and had greater early maladaptive schema scores compared to the controls. Higher increases in paranoia following social stress were accounted for by higher EMS total scores; the defectiveness/shame and enmeshment/undeveloped self-schemas were associated with increases in paranoia.

In a larger non-clinical study, Boyda et al. (2018) examined whether EMS potentially acted as a mediating pathway between early trauma and psychotic-like experiences. Specific types of childhood maltreatment were significantly associated with unusual experiences and particular dimensions of early maladaptive schemas. Dependency EMS mediated the relationship between emotional and sexual abuse and psychotic-like experiences (as measured by the Community Assessment of Psychic Experiences).

We conducted a qualitative investigation asking people about their core beliefs, schemas and psychotic experiences (Taylor, Haddock, et al., 2020). Four emergent themes were identified: the solidity and permanency of core beliefs, the synergy between beliefs and symptoms, the concordance between life events and interpersonal relationships and links between beliefs and images. Taken together, these studies highlight how early childhood trauma and negative experiences can lead to the development of unhelpful schemas in people with psychosis and suggest that these might drive symptoms such as hallucinations and delusions. The evidence of early maladaptive schemas in people with psychosis suggests that a therapeutic approach targeting these directly could be relevant and helpful, with imagery focused therapy being one such targeted approach.

Attachment-focused iMAgery therapy for PSychosis

The development of schemas and attachment style early in life helps individuals to make sense of their world, affecting the interpretation of subsequent life events. Thus, these elements are essential to consider when formulating problems and understanding the appraisals of potentially traumatic experiences. The A-iMAPS protocol brought together the components of imagery, schemas and attachment into an intervention (Airey et al. 2023), by adapting Taylor et al.'s (2019) iMAPS formulation and therapy protocol. There were three key adaptations to the iMAPS therapeutic model: introduction of attachment considerations, instilling 'felt security' and focus on psychosis-related trauma. A range of imagery strategies were used, from both change-focused and positive-generation approaches described in Table 6.1. Table 6.2 provides an overview of the adapted therapy model. The A-iMAPS case series (Airey et al., 2023), included two to five assessment sessions, six sessions of therapy and an end of therapy assessment.

While maintaining a focus on imagery, the intervention was designed to hold attachment security at its core, remaining mindful that psychosis populations often have insecure attachment patterns. The therapist aimed to model a secure base, drawing on qualities that are important in therapeutic alliance development, including being attuned, sensitive and responsive to a client's needs. Specific examples include the therapist being genuine, expressing their full range of feelings and establishing a trusting relationship prior to engaging in other therapeutic tasks. The baseline assessment sessions provided an opportunity for the participants to familiarise themselves with the therapist and begin to develop a therapeutic alliance.

The concept of attachment was introduced in session one when relating style and quality of relationships were explored, along with a brief history, exploration of schemas, imagery and psychosis-related trauma. Attachment

Table 6.1 Common imagery techniques

Imagery approach	Description
Imagery change techniques	
Imagery control (thought suppression)	Many people with intrusive images tend to try and suppress the intrusive images. By engaging participants in a thought suppression experiment with a non-threatening image (e.g. a white polar bear), participants are able to recognise that their suppression strategy can maintain the presence of intrusive imagery.
Manipulation of images	Imagine the intrusive image on a television screen, cinema screen, YouTube computer browser or other preferred screen. Participants are requested to fast-forward, rewind, pause, change the channel, insert advertisement breaks.
Imagery rescripting	Problematic intrusive image is identified, an alternative outcome was developed and imagined. This supported the new image to be transformed into something non-threatening or positive.
Introducing new helpful figures	An adaptation to imagery rescripting was to introduce a trusted person into the image to help to change the outcome. In some cases, this may be the individual's adult self entering the image and intervening to enable them to get their needs met.
Generating positive imagery	
Positive other ('felt security') imagery	Deliberate generation of a positive other (person or animal) may include focus on a memory, where they feel safe and secure, or generation of a new imagined compassionate figure. This imagery could be drawn on voluntarily as a grounding exercise or to reduce distress.
Safe place imagery	Similar to positive other imagery, safe place imagery is constructed or recalled imagery of a place in which the individual feels safe and secure.
Positive images of the future	Generating positive images of desired outcomes and the future, drawing on remembered images and enhancing these with imagined elements.

was included within the formulation alongside core beliefs/schemas following early experiences; this supported the participant to recognise a potential role of attachment style in the development and maintenance of presenting difficulties (Figure 6.1). In session two, participants were introduced to the concept of 'felt security' and the 'felt security prime' described by Newman-Taylor (2020); participants were guided to develop positive interpersonal imagery which elicited feelings of safety and security, typically from drawing on a memory with a family member or friend. In cases where participants

Table 6.2 Overview of techniques

Session	Focus	Strategy	Attachment focus
Session 1	Assessment	Assessing imagery use, History, Schemas, Attachment style, Experience of psychosis diagnosis and treatment	
	Goals	Elicit what client would like to achieve within the limits of the intervention	
	Psychoeducation	Around imagery, relating styles	
Session 2	Formulation	Draw together information into adapted iMAPS imagery formulation, with attachment focus	
	Security prime	Felt security imagery	Prime participants to feel safe & unthreatened.
Sessions 3, 4, 5	Reorient to imagery and check in		
	Prime felt security	Felt security imagery	Prime participants to feel safe & unthreatened in session.
	Imagery change strategy	Image suppression and responding differently	Observe imagery/ memories of relational trauma or psychosis-related trauma from observer perspective. Stop attempts to suppress or engage intensely with the imagery.
		Manipulation of images	Use external stimuli (a screen) to observe memories, imagine felt security figure sat with them for added feelings of safety.
		Imagery rescripting	Helpful figure will be introduced into imagery who generates feelings of safety and security.

(Continued)

Table 6.2 (Continued)

Session	Focus	Strategy	Attachment focus
		Night-time imagery	Helpful figure or felt security figure to support them within the dream – rescript this.
		Generate positive images of the future	Elicit imagery of positive relational moments, a positive rescript of a negative memory or new imagery of them relating positively with someone and gaining feelings of comfort and security.
	Prime felt security	Felt security imagery	Return to feelings of safety and security.
Session 6	Therapy summary	Review Provide resources	Draw on strengths – highlight positive imagery, progress and felt security imagery.

struggled with this, safe place or compassionate figure imagery was utilised, dependent on participant preference.

The intervention focused on psychosis-related trauma. While some direction was provided, the primary image target for intervention was guided by participant preference and could integrate a traumatic memory or psychotic symptom that had become traumatic (e.g. a delusion or hallucination with an associated intrusive image). Similarly, when determining imagery change techniques, participants were given choices (e.g. imagery manipulation or imagery rescripting). Imagery rescripting focused on new narratives of preferred outcomes, often where the participant felt they were being treated better. For imagery manipulation, participants were guided to imagine the image on a screen (e.g. television, projector, YouTube screen) and control the video (Taylor et al., 2019). Initially participants tended to defer to therapist discretion regarding preferred technique; the therapist described the rationale for the chosen technique to facilitate openness and understanding from the participant.

Adaptations were used to remain person-centred and flexible. This included the language used in the formulation: for example, one participant disagreed with their psychosis diagnosis but recognised their tendency to be paranoid or suspicious, so this was reflected in the formulation by referring to general 'distressing symptoms' as opposed to psychotic experiences. Moreover, some participants struggled to generate or hold mental imagery in mind; this was more

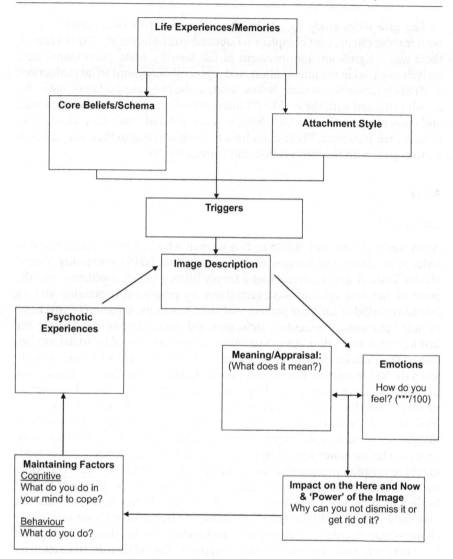

Figure 6.1 Adapted imagery formulation.

(adapted from Taylor et al., 2019).

notable for participants who, in particular, experienced thought disorder. In these cases, strategies were used to refocus attention (e.g. a short, clear agenda and more specific questioning) and visual prompts were used to support their visual representation of the imagery (e.g. a photo of the hospital where the trauma took place).

The case series study found the six-session A-iMAPS intervention to be both feasible (80 per cent completion rate) and safe (Airey et al., 2023). Overall, there was a significant improvement in felt security when participants were actively engaged in the intervention, and a general downward trend (reduction) in PTSD symptoms was seen. Below, we describe two case studies of individuals who engaged with the A-iMAPS intervention: pseudonyms have been used and consent given for inclusion here, and some details have been changed to protect their identities. These cases have been chosen due to their varying ability to engage with the intervention and various results.

Anna

Background

Anna was a 29-year-old White British woman who had experienced two episodes of psychosis and was now under the care of an NHS Community Mental Health Team (CMHT). Anna had a family history of schizophrenia, and the onset of her first episode was precipitated by post-natal depression and an extended period of intimate partner violence. Anna's presentation of psychosis included paranoia, persecutory delusions and malevolent voices. During her first inpatient admission, Anna's daughter had been removed by social services due to her deterioration in mental health. Anna was able to regain custody when she had recovered, but she stopped her medication in the community, due to feeling well, not recognising the potential consequences of this. Anna unfortunately started to relapse but contacted her care team for support as she recognised her deterioration and did not want this to adversely affect her daughter. She did not anticipate that upon calling her CMHT, they would contact social services. Her daughter was abruptly removed from her care, and she was readmitted to hospital to restabilise on medication. Despite a quick recovery, Anna was told that her daughter had been placed into foster care, and over the following months her visits were reduced, for which the rationale was not explained to Anna. While Anna was managing well now, with no active psychotic symptoms, she had regular flashbacks relating to her daughter's removal from her care. Anna was keen to engage in psychological therapy to develop an understanding of her development of psychosis and to reduce the impact of her symptoms on her life. She was petitioning for her daughter to return to her care and hoped that engaging in psychological therapy would also support this.

Imagery therapy

Anna engaged well with formulation and was able to independently link historical experiences, core beliefs and relating style to factors and beliefs that maintained her distress (see Figure 6.2). She chose to utilise a memory with her daughter and her own mother for her 'felt security' imagery; Anna

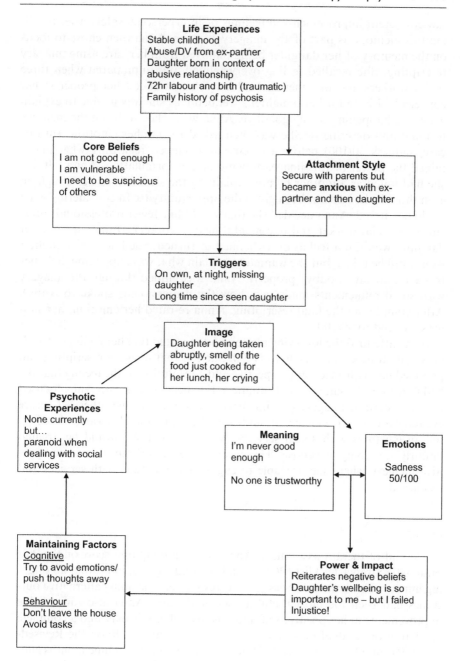

Figure 6.2 Adapted A-iMAPS formulation for Anna.

saw consistent improvements in feelings of interpersonal safety after recalling this memory as part of the imagery exercise. Anna then chose to focus on the memory of her daughter being removed from her care using imagery rescripting. She recalled feeling overwhelmed and unprepared when three social workers and one mental health worker attended her property; her concern had been for her daughter's wellbeing as she was unable to explain what was happening or say goodbye. Anna was asked to bring the memory to mind and describe it. She was then asked to rate her emotions (in this case, sadness 50/100) before a discussion occurred regarding what maintained the power of this image, drawing on her formulation. Anna felt like she had failed as a mother by not explaining the situation to her daughter, even though she had not been given the opportunity to. In considering what could be altered, Anna decided she that would like fewer professionals present (one social worker and one mental health worker) so that she and her daughter would not feel as overwhelmed or rushed. She knew her daughter would still be taken, but she wanted to explain what was happening, help her to pack and say goodbye properly. Anna was guided through the imagery with small refinements made (e.g. how the professionals spoke to Anna). After completing the final rescripting, Anna re-rated her emotion; her sadness reduced to 30/100.

Anna attended the following session and reported that her feelings of sadness had reduced completely to 0/100. She felt that imagery rescripting had provided her with a clearer perspective and a resolution to the feeling that she had failed her daughter in that situation. Further sessions with Anna focused on flash-forward imagery (i.e. intrusive imagery about hypothesised future events) with intrusive images about being afraid and unable to articulate herself in meetings with social services, where she felt she would be 'treated unfairly' due to her psychosis. These were targeted with future-oriented positive imagery where she was able to engage meaningfully with services and feel heard.

Ending

By the end-of-therapy assessment, Anna's trauma symptoms score on the Post Traumatic Stress Checklist (PCL-5) had reduced to zero, indicating no ongoing impact of trauma memories. She expressed that imagining alternative outcomes had been the most useful aspect of therapy. Anna also saw reliable improvements in her positive-self and positive-other schemas, and a complete resolution of residual persecutory beliefs from 6/40 to 0/40 on the Revised-Green Paranoid Thoughts Scale. When Anna was contacted nine months later for consent for inclusion in this book, she reported that her progress had been maintained. Anna had been able to adopt a more assertive approach to services and had gained increased contact with her daughter.

Andy

Background

Andy was a 45-year-old White British man under the care of a CMHT. He had his first episode of psychosis at university, secondary to substance misuse; he was sectioned under the Mental Health Act following some unusual behaviour, which led to an arrest by Police. Andy felt that he had been 'targeted' and that he did not have psychosis. Andy had been bullied at school and felt he was 'worthless' and 'not good enough,' others were 'judgemental' and the world was 'evil'. During his first admission, he was restrained and forcibly given anti-psychotic medication. He described regular flashbacks including visual images of his experiences in hospital, and felt that others were not trustworthy and the world was against him. There had been several subsequent inpatient admissions, and he now resided in supported accommodation. He was stable on anti-psychotic medication, but had some residual negative symptoms and a hostile attribution bias (i.e. a tendency to interpret the behaviour of others as having hostile intent, even when the behaviour is benign or ambiguous).

Initial engagement

Andy was sceptical about engaging in therapy, and initially only wanted to liaise via email. By allowing Andy to take the lead on engagement and appointment scheduling, he reported feeling some control over the interaction. Andy was reminded of his right to withdraw (at any time, without giving a reason) and his scepticism was validated and gently challenged by providing examples of how therapy can be flexible and useful for people with psychosis. Through formulation and psychoeducation, Andy was able to link his early experiences to his relating style and his tendency to view others and the world negatively.

Difficulties working with imagery

Andy demonstrated difficulties in working with imagery, when positive felt security imagery was introduced at session two; he felt that he had few positive memories in his life that were not 'tainted with negativity,' thus compassionate figure imagery was collaboratively developed. Andy was supported to build an image of an individual (he chose a female) in his mind who he felt looked trust-worthy and supportive; he was encouraged to consider how the figure would act toward him (gestures, mannerisms), what they would say and what their voice would sound like (e.g. soothing). He also struggled to hold imagery in mind, without his mind wandering. Andy selected a negative memory to focus on using imagery rescripting: this was a memory where he was forcibly restrained and injected with an antipsychotic drug. In order to support Andy to remain ori-ented to the imagery, an image of the hospital was printed and used in session.

He required a more directive approach to reflecting on the image and how he would like different outcomes, with structured, Socratic dialogue about the image, what was acceptable and what he would want to change and how. Andy was provided with examples and options to support him to consider different outcomes. This was mapped out in detail on paper, so that additional scaffolding could be provided as Andy imagined the events.

Ending

Andy remained apprehensive about engaging throughout the course of therapy, but he attended all sessions. When unable to attend, he requested for the appointments to be rearranged. He expressed that he benefitted from working consistently with one person. Andy's most notable scores at commencement were high paranoia scores, and these were the scores he saw reliable reductions in at his end of therapy assessment (from 20/40 to 11/40 for referential ideas and from 33/40 to 21/40 for persecutory beliefs). Andy's PCL-5 score decreased by 12 points (to 2/80), indicating a reliable improvement in trauma symptoms. His schema scores remained consistent at baseline and end of therapy assessment. Andy said he would consider engaging with psychological therapy again if an opportunity arose, suggesting that while he had difficulties in engagement, he recognised some benefit from therapy.

Conclusion

As demonstrated in this chapter, there is a promising role for imagery therapy in working with psychosis. While the cases described here were focused on psychosis-related trauma, this intervention could be useful when targeting any manner of distressing images, due to the focus on enhancing relational security interpersonally (through the therapeutic relationship) and intra-personally (through imagery). We have presented further evidence for the use of imagery when working with psychosis, in order to reduce the impact of distressing images and also to enhance feelings of safety and security. Attachment theory is relevant to psychosis development, maintenance and treatment (Berry et al., 2019); hence its integration should be considered in care provision and therapeutic intervention. Moreover, while the present research is limited by some design considerations (unblinded assessments, no control group, small sample), there is preliminary evidence that imagery-focused attachment-informed therapy is acceptable and safe, and can result in shifts in core schemas, paranoia and attachment style, even in short intervention periods. Much of the current research examining therapy using imagery is in case series or case study form, and larger evaluation through trials is required. At present, a feasibility randomised controlled trial of the iMAgery therapy for PSychosis (iMAPS) model is being undertaken, using an extended 12-session framework. It is hoped that this will provide sufficient evidence to warrant progressing to a fully powered randomised controlled trial to evaluate imagery therapy for use with people with psychosis compared to routine care.

References

Ainsworth, M. S. (1979). Infant–mother attachment. *American Psychologist, 34*(10), 932. https://doi.org/10.1037/0003-066X.34.10.932

Airey, N. D., Berry, K., & Taylor, C. D. J. (2023). Attachment-focused iMAgery therapy for PSychosis (A-iMAPS): A case series targeting psychosis-related trauma. *British Journal of Clinical Psychology.* https://doi.org/10.1111/BJC.12433

Bailey, T., Alvarez-Jimenez, M., Garcia-Sanchez, A. M., Hulbert, C., Barlow, E., & Bendall, S. (2018). Childhood trauma is associated with severity of hallucinations and delusions in psychotic disorders: A systematic review and meta-analysis. *Schizophrenia Bulletin, 44*(5), 1111–1122. https://doi.org/10.1093/schbul/sbx161

Berry, K., Bucci, S., & Danquah, A. N. (2019). *Attachment theory and psychosis: Current perspectives and future directions.* Routledge.

Berry, K., & Danquah, A. (2016). Attachment-informed therapy for adults: Towards a unifying perspective on practice. *Psychology and Psychotherapy: Theory, Research and Practice, 89*(1), 15–32. https://doi.org/10.1111/papt.12063

Berry, K., Ford, S., Jellicoe-Jones, L., & Haddock, G. (2013). PTSD symptoms associated with the experiences of psychosis and hospitalisation: A review of the literature. *Clinical Psychology Review, 33*(4), 526–538. https://doi.org/10.1016/j.cpr.2013.01.011

Bortolon, C., Capdevielle, D., Boulenger, J.-P., Gely-Nargeot, M.-C., & Raffard, S. (2013). Early maladaptive schemas predict positive symptomatology in schizophrenia: A cross-sectional study. *Psychiatry Research, 209*(3), 361–366. https://doi.org/10.1016/j.psychres.2013.03.018

Bowlby, J. (1969). *Attachment* (Vol. 1). Hogarth Press and The Institute of Psychoanalysis.

Bowlby, J. (1988). *A secure base.* Routledge.

Boyda, D., McFeeters, D., Dhingra, K., & Rhoden, L. (2018). Childhood maltreatment and psychotic experiences: Exploring the specificity of early maladaptive schemas. *Journal of Clinical Psychology, 74*(12), 2287–2301. https://doi.org/10.1002/jclp.22690

Brand, R. M., Bendall, S., Hardy, A., Rossell, S. L., & Thomas, N. (2021). Trauma-focused imaginal exposure for auditory hallucinations: A case series. *Psychology and Psychotherapy: Theory, Research and Practice, 94*, 408–425. https://doi.org/10.1111/papt.12284

Buswell, G., Haime, Z., Lloyd-Evans, B., & Billings, J. (2021). A systematic review of PTSD to the experience of psychosis: Prevalence and associated factors. *BMC Psychiatry, 21*(1), 1–13. https://doi.org/10.1186/s12888-020-02999-x

Cairns, A., Kelly, J., & Taylor, C. D. J. (2023). Assessing delivery of iMAgery focused therapy for PSychosis (iMAPS) via Telehealth. *Psychology and psychotherapy: Theory, research and practice.* https://doi.org/10.1111/papt.12463

Carr, S., Hardy, A., & Fornells-Ambrojo, M. (2018). Relationship between attachment style and symptom severity across the psychosis spectrum: A meta-analysis. *Clinical Psychology Review, 59*, 145–158. https://doi.org/10.1016/j.cpr.2017.12.001

Clarke, R., Kelly, R., & Hardy, A. (2022). A randomised multiple baseline case series of a novel imagery rescripting protocol for intrusive trauma memories in people with psychosis. *Journal of Behavior Therapy and Experimental Psychiatry, 75*, 101699. https://doi.org/10.1016/j.jbtep.2021.101699

Cohen, L. H. (1938). Imagery and its relations to schizophrenic symptoms. *Journal of Mental Science, 84*(349), 284–346. https://doi.org/10.1192/bjp.84.349.284

Edwards, D. (2011). Invited essay: From ancient shamanic healing to twenty first century psychotherapy: The central role of imagery methods in effecting psychological change. In A. Hackmann, J. Bennett-Levy, & E. A. Holmes (eds), *Oxford guide to imagery in cognitive therapy* (pp. xxxiii–xlii). Oxford University Press Oxford.

Feeney, B. C., & Van Vleet, M. (2010). Growing through attachment: The interplay of attachment and exploration in adulthood. *Journal of Social and Personal Relationships*, *27*(2), 226–234. https://doi.org/10.1177/0265407509360903

Gilbert, P. (2009). *The compassionate mind*. Robinson.

Hackmann, A., & Holmes, E. (2004). Reflecting on imagery: A clinical perspective and overview of the special issue of memory on mental imagery and memory in psychopathology. *Memory*, *12*(4), 389–402. https://doi.org/10.1080/09658210444000133

Hutton, J., Ellett, L., & Berry, K. (2017). Adult attachment and paranoia: An experimental investigation. *The Cognitive Behaviour Therapist*, *10*, e4. https://doi.org/10.1017/s1754470x17000058

Ison, R., Medoro, L., Keen, N., & Kuipers, E. (2014). The use of rescripting imagery for people with psychosis who hear voices. *Behavioural and Cognitive Psychotherapy*, *42*(2), 129–142. https://doi.org/10.1017/s135246581300057x

Ji, J. L., Kavanagh, D. J., Holmes, E. A., MacLeod, C., & Di Simplicio, M. (2019). Mental imagery in psychiatry: Conceptual & clinical implications. *CNS Spectrums*, *24*(1), 114–126. https://doi.org/10.1017/s1092852918001487

Keen, N., Hunter, E. C. M., & Peters, E. (2017). Integrated trauma-focused cognitive-behavioural therapy for post-traumatic stress and psychotic symptoms: A case-series study using imaginal reprocessing strategies. *Frontiers in Psychiatry*, *8*, 92. https://doi.org/10.3389/fpsyt.2017.00092

Kosslyn, S. M., Ganis, G., & Thompson, W. L. (2001). Neural foundations of imagery. *Nature Reviews Neuroscience*, *2*(9), 635–642. https://doi.org/10.1038/35090055

Main, M., & Solomon, J. (1986). Discovery of an insecure-disorganized/disoriented attachment pattern. In T. B. Brazelton & M. W. Yogman (eds), *Affective development in infancy* (pp. 95–124). Ablex Publishing.

Martland, N., Martland, R., Cullen, A. E., & Bhattacharyya, S. (2020). Are adult stressful life events associated with psychotic relapse? A systematic review of 23 studies. *Psychological Medicine*, *50*(14), 2302–2316. https://doi.org/10.1017/s0033291720003554

Mikulincer, M., & Shaver, P. R. (2010). *Attachment in adulthood: Structure, dynamics, and change*. Guilford Publications.

Morrison, A. (2004). The use of imagery in cognitive therapy for psychosis: A case example. *Memory*, *12*(4), 517–524. https://doi.org/10.1080/09658210444000142

Morrison, A. P. (2001). The interpretation of intrusions in psychosis: An integrative cognitive approach to hallucinations and delusions. *Behavioural and Cognitive Psychotherapy*, *29*(3), 257–276. https://doi.org/10.1017/s1352465801003010

Morrison, A. P., Beck, A. T., Glentworth, D., Dunn, H., Reid, G. S., Larkin, W., & Williams, S. (2002). Imagery and psychotic symptoms: A preliminary investigation. *Behaviour research and therapy*, *40*(9), 1053–1062. https://doi.org/10.1016/s0005-7967(01)00128-0

Morrison, A. P., Frame, L., & Larkin, W. (2003). Relationships between trauma and psychosis: A review and integration. *British Journal of Clinical Psychology*, *42*(4), 331–353. https://doi.org/10.1348/014466503322528892

Newman-Taylor, K. (2020). 'Felt security'as a means of facilitating imagery rescripting in psychosis: A clinical protocol and illustrative case study. *The Cognitive Behaviour Therapist*, *13*, e24. https://doi.org/10.1017/s1754470x20000288

Paulik, G., Steel, C., & Arntz, A. (2019). Imagery rescripting for the treatment of trauma in voice hearers: A case series. *Behavioural and Cognitive Psychotherapy*, *47*(6), 709–725. https://doi.org/10.1017/s1352465819000237

Pitfield, C., Maguire, T., & Newman-Taylor, K. (2020). Impact of attachment imagery on paranoia and mood: Evidence from two single case studies. *Behavioural and Cognitive Psychotherapy*, *48*(5), 572–583. https://doi.org/10.1017/s1352465820000351

Schäfer, I., & Fisher, H. L. (2011). Childhood trauma and psychosis-what is the evidence? *Dialogues in clinical neuroscience*, *13*(3), 360–365. https://doi.org/10.31887/dcns.2011.13.2/ischaefer

Schulze, K., Freeman, D., Green, C., & Kuipers, E. (2013). Intrusive mental imagery in patients with persecutory delusions. *Behaviour research and therapy*, *51*(1), 7–14. https://doi.org/10.1016/j.brat.2012.10.002

Serruya, G., & Grant, P. (2009). Cognitive-behavioral therapy of delusions: Mental imagery within a goal-directed framework. *Journal of Clinical Psychology*, *65*(8), 791–802. https://doi.org/10.1002/jclp.20616

Shapiro, F. (2001). *Eye movement desensitization and reprocessing (EMDR): Basic principles, protocols, and procedures*. Guilford Press.

Sheaves, B., Onwumere, J., Keen, N., & Kuipers, E. (2015). Treating your worst nightmare: A case-series of imagery rehearsal therapy for nightmares in individuals experiencing psychotic symptoms. *The Cognitive Behaviour Therapist*, *8*, e27. https://doi.org/10.1017/s1754470x15000665

Smith, K., Goodby, E., Hales, S., & Johns, L. (2022). Enhancing future-directed thinking in people with first-episode psychosis using a guided imagery intervention. *Journal of Behavior Therapy and Experimental Psychiatry*, *76*, 101738. https://doi.org/10.1016/j.jbtep.2022.101738

Sood, M., Carnelley, K., & Newman-Taylor, K. (2021). How does attachment imagery for paranoia work? Cognitive fusion and beliefs about self and others mediate the impact on paranoia and anxiety. *Psychology and Psychotherapy: Theory, Research and Practice*, *94*(4), 973–993. https://doi.org/10.1111/papt.12354

Steel, C., Hardy, A., Smith, B., Wykes, T., Rose, S., Enright, S., Hardcastle, M., Landau, S., Baksh, M. F., & Gottlieb, J. D. (2017). Cognitive–behaviour therapy for post-traumatic stress in schizophrenia. A randomized controlled trial. *Psychological Medicine*, *47*(1), 43–51. https://doi.org/10.1017/s0033291716002117

Sundag, J., Ascone, L., de Matos Marques, A., Moritz, S., & Lincoln, T. M. (2016). Elucidating the role of early maladaptive schemas for psychotic symptomatology. *Psychiatry Research*, *238*, 53–59. https://doi.org/10.1016/j.psychres.2016.02.008

Sundag, J., Ascone, L., & Lincoln, T. M. (2018). The predictive value of early maladaptive schemas in paranoid responses to social stress. *Clinical Psychology & Psychotherapy*, *25*(1), 65–75. https://doi.org/10.1002/cpp.2128

Taylor, C. D. J., Bee, P. E., Kelly, J., Emsley, R., & Haddock, G. (2020). iMAgery focused psychological therapy for persecutory delusions in PSychosis (iMAPS): A multiple baseline experimental case series. *Behavioural and Cognitive Psychotherapy*, *48*(5), 530–545. https://doi.org/10.1017/s1352465820000168

Taylor, C. D. J., Bee, P. E., Kelly, J., & Haddock, G. (2019). iMAgery-focused psychological therapy for persecutory delusions in psychosis (iMAPS): A novel treatment approach. *Cognitive and Behavioral Practice*, *26*(3), 575–588. https://doi.org/10.1016/j.cbpra.2018.10.002

Taylor, C. D. J., Haddock, G., Speer, S., & Bee, P. E. (2020). Characterizing core beliefs in psychosis: A qualitative study. *Behavioural and Cognitive Psychotherapy*, *48*(1), 67–81. https://doi.org/10.1017/s1352465819000274

Taylor, C. D. J., & Harper, S. F. (2017). Early maladaptive schema, social functioning and distress in psychosis: A preliminary investigation. *Clinical Psychologist*, *21*(2), 135–142. https://doi.org/10.1111/cp.12082

van den Berg, D. P. G., de Bont, P. A. J. M., van der Vleugel, B. M., de Roos, C., de Jongh, A., Van Minnen, A., & van der Gaag, M. (2015). Prolonged exposure vs eye movement desensitization and reprocessing vs waiting list for posttraumatic stress disorder in patients with a psychotic disorder: A randomized clinical trial. *JAMA Psychiatry*, *72*(3), 259–267. https://doi.org/10.1001/jamapsychiatry.2014.2637

Varese, F., Sellwood, W., Pulford, D., Awenat, Y., ... Bentall, R. P. (2023). Trauma-focused therapy in early psychosis: Results of a feasibility randomised controlled trial of EMDR for Psychosis (EMDRp) in early intervention settings. *Psychological Medicine*, 1–12.

Varese, F., Smeets, F., Drukker, M., Lieverse, R., ... Bentall, R. P. (2012). Childhood adversities increase the risk of psychosis: A meta-analysis of patient-control, prospective-and cross-sectional cohort studies. *Schizophrenia bulletin*, *38*(4), 661–671. https://doi.org/10.1093/schbul/sbs050

Young, J. E. (1990). *Schema-focused cognitive therapy for personality disorders: A schema focused approach*. Professional Resource Exchange.

Young, J. E., & Brown, G. (2003). *Young schema questionniare-L3a*. Cognitive Therapy Centre of New York.

Young, J. E., Klosko, J. S., & Weishaar, M. E. (2003). *Schema Therapy: A practitioner's guide*. Guilford.

Chapter 7

Imagery rescripting in trauma-affected voice hearers

By Georgie Paulik*

Imagery rescripting can be a powerful experiential therapeutic tool when working on memories to help shift associated schemas, modes or voices: either within Schema Therapy or as a stand-alone treatment for voices and underlying trauma (that is, trauma directly or thematically linked to the content of voices) and related post-traumatic stress symptomatology (e.g. intrusive memories and negative appraisals). This chapter reviews the association between voice hearing and childhood trauma, and ways of addressing trauma and resulting traumatic cognitive intrusions in this clinical population. The chapter presents clinical protocols for the delivery of imagery rescripting when working with trauma-affected voice hearers, and provides case illustrations and an example of a therapeutic transcript. The chapter also details how to amend protocols when working with clients who are dissociation prone and outlines an adaptation of the delivery via telehealth.

Introduction

Voice hearing as a transdiagnostic experience

Voices (also known as 'auditory verbal hallucinations') vary considerably in the things they say, the way they are perceived (e.g. location, loudness) and the way they are made sense of by the individual. Those, however, who seek help around their voices typically report that the experience is distressing and highly personal in nature, often targeting the things they feel most insecure about. When people think of voice hearing, they typically think of psychotic disorders. Indeed, approximately two-thirds of people with a schizophrenia-spectrum disorder will hear voices at some stage in their lives. However, voice hearing is common in the general population also, with the lifetime prevalence

---

* Georgie Paulik is a clinical psychologist, adjunct associate professor and research practitioner who is passionate about developing and delivering effective psychological therapies (including Relating Cognitive Behavioural Therapy, imagery rescripting, and Schema Therapy) to people who have distressing hallucinatory experiences and underlying trauma.

DOI: 10.4324/9781003350583-7

of voice hearing being estimated between 10 to 25 per cent, and approximately 4 to 8 per cent of the population hearing voices at any given time (Johns & van Os, 2001). Thus, the majority of voice hearing (over 65 per cent) occurs in the context of other mental health problems, including personality disorders, post-traumatic stress disorder (PTSD), depression, dissociative identity disorder (DID), as well as in individuals without a mental health disorder (de Leede-Smith & Barkus, 2013).

Voice hearing and trauma

The most common vulnerability factor for voice hearing, regardless of diagnosis or presenting problems, is a history of childhood trauma, with a striking prevalence of childhood sexual abuse being reported (e.g. McCarthy-Jones & Longden, 2015). The prevalence of traumatic life events reported by people who have been diagnosed with a psychotic disorder is approximately 75 per cent, and between 2 to 16 per cent meet criteria for PTSD (de Bont et al., 2015; Hardy et al., 2016).

Cognitive Behavioural models that attempt to explain how early traumatic experiences result in voice hearing suggest that childhood trauma can lead to insecure attachment styles and/or produce neurodevelopmental changes that increase the likelihood of voices (see Strachan, Paulik, & McEvoy, 2022, for a narrative review of psychological theories of PTSD and voice hearing). These changes include the development of information processing dysfunction, maladaptive trauma-influenced appraisals, and maladaptive coping strategies (including dissociation) (e.g. Berry, Varese, & Bucci, 2017; Longden, Madill, & Waterman, 2012; Hardy, 2017; see Strachan et al., 2023b for a comprehensive trauma-informed model of voice hearing). In Schema Therapy terms, early childhood trauma leads to the development of negative schemas, which shape a person's everyday appraisals, including the way the individual makes sense of their voices (e.g. their beliefs around the voice's intent, power, knowledge, control) and also shape the content of the voices (e.g. the voices commonly say things to reinforce their schematic beliefs about self and others, such as 'you're pathetic'). Also, the child develops maladaptive coping modes in response to trauma and insecure attachment, in particular dissociation-based coping modes, such as detached protector and detached self-soother. Research is currently being done by our group to explore whether voices in fact represent specific modes, with our clinical observation being that people's dominant voice often presents as a punitive or demanding parent mode. In Schema Therapy we think of the dysfunctional parent modes as internalisations of parents or other key adult figures, who are often, for those with trauma, also the perpetrators. For voice hearers, this dysfunctional parent mode may be heard as a voice, and may even sound like the voice of the perpetrator (and/or parent). This mode may be experienced as a voice (rather than part of the self) due to incomplete or fragmented contextual information bound to the related traumatic memories on retrieval (see Steel, 2015 for more on this context binding theory of trauma-related voices).

Given that trauma plays a critical role in the development of voices for the majority of voice hearers, it makes sense that therapeutically addressing the underlying trauma may have benefits to the client, both with regards to lessening PTSD symptoms but also potentially ameliorating or changing the voice hearing experience. Brand et al. (2018) reviewed the outcomes of trauma-focused randomised controlled trials in people with psychosis, both with regards to treatment effects on PTSD symptoms and positive symptoms (voices and delusions). They found that both Eye Movement Desensitisation and Reprocessing (EMDR) and Prolonged Exposure (PE) resulted in small to moderate reductions in PTSD (while cognitive restructuring did not achieve this), while none of the intervention types included led to significant reductions in voice severity. This may have been because the studies included were mostly looking at changes in positive symptoms more broadly, which meant that they often did not administer especially sensitive measures of voice severity, and the protocols often did not include targeting memories directly or thematically linked to voice content or appraisals. However, it may also be because these three types of trauma-focused therapies are not best suited to treating trauma in voice hearers. Our research group instead wish to suggest that imagery rescripting (ImRs) is best suited to treating related traumas in voice hearers. In our two studies of imagery rescripting in trauma-affected voice hearers (in a case series of 12 participants, Paulik, Steel, & Arntz, 2019; and a larger naturalistic, multiple-baseline study of 42 participants, Strachan et al., 2023a), and another small case series (of 4 participants, Ison et al., 2014), imagery rescripting had large effects (reductions) on both PSTD symptoms and voice distress and frequency, which were maintained at three month follow-up.

Imagery rescripting for trauma-affected voice hearers

Imagery rescripting is a powerful trauma-focused therapeutic tool and a key experiential technique used in Schema Therapy. In this context it is used to help shift negative schemas and dysfunctional modes, and build the healthy adult mode, by processing key underlying memories (e.g. targeting memories where that schema and/or modes were developed or strengthened). However, imagery rescripting has also been developed as a stand-alone therapy, initially intended to reduce reliving cognitions in people with PTSD, but also adapted to targeting a range of different intrusive cognitions (including flashbacks, nightmares, mental images, voices, obsessions) in a range of different presenting problems (including PTSD, depression, social phobia, snake phobia, obsessive compulsive disorder, body dysmorphic disorder, eating disorders, paranoia, trauma-affected voice hearers and personality disorders; for a literature review and meta-analysis, see Morina et al., 2017). Broadly speaking, imagery rescripting involves the client reliving the initial part of a traumatic memory, but together with the therapist, then changing the ending of the memory or 'script' to help get the client's needs met. There are several different styles of imagery rescripting; however, in this chapter we will focus on that developed by Arnoud Arntz, which is the style of rescripting most studied to treat PSTD, and that which has been incorporated into Schema Therapy (other pioneers of different styles of imagery rescripting include Emily Holmes and Mervyn Schmucker).

In Arntz and Weertman's (1999) initial description of imagery rescripting, they outlined a three-stage approach. In the first stage, the memory is visualised from the perspective of the child (the age of the client in the memory), and the therapist enters the image once the client's distress levels have risen (right before or at the initial 'hot' part of the trauma) to help the client get their needs met. This serves several functions. First, it helps the client connect with and identify the needs of the vulnerable child. Second, it models for the client the intervening of the healthy adult – a target of Schema Therapy. Third, it helps shift schemas by changing the meaning obtained from the memory (e.g. shifting the blame and shame from the child to the perpetrator, which may help to shift a defectiveness and shame schema). This first stage is often used for the first six or so sessions of rescripting, with this stage being longer in clients with more complex trauma and a more underdeveloped healthy adult mode, as typically they struggle to know what their needs are or how to go about getting them met, just as they struggled when children. The second stage involves the client visualising the event from their child-self perspective but then shifting to their healthy adult-self perspective once they have commenced the rescript, with their adult-self entering the image to help their child-self get their needs met. The third stage is typically done right after the second stage (in the same session), but this time the client visualises the event from the perspective of the child-self, watching their adult-self helping them get their needs met. The second and third stage of imagery rescripting have the same functions as the first, but also help build the skills of the healthy adult mode. In all stages of imagery rescripting, the new 'rescripted' image focuses on the unmet needs of the child (e.g. involving emotional validation, gaining control over the situation, empowerment and perpetrators being held accountable for their actions), which will differ from person to person and memory to memory, but can be informed by a client's schema mode formulation. There is also evidence that inner dialogue, self-compassion, emotional self-efficacy (or a person's perceived abilities to self-regulate their emotions), emotion regulation skills, dissociation and self-beliefs in trauma-affected voice hearing populations are modified by imagery rescripting (e.g. Strachan et al., 2023).

There are four main reasons why imagery rescripting may be more effective at treating trauma-affected voice hearing than other trauma-focused therapies (such as PE, EMDR or cognitive restructuring). In Schema Therapy, the memories to be rescripted are selected based on their link to a certain schema or mode being worked on in therapy, making it most relevant and helpful in treating targeted beliefs or behaviours. Likewise, in imagery rescripting when delivered as a standalone therapy for trauma-affected voice hearers, the memories are selected based on either direct (e.g. the voice says the exact same things as their perpetrator) or indirect (e.g. the voice bullies the client, much like the bullies did at school, but not the same identity or words as the bullies) links to the voices. This allows the formulation to target and prioritise addressing the traumatic memories most centrally connected to the voice hearing experience. Second, imagery rescripting can target negative schemas/beliefs more directly than say in PE, as the therapist can take targeted steps to address different needs and beliefs linked to these schemas. For instance, for people who have a strong defectiveness and shame schema, the therapist in the rescript can directly reassure the child that the abuse was not their fault and shift blame to the perpetrator when reprimanding them. Third, imagery rescripting generalises well between similar memories either involving the same perpetrator(s) in the same location or with the same/similar underlying schema being targeted. This is essential for voice hearers, as they typically have very complex trauma, with many different trauma clusters (e.g. they may have histories of childhood neglect, family violence, repeated sexual abuse, and school bullying, and then have gone on to be in domestically violent relationships in adulthood), and thus doing a trauma-focused therapy that does not generalise well would take too long and likely have higher dropouts. Finally, imagery rescripting also has lower dropouts than other trauma-focused therapies because it does not always entail the reliving of the 'hot' part of the trauma memory, which is reported to be the main reason for withdrawing from trauma-focused therapies as this is often highly distressing and thus avoided.

How to deliver imagery rescripting to trauma-affected voice hearers

I will now talk about the protocols developed together with Arnoud Arntz and Craig Steel (protocols available on request from the author of this chapter), which were evaluated in our two naturalistic treatment studies (Paulik et al., 2019; Strachan et al., 2023a). As these studies were the first to use imagery rescripting as a trauma-focused treatment in transdiagnostic trauma-affected voice hearers, caution must be taken not to assume these guidelines are the most effective way to deliver imagery rescripting, and to use clinical judgment in doing this work. In the following I shall write about imagery rescripting as a standalone intervention; however, the approach outlined is, I believe, suitable and beneficial for use in Schema Therapy for voice hearers, as I have found in my own application of Schema Therapy in this area. It is advisable to allow 90 minutes per session when doing imagery rescripting; however, for stage one (where the therapist guides the rescript) these sessions often only take 60 minutes, and for many voice hearers 90 minutes may exceed the limits of their window of attention. It is recommended that sessions are conducted weekly to biweekly to get the best outcomes, and to allow 10 to 20 sessions to complete therapy (depending on the complexity of a person's mental health and trauma background). Clinicians should receive formal training in the delivery of imagery rescripting (this chapter does not provide enough detail on the basics of imagery rescripting to replace this) and make use of appropriate supervision when applying imagery rescripting to voice hearers, given the complexity of trauma and proneness to dissociation in this population (Longden et al., 2012; Pilton, Varese, Berry, & Bucci, 2015) – see the end of this section on ways to manage dissociation.

The assessment should entail a thorough evaluation of their developmental history, their voices, and their trauma, and the therapist should ask questions that assist in understanding the links between the client's voices and trauma. Van den Berg et al. (2023) developed a series of questions to ask clients to explore this:

- 'Did the voices first start directly after experiencing one of these [traumatic] events?'
- 'Do the voices sound like or belong to people involved in any of the events?'
- 'Do the voices say things (to or about you) that are similar to the things that were said (to or about you) during any of the events?'
- 'Do the voices ever say *exactly* the same things that were said to you during the events?'
- 'Is the way the voices treat you or the way that they behave similar to the way people treated you during any of the events?'
- 'Do the voices ever say or do things that you fear might have happened during any of the events?'
- 'Do you react to or cope with the voices in a similar way to how you reacted or coped during any of the events?'
- 'Do the voices make you feel similarly to how you felt during the events?'
- 'Do you sometimes say negative things about yourself in a similar way to how the voices say negative things about you?'
- 'Do you agree with the negative things that the voices say about you, or believe them to be true?'
- 'Are the voices more severe when you feel tense, on edge, stressed or aroused?'
- 'Are the voices more severe when you're trying to avoid or when you feel shut-off, numb, blanked out or unreal?'

These can be used to help develop a shared formulation or understanding of the way the client's voices relate to their trauma histories, including their shared links to schemas and modes if you are doing imagery rescripting in the context of Schema Therapy.

The first session after assessment and formulation helps set the stage for therapy, and includes setting goals, discussing expectations, providing psychoeducation on what imagery rescripting is and how it works, doing a practice rescript with a mild to moderately negative childhood memory (although we did not find this was essential), and developing a hierarchy or plan of which memories to rescript and roughly in what order. We help guide the client to make an informed decision about the latter, by advising them that memories are typically rescripted in roughly chronological order, and that it is best to target the memories where the schemas and modes first started to develop prior to working on memories where the schemas and/or modes were subsequently strengthened. It is also advised not to avoid or leave more severe traumas – or traumas the person is having the most nightmares or flashbacks of – to the end of therapy, to ensure adequate time is given to these memories. In addition, these traumatic memories may be the greatest contributors to the client's PTSD symptom severity, so targeting them early on may help the client to improve more rapidly. Conversely, often it is best not to work on the most distressing memory in the first rescript, as the client will already be feeling more anxious than in subsequent rescripts, and given that they are unsure of the process in the first session, and experience more anxiety, they may be more vulnerable to dissociation or panic. It is also important to prioritise memories that are directly or thematically linked to their current distressing voices. For example, Bill grew up with a mother who was overly critical and punitive, often calling him derogatory names such as 'lazy,' 'pathetic' and 'stupid.' Bill was now hearing a middle-aged, female voice that frequently calls him 'stupid,' which he found highly distressing. When choosing memories around his relationship with his mother to rescript, we prioritised memories where she used the word 'stupid' when addressing him over other equally critical and punitive memories, and consequently saw an immediate reduction in the frequency with which the voices called him this (and related) names. One client, Susan, had heard the voice of her step brother who had sexually assaulted her in childhood almost continually for over 35 years (a direct relationship between voice and trauma). After rescripting several instances of sexual abuse, as well as rescripting memories surrounding the abuse involving her parents' treatment of her relative to her step brother, Susan reported that this voice 'just left.'

Towards the end of therapy, you can also choose to rescript memories of the actual trauma of a distressing voice hearing – or other hallucination modality – episode (e.g. a memory of hallucinating a lion roaring at them in their living room), especially if the client is having flashbacks of this memory. In keeping with the recommendations around how to rescript adult traumatic memories, we suggest that here the therapist does not need to enter the image to help get the client's needs met but rather have the client and other safe people in their lives help them to get their needs met (unless the client specifically feels they need you to assist). The rescript may include imagining addressing the hallucination in a way that gets it to dissipate promptly (e.g. being assertive with the voice, and it responding well to this; or vacuuming up a visual hallucination like in a scene from *Ghostbusters*); coping with the experience and resulting emotions better; seeking and getting help from mental health services or others more promptly and effectively; and finally, ending the image feeling soothed and safe. Together with Chris Taylor (author of the chapter in this book on working with paranoia), we have just completed a case series of imagery-focused CBT for working with visual hallucinations (with ten participants), which showed promising results. This approach (which can be adapted when working with voices in imagery rescripting) included Arntz's rescripting technique (as described here, and see Arntz, 2011), combined with Holmes' approach (where the client and therapist find the meaning of the vision and then work to come up with the antithesis of this meaning using mental imagery; see Hackmann, Bennett-Levy, & Holmes, 2011). Meta-cognitive strategies were also used to increase a sense of control over the image (e.g. by putting the vision onto a television screen and using a remote control to change the image).

The rescripting instructions

In our previous treatment trials of imagery rescripting in trauma-affected voice hearers, we only used stage one of Arntz and Weertman (1999)'s procedure, that is, for all memories the therapist entered the image to help get their client's needs met (with the exception of adult memories, where the procedure is that the client has their needs met by themselves and/or others in the image). This was chosen primarily because our initial experiences of doing stages two and three, especially for clients with a psychotic illness, was that there was an increase in dissociation and confusion during rescripting, e.g. jumping between the perspective of their child-self, their healthy adult-self and even the perspective of the perpetrator. We think this was likely, in part, because this client group tends to have very complex childhood trauma histories and thus very under-developed healthy adult modes, so more modelling is required of how to identify and meet their needs. While I would recommend clinicians use their clinical judgement as to whether or not they proceed to stages two and three of imagery rescripting with this client group, I would advise that they spend more sessions initially in stage one than when working with clients with less complex trauma presentations.

The instructions our therapists used were to proceed as follows. At the start of each session, after discussing how the client's week was, allow time for clients to reflect on the rescript in the last sessions, including what they liked and didn't like, or what bits were triggering or did not feel natural. This information can be useful to shape the next rescript. Following this, select the memory to rescript that session. If you have set up a list of memories to rescript in the first or second session, then this will likely not be a difficult task. However, if the client is having difficulty identifying a significant memory to rescript, the therapist can get the client to use a recent event of hearing distressing voices as an emotional bridge to help select which memory to rescript in that session. When doing this, get the client to close their eyes and recall a time in the past week when they felt distressed by their voices. Use the first part of the rescripting procedure to help them reconnect to that memory (e.g. where they were, what they could see, hear, etc.), and recall what the voices were saying and how they were feeling. Once they are reconnected emotionally to that memory, encourage them to sit with their discomfort for a few moments until an adverse childhood memory arises. Ideally, once the memory arises, commence the rescript (eyes to remain closed throughout the process if they feel comfortable to do so), rather than bringing them back to the room and discussing it first. This allows them to stay connected to the associated beliefs and feelings.

When a memory has been chosen from the hierarchy, discuss the memory and some aspects of the rescript with the client prior to commencing. In this discussion, explore the links to their voices, and their schemas and/or modes being worked on if doing imagery rescripting in the context of Schema Therapy. Even if not doing the rescript as part of Schema Therapy, it is still helpful to ask clients 'what was the belief about yourself that started to develop from this memory?' (or 'how did this [memory] make you feel about yourself?'), and 'what was the belief about others that started to develop from this memory?' (or 'how did this [memory] make you feel about the people around you?'). This will help you better understand the unmet needs of the client, and to guide you around the language to be used when addressing the child image of the client and others in the rescript. For instance, for a client that believes the memory is an example of them being a 'failure,' the therapist can explicitly tell the child in the image that they are not a failure, and that all children make mistakes, especially in their given context, and then reprimand the parent/caregiver/other for speaking to the child in a way that fosters this feeling or belief (shifting the blame). By asking the client to rate their chosen belief 0–10 before the rescript and again the following week, we can track changes in belief conviction and gauge whether the client is ready to move onto targeting a different belief/schema.

For clients who are dissociation prone (which is many, if not most, voice hearers), it is advisable to discuss with the client where in the memory the therapist will enter (though if the client is clearly getting distressed or starting to dissociate early in the memory, always offer to enter earlier than planned) and agree to the first few things that will happen in the rescript (e.g. that you will enter the image with three police officers, and then you will go to the child and assure them that they are safe while the police officers arrest the perpetrator, etc.). This helps to reduce anxiety (a primary trigger of dissociation) as the client knows what to expect. Choose the steps of the rescript together with the client, asking them what they think their child self would have needed. As many clients with complex trauma often have an underdeveloped healthy adult mode, you may need to make suggestions around the initial steps of making sure the child is safe, de-shaming and reassuring the child, and reprimanding the perpetrator. These steps can be modified in the rescript based on feedback from the client around their needs once connected to their child self. Once the initial steps have been decided upon, you are ready to commence the rescript.

The stages of the rescript are: (1) connect the client to the initial part of the memory by asking where they are, what they can see, hear, smell, feel, etc.;

(2) play out the first part of the memory (from first person, present tense per-spective, as in the transcript example below); (3) the therapist enters the image at the point where the child (client) is starting to feel unsafe or upset but ideally before the child is hurt. You then describe to the client what you are doing and saying to make them safe and have their needs met, checking other relevant needs by asking the client questions such as 'what else you do need?' and encouraging them to envisage the needs being met ('OK, make that happen...,' 'what is happening now?,' 'how is mum/dad/other responding?' etc.); (4) con-tinue the rescript until all needs have been met. In the final stage of the rescript, ensure the child is starting to feel calm and soothed. To achieve this, you may need to guide the child through two minutes of slow breathing in the image (and actually have the client do this) and have the child (together with safe other(s)) engage in soothing and/or happy activities (e.g. cuddling a pet, watch-ing a movie or eating their favourite meal with the family, playing games with a sibling, or going to the park or the beach). For a more detailed description of the imagery rescripting procedure, see Arntz (2011).

Case illustration and transcript

This client is an amalgamation of two different clients to ensure confi-dentiality.

Vanessa was a 34-year-old Caucasian cis-female who presented for therapy around her distressing voices in the context of complex PTSD and borderline personality disorder (BPD) with psychotic features. She had been hearing three distinct voices and one group of voices since the age of 7 (though the group only commenced at age 16), around three months after her stepfather started sexually assaulting her at night. The abuse lasted almost two years, and it ended because her mum left her partner following a 'terrible fight' which 'landed Mum in hospital.' Vanessa also experienced moderate emotional neglect and occasional verbal abuse from her mother, school bullying in early high school and had been in a four-year domestically violent relationship in adulthood. She had been single over the past eight years due to difficulties trusting others (and herself). She heard the voice of her mother (which often said similar hurtful and critical things as her mother had said, such as 'you stupid, stupid girl'), an unknown male voice (which often said sexual and abu-sive things to her which were similar to things that her stepfather used to say) and the voice of her deceased grandmother (which was supportive and reassur-ing, but would only appear when she was highly distressed). She reported that the group of voices sounded much like the girls who bullied her in high school, and they spoke together to either bully her directly (calling her hurtful names, as the girls did in high school) or to say nasty things about her to each other. The group of voices were often triggered by her social anxiety.

Following assessment, I explored with her the links between her past trauma and her voices (including their content, identity, beliefs about them, evoked emotions and her pattern of behavioural responding). We then proceeded to prepare for imagery rescripting, developing a hierarchy of memories to rescript, choosing to work on trauma 'clusters' in chronological order (e.g. memories pertaining to her mother first, then the sexual and physical abuse by her step-father, then school bullying, then the abusive adult relationship), and chose a few key memories to work on in the first cluster – which were most strongly linked to her 'mother voice,' and which she was having the most intrusive memories of – before the first rescripting session.

In the first rescripting session, Vanessa chose to rescript a memory at age four where her mother had yelled at her 'you stupid, stupid girl' after she had spilled her cereal on the couch. We started by discussing her beliefs around this memory ('I am stupid' and 'others will judge me harshly,' both which were linked to her failure schema), her unmet needs and steps we could take in the rescript to correct these. Below is the transcript from this first rescript:

Therapist [Th]:	OK Vanessa, I am going to get you to now close your eyes and go back to being four-year-old you, sitting on the couch eating your cereal. [pause]. Are you there?
Client [C]:	Yes.
Th:	Good. Take a look around the room and tell me what you can see.
C:	I can see the TV in front of me. The couch I am sitting on – which is brown leather. The windows to my right. The hallway off to my left. The kitchen bench behind me.
Th:	What can you hear around you?
C:	Umm, I can hear the TV going. Cartoons I think. And the sound of my mum entering the kitchen.
Th:	What are you feeling?
C:	I'm feeling OK. Enjoying watching my morning cartoons.
Th:	What's happening now?
C:	I'm laughing at my TV show. I'm not paying attention to my cereal, and then it spills in my lap and all over the couch, right as Mum enters the room.
Th:	What's happening now?
C:	She stares hard at me. I know she is mad by the look on her face. She yells at me 'you stupid, stupid girl!!'
Th:	How do you feel?
C:	I feel scared, and a bit sad
Th:	Where do you feel this in your body?
C:	Mostly in my chest. It's tight. And my heart is racing.
TH:	Are you ready for me to enter the rescript?
C:	Yes.
Th:	OK, I want you to see me walk into the room from the hallway. I'm standing between you and Mum – can you see me?

C:	Yes.
Th:	Good. I turn to you and crouch down next to the couch and say to you 'oops, it looks like you've had an accident.' I am now mopping up the spill with a towel, and I say 'I often spill things too when I'm laughing at funny cartoons. It's not a big deal, it happens to all of us. You are not a stupid girl. You are a smart, curious and kind little girl, and one that likes to laugh at cartoons. I really like that about you. I'm sorry that Mum yelled at you. That's not OK. It was just a mistake. I'm going to talk to Mum and help see that she doesn't get so cross next time, is that OK?'
C:	OK.
Th:	I now turn to Mum and say 'Elenore, you cannot yell at your child like that. Vanessa is only four years old. She is just a small child. How can she be expected to eat a messy meal like cereal on the couch and not have an accident? Accidents happen. It does not make her stupid. Making her feel like there is something wrong with her – that she is stupid or not good enough – just because she has a small accident is not OK. She is a wonderful little child. She needs you to help her with things, like breakfast, as she is still little. She also needs patience from you, as children learn through trial and error. I'm not going to let you keep treating Vanessa this way.' How is Mum responding to me? How do you need her to be responding to me?
C:	She is looking ashamed.
Th:	Yes, I can see she is struggling to make eye contact. I add 'Elenore, I can assist you to get help with your anger management and parenting skills, but you have to want to do better, for Vanessa.' I can see she is nodding her head. Do you want her to apologise to you?
C:	Umm, yes, but I'm not sure she would.
Th:	OK, you tell me what she is doing and saying now.
C:	She is coming over to me and takes the bowl and places it on the coffee table. She says 'sorry, I shouldn't have yelled at you. We all make mistakes. Next time I will help you eat breakfast in the kitchen, at the table.'
Th:	Good. How does that feel?
C:	Strange, but good.
Th:	What else do you need?
C:	I think I want Mum to give me a hug.
Th:	OK, make it happen. [pause] What's happening?
C:	She sits next to me on the couch and puts her arms around me.

Th:	Can you feel your head against her chest?
C:	Yes, it feels nice.
Th:	What else do you need?
C:	I want to know that Mum will stop yelling at me and that I'm not alone.
Th:	OK, so I come sit on your other side, and I take a mobile phone from my pocket. What colour is it?
C:	It's pink.
Th:	I put the pink phone in your hand and I say 'this is for you. You see this number 1 button? When you press this I will come instantly. You can press this any time Mum is not keeping up her word and is getting cross with you. Or really any time you feel scared, unsafe or lonely. I will be here to protect you and to make sure that Mum is learning how to be the mum that you need her to be. How does that feel?
C:	Yeah, good.
Th:	What else do you need?
C:	I think I just want Mum to do something with me, maybe take me to the park.
Th:	OK, make that happen. [pause] What's happening now?
C:	Mum suggests that we go across the road to the park, which I have been bugging her about for ages now.
Th:	What's happening now?
C:	Mum is leading the way through the living room, towards the front door. She puts a hat on my head and we start walking towards the park.
Th:	What's happening now?
C:	We arrive and I run up to the swings and ask Mum to push me on them. She helps me onto it and then starts to push.
Th:	Can you feel the cool air against your skin?
C:	Yes, it feels lovely.
Th:	How do you feel?
C:	Happy. Safe.
Th:	Is there anything else you need?
C:	No, I think that's it.
Th:	OK, I'm going to get you then to slowly expand your awareness to become aware of your body sitting in the therapy chair. [pause] Now expand your awareness to become aware of the sounds around us. [pause]. When you're ready, open your eyes and look around the therapy room, noticing all the colours, shapes and objects around us. [pause]. How did you go with that?
C:	It felt really strange to have Mum accept some responsibility for the way she treated me. Strange, but in a good way.

	I always believed she treated like that because there was something wrong with me, like I wasn't good enough, or just 'bad.' Maybe that wasn't the case.
Th:	Yeah, it's interesting how during a rescript we see things more clearly, like a bystander might, but we are also able to emotionally connect to it, not just on a cognitive level.
C:	Yeah, that's how it felt.

Managing dissociation

Voice hearing itself has been conceptualised as a dissociative experience (e.g. Longden et al., 2012). With this in mind, it is perhaps not surprising that trauma-affected voice hearers are prone to various forms of dissociation, including experiences of depersonalisation, derealisation, dissociative amnesia, identity confusion and identity alteration (Pilton et al., 2015). In our clinical case series, we found that clients who more frequently dissociated during a rescript took a greater number of sessions before starting to report symptom reduction than those who did not dissociate. They were, however, able to reach the same level of symptom reduction by session ten (Paulik, Newman-Taylor, Steel, & Arntz, 2022). The most common types of dissociation we saw in our case series were flashbacks, going into a dissociative-like trance (where the client became non-responsive to the therapist), losing connection to the image being described by the therapist, and the imagery starting to change of its own accord (like their imagination was getting away from them) and becoming emotionally disconnected from the image. It is better to prevent an episode of dissociation than to have to bring someone back from dissociation. However, if the client does dissociate, it is best to try bringing them back to the image and continuing the rescript rather than getting them to stop the rescript and open their eyes, as the latter is likely to result in a higher level of distress associated with the disturbing memory. Below are some recommendations for preventing and reducing dissociation during an imagery rescript in voice hearers for those individuals who are particularly dissociation prone (see Paulik et al., 2022, for more information on managing dissociation in this clinical group):

- Discuss the first few steps of the rescript before commencing (i.e. roughly when in the memory you will start the rescript and what will happen in the first few steps of the rescript) to help reduce anxiety and, thus, dissociation.
- Reduce anxiety prior to commencing the rescript by using slow breathing or safe place imagery immediately prior to starting the rescript.
- Progress through the memory more quickly than one might for other clients (e.g. not ask as many sensory grounding questions at the commencement and have them describe each action taking place in less detail), and have the

rescript commence earlier in the memory. Conversely, if a client is emotionally detached from the image, spend longer in the original memory, and ask them questions which heighten emotions (e.g. 'what are you feeling? Where do you feel this in your body?').

- It is helpful if the therapist leads most of the rescript (at least for the first few significant steps to get the client safe and comforted) and to ensure that the client is present in the image by continually asking them to describe what is happening (e.g. 'the police are now forcing him to the ground. Describe to me what's happening now…').
- Therapist and client each hold one end of a scarf and the therapist tugs on it if the client goes silent and the client is asked to respond by tugging back. This also reminds the client they are in the therapy room with the therapist where they are safe.
- Use sensory items (e.g. Tiger Balm, fidget cube) to help ground the client during the rescript if needed.
- If the client begins to dissociate during the rescript, assure them they are safe by saying 'you are safe with me here in the therapy room, this image cannot hurt you and there is no need to dissociate. Come back to the image now…'
- If needed, ask the client to open their eyes and focus on present stimuli (grounding; looking at a specific object and asking the person to then describe it), then start again or resume where you left off.

Delivering imagery rescripting via telehealth

Imagery rescripting can also be safely delivered via telehealth. Our recent study showed no differences in outcomes between voice hearers who underwent imagery rescripting face-to-face or via telehealth during COVID-19 (Paulik et al., 2021). To proceed with imagery rescripting via telehealth, however, clients need both real and perceived safety and privacy. Some of the modifications to the protocols include ensuring the client has set up a space that feels safe, comfortable and without distractions; has grounding items on hand; has requested that others in the house do not disturb them during sessions; has a full battery (or device on charge) and strong internet connection; has a back-up plan in case the device disconnects (e.g. that the therapist will call the client on the phone to continue the rescript if the internet connection fails); and has a plan to separate their therapy session from the rest of their day (e.g. to pack up all therapy-related items after the session and then do an activity elsewhere).

Conclusion

Imagery rescripting can be a powerful experiential tool when working on memories to help shift associated schemas, modes or voices within Schema Therapy, or as a stand-alone treatment for voices and processing of underlying trauma and associated post-traumatic symptomatology. As reviewed here, some modifications to the protocols are needed when working with trauma-affected voice hearers, especially given their proneness to dissociation, and their often underdeveloped healthy adult mode due to complex childhood trauma. Selecting memories that are directly or thematically linked to the client's voices is also likely to get the best outcomes with regards to shifts in their voice severity, distress and content. The majority of the clients who did imagery rescripting at our service reported significant improvements in their PTSD symptoms, and often dramatic reductions in their voices' severity (frequency and intensity) and distress. While there are now several published evaluations, and reported clinical work, further research is still needed, and we hope that next steps will include randomised controlled trials.

References

Arntz, A. (2011). Imagery rescripting for personality disorders. *Cognitive and Behavioral Practice, 18*, 466–481. https://doi.org/10.1016/j.cbpra.2011.04.006

Arntz, A., & Weertman, A. (1999). Treatment of childhood memories: Theory and practice. *Behaviour Research and Therapy, 37*(8), 715–740. https://doi.org/10.1016/S0005-7967(98)00173-9

Berry, K., Varese, F., & Bucci, S. (2017). Cognitive attachment model of voices: Evidence base and future implications. *Frontiers in Psychiatry, 8*, 111. https://doi.org/10.3389/fpsyt.2017.00111

Brand, R. M., McEnery, C., Rossell, S., Bendall, S., & Thomas, N. (2018). Do trauma-focussed psychological interventions have an effect on psychotic symptoms? A systematic review and meta-analysis. *Schizophrenia Research, 195*, 13–22. https://doi.org/10.1016/j.schres.2017.08.037

de Bont, P. A. J. M., van Den Berg, D. P. G., van Der Vleugel, B. M., de Roos, C., de Jongh, A., van Der Gaag, M., & van Minnen, A. (2015). Predictive validity of the Trauma Screening Questionnaire in detecting post-traumatic stress disorder in patients with psychotic disorders. *The British Journal of Psychiatry, 206*(5), 408–416. https://doi.org/10.1192/bjp.bp.114.148486

de Leede-Smith, S., & Barkus, E. (2013). A comprehensive review of auditory verbal hallucinations: Lifetime prevalence, correlates and mechanisms in healthy and clinical individuals. *Frontiers in Human Neuroscience, 7*, 367–367. https://doi.org/10.3389/fnhum.2013.00367

Hackmann, A., Bennett-Levy, J., & Holmes, E. A. (2011). *Oxford guide to imagery in cognitive therapy*. Oxford Academic. https://doi.org/10.1093/med:psych/9780199234028.001.0001

Hardy, A. (2017). Pathways from trauma to psychotic experiences: A theoretically informed model of posttraumatic stress in psychosis. *Frontiers in Psychology 8*, 697. https://doi.org/10.3389/fpsyg.2017.00697

Hardy, A., Emsley, R., Freeman, D., Bebbington, P., Garety, P. A., Kuipers, E. E., Dunn, G., & Fowler, D. (2016). Psychological mechanisms mediating effects between trauma and psychotic symptoms: The role of affect regulation, intrusive trauma memory, beliefs, and depression. *Schizophrenia Bulletin, 42*(Suppl. 1), S34–S43. https://doi.org/10.1093/schbul/sbv175

Ison, R., Medoro, L., Keen, N., & Kuipers, E. (2014). The use of rescripting imagery for people with psychosis who hear voices. *Behavioural and Cognitive Psychotherapy*, *42*(2), 129–142. https://doi.org/10.1017/s135246581300057x

Johns, L. C., & van Os, J. (2001). The continuity of psychotic experiences in the general population. *Clinical Psychology Review, 21*, 1125–1141.

Longden, E., Madill, A., Waterman, M. G. (2012). Dissociation, trauma, and the role of lived experience: Toward a new conceptualisation of voice hearing. *Psychological Bulletin, 138*(1), 28–76. https://doi.org/10.1037/a0025995

McCarthy-Jones, S., and Longden, E. (2015). Auditory verbal hallucinations in schizophrenia and post-traumatic stress disorder: Common phenomenology, common cause, common interventions? *Frontiers in Psychology, 6*, 1071. https://doi.org/10.3389/fpsyg.2015.01071

Morina, N., Lancee, J., & Arntz, A. (2017). Imagery rescripting as a clinical intervention for aversive memories: A meta-analysis. *Journal of Behavior Therapy and Experimental Psychiatry*, *55*, 6–15. https://doi.org/10.1016/j.jbtep.2016.11.003

Paulik, G., Maloney, G., Arntz, A., Bachrach, N., Koppeschaar, A., & McEvoy, P. (2021). Delivering imagery rescripting via telehealth: Clinical concerns, benefits, and recommendations. *Current Psychiatry Reports*, *23*(5), 24. https://doi.org/10.1007/s11920-021-01238-8

Paulik, G., Newman-Taylor, K., Steel, C., & Arntz, A. (2022). Managing dissociation in imagery rescripting for voice hearers with trauma: Lessons from a case series. *Cognitive and Behavioral Practice*, *29*(2), 434–445. https://doi.org/10.1016/j.cbpra.2020.06.009

Paulik, G., Steel, C., & Arntz, A. (2019). Imagery rescripting for the treatment of trauma in voice hearers: A case series. *Behavioural and Cognitive Psychotherapy*, *47*(6), 709–725. https://doi.org/10.1017/s1352465819000237

Pilton, M., Varese, F., Berry, K., & Bucci, B. (2015). The relationship between dissociation and voices: A systematic literature review and meta-analysis. *Clinical Psychology Review, 40*, 138–155. https://doi.org/10.1016/j.cpr.2015.06.004

Steel, C. (2015). Hallucinations as a trauma-based memory: Implications for psychological interventions. *Frontiers in Psychology, 6*, 1262. https://doi.org/10.3389/fpsyg.2015.01262

Strachan, L. P., McEvoy, P. M., Arntz, A., Steel, C., & Paulik, G. (2023a). *Effectiveness and change mechanisms of imagery rescripting for trauma-affected voice hearers: An open trial* [Manuscript submitted for publication]. School of Psychology, Curtin University.

Strachan, L. P., Paulik, G., & McEvoy, P. M. (2022). A narrative review of psychological theories of post-traumatic stress disorder, voice hearing, and other psychotic symptoms. *Clinical Psychology & Psychotherapy*, *29*(6), 1791–1811. https://doi.org/10.1002/cpp.2754

Strachan, L. P., Paulik, G., & McEvoy, P. M. (2023b). *The trauma-related voices model: An integration of auditory verbal hallucinations and posttraumatic stress* [Manuscript submitted for publication]. School of Psychology, Curtin University.

Van den Berg, D., Tolmeijer, E., Jongeneel, A., Staring, A. B., Palstra, E., Van Der Gaag, M., & Hardy, A. (2023). Voice phenomenology as a mirror of the past. *Psychological Medicine, 53*(7), 2954–2962.

Chapter 8

Psychosis and Schema Therapy

This chapter will explore how Schema Therapy can be applied in working with clients experiencing psychosis, in particular those suffering from delusions and delusion related experiences. We propose that modes that express states such as self-attack or fear might amplify feelings of persecution or defectiveness; a core aim in therapy is to help the person to develop a new relation to these states by accessing and augmenting a realistic and caring self. The first section looks at assessment and the planning of sequences of work, on developing formulations, borrowing from other relevant therapies and an outline of the basic approach. The latter half of the chapter gives a series of detailed case studies illustrating how to work with modes in these contexts.

Assessment and planning of phases of therapy

Schema Therapy is complex and is not usually recommended as the first line therapy for psychosis; in general it would seem better that Schema Therapy is considered once other more specific therapies, for example, a version of cognitive behaviour therapy for delusions or voices, has been attempted or completed. It is also essential that either before Schema Therapy, or in its own initial stages there has been a phase of stabilisation with the aim of building the client's capacity to cope with challenges and to establish a sense of safety.

Which clients are suitable for Schema Therapy? In general, clients are suitable who have shown a capacity to focus and engage in a regular therapy and are willing to explore and work on emotions and social issues. Schema Therapy is also indicated if the client wishes to explore the influence of the past, or at least acknowledge some possible relevance. It is not a barrier to therapy if the client has active delusions or voices, or feels depressed or anxious. This is the case even where the client is, for example, utterly convinced that they are under the surveillance of a persecutor; if the client wants to work on feelings, and to attempt to make social changes, then there is sufficient ground to explore. It is assumed that working on core fears and extreme mode states can have an effect both on daily living but also the tenacity and extent of delusions and voices.

DOI: 10.4324/9781003350583-8

In general the sequence of work involves the following phases: first, a basic therapy including methods of stabilisation, particularly if it is thought that the work will need to address memories of trauma. Second, the focus can move to working with schemas and modes. In the final phase, the foundational work can be extended to wider issues in the client's life, such as work, education and a range of relationships, as the client takes on greater autonomy and nears readiness to end therapy.

Once an agreement has been reached to carry out a version of Schema Therapy, further assessment is required, particularly to conceptualise schemas and modes; here it is informative to use the schema and mode questionnaires and other methods as described in Chapter 5. Over time a formulation is developed: this, at a minimum, should include a basic map of the client's modes and how these relate to their current problems, symptoms and history.

Formulation

In putting together a formulation using modes and schemas, information is collected from the questionnaires but also directly from the client and from observations made in the sessions. The formulation normally consists of listing the main relevant modes, preferably using words or expressions which the client has suggested themselves. In conventional Schema Therapy, everything is typically brought together in one written formulation, which might include a diagram listing the states, their origin, and how they relate to and illuminate the specific problems. This is shared with the client early in therapy. Our preference for schema work with psychosis, however, is to move towards these understandings in slow and small steps. Typically, a small and specific selection of relevant modes is presented to the client and discussed; it may then be appropriate to enquire about links, for example between the feelings of a vulnerable child self and current experiences of terror in public. The extent to which one might do this depends on the degree of willingness of clients to consider these connections, even if they still believe that their fear is caused by the actions of real persecuting entities outside themselves.

With some clients it is possible to maintain two areas of discourse, in which one explores meanings within a delusional system, while the other addresses how the person's feelings can be linked to the experience of modes. For example, one might discuss with the client their experience of others in a work setting thinking terrible thoughts about them, but then in another session link the person's patterns of distress to reminders of earlier times when they were attacked at school. It is not necessary to point out the parallels between these two topic areas, and in fact it is often better to let the client begin to consider these possibilities in their own time and in their own words. The formulation is revisited each time specific problematic situations and coping are discussed. Discussion of the formulation, whether making connections with the distant past or recent emotions, is a linchpin of the work and repeatedly returned to. Examples of formulations will be given in the case studies to follow.

The basic elements of the approach

Having finished an initial exploration of the client's different modes and reached an agreement on which seem to be the most frequent and distressing, the work can move towards exploring the most relevant modes. A very small number of modes, even just one, might be the most important in early stages; over time, a wider range of mode states are usually addressed. A feature of Schema Therapy is the scope to specify a range of areas to work on, which can then be looked at flexibly, according to how they manifest in the life of the person. For most, if not all clients, vulnerable child modes are the single most important area of focus. This can include discussion, imagery, chair work; all of these being carried out in order to give care and compassion, and to consider what the child might have needed and should have received from caring adults in the past. The development and maintenance of a strong and supportive therapeutic relationship is a key priority throughout sessions.

In addition to the sort of work carried out with the vulnerable child, specific approaches can be needed for each mode. For example, if a client is very detached, then exploration is warranted of why this occurs, its function and any negative consequences; following this, methods might be developed to try moving out of detachment. For angry modes, there may be a focus on expression of the feeling, and how this can be constructively employed in a client's life. To address frequent occurrences of a demanding or critical mode, the therapist might explore the origin of such criticism or demands, and then aim to help the client to renegotiate their relationship with these parts, such that they no longer dominate or terrify the client; instead they may even find constructive expression for desires such as self-improvement. As in all Schema Therapy, the aim is to help the person to build a more confident, caring, and reasonable adult self.

Components in common with related therapies

The following case studies illustrate applying Schema Therapy flexibly, modifying and simplifying as appropriate, in working with people experiencing psychosis. Within the framework of Schema Therapy the case illustrations will also include compatible questions and ideas taken from Internal Family Systems (IFS; Schwartz, 1995) and Sensorimotor Therapy (Fisher, 2017). Rather than seeking to present one pure applied model, ideas have cross-pollinated here and elsewhere which we believe to be compatible and mutually beneficial. Briedis and Startup (2020), for example, have illustrated how Schema Therapy can be combined in various ways with sensorimotor work, particularly when trauma is a focus. As summarised in Chapter 4, Schema

Therapy, IFS and sensorimotor therapy all offer overlapping but somewhat different conceptualisations of parts of the self that can in fact complement each other.

Since its original conception, Schema Therapy has aimed to form an integrative framework, and the illustrations in this chapter continue in that spirit. As stated, it is also assumed in this book that specific use of Schema Therapy is often preceded by therapies such as CBT or solution orientated therapies. The following case illustrations are composites of several cases and have been altered for anonymity.

Case illustrations

Carl

Carl was diagnosed with a schizoaffective disorder and obsessive-compulsive disorder (OCD): he held a series of delusional beliefs that people were following him, and for a period he believed that an East European gang had put him under surveillance, placing a camera outside his house. He feared that they might kidnap him to extract money or rights to his house. Carl had also had OCD rituals which in fact incapacitated him from carrying on with everyday living. These included specific ways of breathing, as well as repetitive mental rituals to ward off danger. When starting therapy, he was stable in the community and had already received a treatment of CBT for his OCD, whose impact was reduced, though some rituals were still present. He scored very highly on measures of anxiety and depression.

Carl was living alone, although he often visited his mother and two sisters; his father had died several years earlier. The family history was complex: he expressed clear affection for his mother and father, but growing up had been extremely difficult. There was no suggestion of physical or sexual abuse; however, the effects of his father's drug addictions were such that Carl was often put in dangerous situations that were traumatic or emotionally neglectful.

The therapy consisted of several phases: we began by looking at his current life circumstances using narrative CBT, in this case focusing on his immediate goals such as exercise and looking for work; exploring exceptions to his problems, particularly in how he coped with his OCD symptoms, and building on these methods. He was encouraged to report his daily experiences in the form of metaphors on a record sheet, the aim here being to allow him to begin a more articulate expression of emotions, something he found very difficult (Rhodes & Jakes, 2009). We also carried out cognitive work, recording some negative thoughts and considering alternatives, both in session and at home; this work was not about delusions, but concerned everyday negative thinking of a depressive and anxious nature. After the narrative CBT, we began schema-focused therapy: in the following we will illustrate key areas of this process.

Formulation

Several of Carl's schemas concerned social connection: namely, emotional deprivation, mistrust, and abuse and abandonment; there were also schemas concerning self-sacrifice, emotional inhibition, unrelenting standards and neg- ativity. This pattern captured well his extreme sense of responsibility for others and his difficult relationships. On the mode scale, he scored very highly for demanding parent, detached protector and detached self-soother but also for modes of angry, enraged and vulnerable child. In terms of expressed thoughts or beliefs, very few were direct attacks on himself; however, many concerned the perceived negative behaviour of others, such as being let down, taken advantage of and being mocked by someone. His patterns of schemas matched very well his presentation of someone who was distant with others, held back from expression of emotion, felt under great pressure to look after others and who reported often having to struggle with feelings of intense anger when he perceived that he was being slighted.

A basic formulation was as follows: while having been loved and cared for, Carl also experienced extreme instability, a lack of support from his mother and father, and in addition he was exposed to neglect and situations of danger. To cope with such an environment, he developed a profound detachment from his emotions and also from others; to deal with feelings of danger, he devel- oped an attitude that he was responsible for looking after his family. Carl sensed within himself deep fear but also anger at his mistreatment: these two powerful emotions were usually ignored and not expressed. Under extreme circumstances such as the death of this father, he tried to fight off the sense of danger by engaging in ever more elaborate thought rituals aimed at preventing harm to his family. A sense of permanent threat fostered a perception of attack and danger from others, and as he broke down these became increasingly per- secutory. His delusions symbolised threats from terrible forces outside himself, that is, of 'demons' and 'government forces.'

Relation to his parents and expressing needs

We explored Carl's relationship with his father and mother following Young et al. (2003). He expressed a mixture of affection, good memories but also great difficulties. He remembered distressing incidents during childhood, and we were able to address these memories using dialogue and imagery. One was of a time when he could not sleep and went downstairs; his father was lying on the floor unconscious with a needle at his side. Carl had felt panic but also worried that his father would disapprove of his son seeing him in this state. In imagery, Carl was encouraged to express his feelings and needs to his father: he said that he wished his father would stop doing drugs, so that they could be a normal family, and added that he was not looking after everyone properly, and was making everyone scared. Prompted as to whether he felt any anger towards his father, Carl asked further: 'why do they have to go through this?' adding that it was not fair. The imagery was extended until the father was awake and Carl asked: 'why do you need drugs?' He expected that his father would eventually say to the young Carl that he should go to bed but would also be angry with himself. Carl recalled happy memories of his father, and he said poignantly: 'he was half a normal father.' The perspective taking in the imagery sought to allow traumatic memories to be viewed from a caring adult perspective, and to encourage compassion and warmth to be expressed towards the younger Carl experiencing difficulties.

Demanding mode and guilt

Carl spent a great deal of time trying to do things for his family, and often this led to conflict when others were not appreciative of his efforts or were critical. As we explored many of his thoughts and actions, it was clear to him that he had a demanding mode linked to a strong feeling of guilt. When asked to focus on this feeling of guilt, he said that he felt he was letting his family down, and that if he didn't look after them, he would be a 'sell-out' and very 'low and selfish.' Asked if he could form an image of what the demanding mode would look like, he said that it would be a strong leader but stern and cold; he explained that he felt intimidated by it. While investigating the origins of this mode, we used imagery to revisit a memory involving his father. Carl had been trying to get various members of the family to do things; at this point his father said 'you're the reason this family is in a mess… you're the problem.' Viewing this interaction from an adult perspective allowed a consideration of how events could have unfolded otherwise, what could have been said to his father, and provided an opportunity for Carl to re-evaluate the sense of blame and guilt that had been induced by it.

Schema Therapy recommends exploring the benefits and drawbacks of modes where these have negative effects or create blocks to recovery (Arntz & Jacob, 2013). When Carl was asked about the advantages of the demanding part, he said that it encouraged him to be strong, organised, more ambitious and motivated. Regarding the negatives, he said that it was stressful, time consuming, tiring, that it ended up making him feel bitter and resentful, and sometimes even led to him being unappreciated and 'mocked' by others. He identified specific problems it created; for example, he had spent far too much time tidying his room recently.

We set up a dialogue using imagery with the mode: Carl was able to ask what it does and why, and what would satisfy it; a key feature was to negotiate with the demanding part to see if it could become less severe. The demanding mode first stated that it wanted everything to be 'perfect,' but when asked to spell this out, suggested simple things like the family having security. It was thus possible to find common aims and to agree to try an adjusted role of being protective and encouraging. From this point Carl was able to be more aware of his demanding part and to try slightly different approaches towards others.

Detached mode and anger

When asked for an image of the part of him that was detached, Carl said: it would be 'blue ice' or like an 'ice sculpture' or 'ice man': he could see through it, and this part was not interested in anything. When asked what he felt towards it he said 'empty:' he added that the detached part was hollow, not in the room, floating and sometimes daydreaming. It stopped him being comfortable when given hugs by his family. For positives, he said it made him stronger and allowed him not to worry about the welfare of others. He thought the detached part was protecting him from fear, and in dialogue when asked about its role at first it said: 'I am you,' 'don't play games with me,' and 'don't wake the demons.' To 'what do you fear most?' it said that if his anger was unleashed, it would hurt others.

Carl, however, wanted to proceed to work with anger in spite of the above. Several precautions were taken, for example, keeping whatever imagery appeared at some distance. He saw an image of an angry child in a sort of underground basement. Carl stated: the detached part is the guard in the corridor, and 'even I'm not allowed to go see the child in the basement.' He spontaneously added that the angry child had changed and had been thinking more over the years. In the next session, we discussed the meanings of this image; Carl suggested that most of his anger was aimed towards his father, and sometimes at other families who had an easy life. Additional work on anger concerned racist insults that a boy at school had made about his ethnic background: imagery allowed Carl to identify and express what he would now like to say to that boy, thus facilitating a practice of expressing anger and standing up for himself. We also negotiated another new role for anger: in directing energy towards starting a business.

Direct work with the fearful child

In the later stages of therapy, we were able to address the fearful child part of Carl more directly. When asked what the fearful part might look like, he said a six-year-old child 'in a corner.' Towards this child he felt sorry and wanted to help him. Carl asked the child what he was afraid of to which he replied 'being alone.' He then had a memory of the time he and his father were arrested and Carl was put in a cell by himself. In the image he comforted the child, although he did find doing this difficult. It is interesting to note how a similar image of a cell was used here for fear and also previously when considering anger.

Imagery was also used to address a memory regarding a drug dealer visiting the house when his father was not here; this man demanded money but took the video player instead. In imagery, the child was at first angry, but on investigating what the younger Carl needed to stop the fear, the child was moved to sit on a new settee playing a computer game. Carl was able to tell his younger self: 'don't worry, those days are over.'

Outcomes

Over the course of therapy, Carl's rituals diminished until they no longer posed a practical problem, and they only occurred for a few seconds now and then. He eventually hardly mentioned his former delusions, which were now of no particular concern, and in fact appeared to have softened into realistic beliefs, such as that there might be criminal gangs in the area. In the first months of therapy, various scores suggested very high levels of clinical anxiety and moderate depression. In the last three assessments, Carl scored as not depressed and just on the border between mild and moderate anxiety. He reported functioning well and feeling better, stating that he thought it was now time for him to really try to find the sort of employment that he had always wanted to do.

Of course, there were many other more subtle changes, such as being able to shift focus from problems connected with the modes of being demanding and detached, over to an expression of a range of emotions in general. Carl was also able to re-evaluate issues relating to feelings of guilt, appraising the causes in his childhood; importantly, he was also able to approach his experiences of anger without being overwhelmed and to realise that this emotion did not have to be out of control or totally destructive. A year later, he had maintained these various gains.

James

James was in his early twenties, and had been diagnosed with psychosis after being brought to hospital, due to his family's concerns about him behaving erratically and shouting at night. He had been withdrawn and low in mood for some time and had become increasingly preoccupied with beliefs that people on the street were mocking him and intended to attack him. James stopped attending university and almost never left his room. He said that he heard his family members belittling him and plotting against him, although they denied this, and while in hospital he perceived other patients and staff as 'actors' playing roles. He was deeply distrustful of others' intentions and felt somehow someone was 'pulling the strings.' He was willing to engage in therapy to try to cope with stress and feel better about himself, although his beliefs about persecution were held with complete certainty.

Sessions initially focused on understanding James' current experiences, and a brief history of his perceptions, feelings and coping responses. The next phase used ideas from narrative CBT (Rhodes & Jakes, 2009) for the purpose of stabilisation, in particular, encouraging ways of coping with stress and emotional difficulties but also any relevant practical and social issues. James already had ways of coping, including exercise and housework; he was encouraged to return to these constructive activities and to consider re-starting his studies with appropriate support and adjustments put in place.

After the stabilisation phase, we built a shared understanding of the factors contributing to James' breakdown. These included stress and a lack of sleep, seeming to hear his name being whispered, an increasing conviction that people knew about the sexual content he had looked at online and were mocking him at university and on the street. As James attempted to hide from the world and gave up his course, the social isolation and lack of routine had allowed the persecutory worries to take over completely.

Assessing and understanding modes

After a few sessions when James felt a bit better able to cope, we introduced the idea of modes of self in a normalised fashion, noting that we all have different states in different circumstances, and discussing some everyday examples. He completed the schema and mode questionnaires and spoke about what he thought his potential states of self were. The questionnaire scores, clinical observations and subjective descriptions were combined to inform a case conceptualisation. Recent examples from James' life also indicated some active modes; for example, he described tolerating a recent trip to the supermarket with great distress, reporting very strong feelings of unease and a sense that others were aware of him, in fact, could 'see through' him, and what they saw was someone 'weird.' This mode of being conspicuous and 'weird' would recur at times of being in public. In terms of schema and mode questionnaires the most relevant schemas were emotional deprivation, mistrust/abuse, subjugation, negativity/pessimism and punitiveness. The main modes were: vulnerable child, enraged child, compliance, detached protector and punitive parent; in addition his scores for contented child and health adult were very negative.

Mapping the modes and accessing a child image

We returned to the idea of different states of the self as a foundation for the first piece of imagery work. James closed his eyes and imagined a peaceful garden. He was asked if any part of him felt threatened by this process and, particularly, any image of himself as a child. He reported that he felt fine but that it was as if part of him was at that very moment hiding and listening. When asked again to try to imagine a younger self in a safe or positive situation the image he generated was of someone about eight years old who was content and just watching. Having achieved that, and checking if he felt he could proceed, we then considered any image of a young self not feeling content; he was able to generate an image of a child in anger, who did not trust, and who was scared. As we proceeded, however, it seemed that James had begun to 'fuse' with the young self, that is, was seeing things through the eyes of the child and experiencing the situation as if the child. He was prompted to step back and see the child from the outside, that is, the third person perspective. He was then able to see the child playing at a distance. James and the therapist were then able to express care and give reassurance to the child image, saying that we would return.

After the imagery, James recalled a time he had got into trouble for damaging a neighbour's trees, breaking some branches on purpose to make swords. He had been made to apologise, feeling full of shame at the time. It is important to note that he was not being asked to give details of any trauma in this phase; memories were occurring spontaneously and were discussed briefly. If he had gone into further details, or had become distressed, the therapist would have suggested stopping and returning to the immediate, noting, however, that we could return to these topics later if needed.

In the next session James reported having had a good week, with no negative effects from the imagery work, and he expressed an interest in doing more and returning to the child image. We went on to list all the different states that he could recognise in himself. He linked the image of feeling 'small and weird' with what he had felt when he had been shouted at and insulted by his father, explaining that this state felt 'stupid,' 'inferior' and that it made him feel 'dull.' James' mode list included a contented child state, fearful, feeling ugly and strange, impulsive, angry and critical. Most of these had a clear equivalent on the mode questionnaire; however, the questionnaire scores also indicated features he had not described, namely detachment and compliance. From clinical observation, we believe these are often not reported spontaneously by clients.

Working with paranoia and the modes of vulnerable child and critic

The therapy went on to directly address the key modes of vulnerable child, punitive parent and compliant surrender. Interspersed with imagery and chair work were reflections connecting the modes with events in James' earlier life; in general, the direction was to help him move away from a negative and damning set of ideas, experiences or interpretations of himself and of what happened, to a more complex and compassionate healthy adult perspective. While direct work concerning his parents tended to be in the later phases of therapy, the actual order of addressing modes was flexible and non-linear; an aspect of Schema Therapy is, in fact, to deal with issues as they arise, and relate these to modes and past events as one proceeds. In the following I will illustrate selected features of the therapy, in particular with the vulnerable child, and with sources of the punitive mode in terms of school and his father.

James would often say that he was 'bad,' or 'a failure.' It became increasingly clear that he had always felt not good enough at school, not good enough for his parents, and in fact that he believed that they saw him as 'bad.' So while he was able to remember many episodes of being rejected or criticised by others, it was also the case that as far as he could remember, there had always been an internal feeling of being 'bad,' which was expressed in the image of looking 'weird.' In one session we wondered whether this image of being small and weird could be a version or expression of shame. He was then able to say that it was always there at a 'ground level' but much less so when he is doing good or pleasant things.

Offering an alternative perspective is of course almost never enough to update a client's beliefs; we needed to return to these topics many times, combining discussion with experiential work. One piece of imagery started from James' memory of showing a piece of writing to his teacher at school and being criticised by her. In the image he saw the situation from the child's point of view. With his agreement, the therapist was able to enter the image and say to the teacher that this was not a way to treat him. She, in return, was very insistent and argumentative; the therapist, however, argued assertively for a better way of treating James, explaining that this would have a more positive impact and that she had not realised the long-term damage she might be doing with her harshness and instant rejection of his work. James reflected afterwards that at first he had been worried about the interaction, but had found it very reassuring how the therapist had stood their ground with the teacher. This had modelled assertiveness, and it had also helped James to see that the teacher was authoritarian and inflexible. He noted that when the teacher had spoken to him in this rejecting way he had felt a 'weight' put on him.

We sought also to address James' criticism of himself, which he explained might occur particularly when feeling angry. He described a sort of critical internal voice, which sounded like a combination of many people who had acted this way towards him. These included multiple teachers but also James' father, who too was critical and often scary, stern and controlling. James had never really felt accepted by him, and sensed he was not quite living up to some standard, despite there also being a great deal of love in the relationship. When James was asked to form an image of the critic as a person, he described a woman screaming and putting him down. Asked what he felt towards this person, he said anger. He was able to put the anger temporarily aside and ask the woman why she engaged in such criticism; to this she explained that he was not looking after himself and was putting too much importance on impressing other people, arguing that she really wanted him to change. This may be an example of how a harsh critic can sometimes change its function, becoming closer to some form of ally.

Later in therapy we were able to address the role of James' father more fully. On returning to an image of being weird and small, and his feelings associated with this, James linked these to the humiliation he felt from his treatment by teachers and peers at school but also the times his father had shouted and insulted him, particularly in front of his friends who were visiting his home. At this point he was finally able to express anger. After the imagery work, we discussed in depth this feeling and what he might do with it, he thought he would not take any particular action. It turned out, however, that James decided to speak calmly to his father about the occasional times when he had been humiliated, and this seemed in fact to bring about a positive change in their relationship. Subsequent sessions similarly addressed the role of James' mother, who had loved him but had not protected him from his father's insults or over-controlling behaviours.

Returning the focus again later to the vulnerable child mode, we sought to explore in imagery why James had sometimes felt 'pity' towards the child self; interestingly, he spontaneously generated an image of a pre-verbal child just beginning to walk. He could see the eyes and face of this child and realised that he was making a big effort, was almost heroic in using all the strength he could. About this image James felt very happy, and when asked what the child might need at this point, he said for the adult James to smile and clap. When asked what else, he said for the child to receive a hug, which he proceeded to do in the image.

Clinical observations and outcomes

The work comprised many sessions spanning two years. After a few months, James' conviction that he was going to be mocked or attacked in the street had ceased. He retained for longer a sense that someday somebody would find something out about him. He was strikingly less depressed and became far more engaged in completing his studies and later in exploring interesting work. We also looked at how he might overcome feelings of being not good enough in order to start a new romantic relationship. He had one serious relapse, during which he thought that a plot against him had started and people were passing messages, some of which he heard; this resolved quickly, and he was able to return to his previous better functioning state.

It seems clear that in the case of James the experience of persecution was based on a sense of shame and feeling himself to be an 'outsider' to others who were potential critics and who might reject him. These initial feelings developed during the complex events of his childhood and school years. He loved his parents; however, there were frequent arguments, a sense of neglect or absence from his mother, and from his father a pressure of over-control and the weight of expectations. He found it difficult to form relationships at school and began to experience himself as being a sort of outsider and different to others. Certain experiences of not succeeding seemed to snowball, until they researched a crisis point. There were themes relating to guilt about childhood misdemeanours that also fed into the more complex paranoid story. It must be emphasised that the therapist never argued that James' delusional beliefs, voices or visual experiences were false. Rather, we tended to focus on other related issues, such as the experience of feeling weird and relevant emotions and social relations.

It is interesting to note how James's attitude both to the past and present changed over time. For example, despite at one point giving extremely clear examples of feeling fear, he subsequently said that he didn't know where this might came from. He also fluctuated in whether he wished to speak about his parents, which was done only with his full consent. Like many individuals experiencing psychosis, he seemed to sometimes see things in a paranoid light but at other times from a more biographic and psychological perspective. As the work proceeded, he tended to feel clearer about the origins of his experiences.

There were of course many key therapeutic ingredients in this work, not least the developing relationship between client and therapist, which here was very positive. Other features included: exploring delusions and voices without any extended focus on their reality status; practical techniques such as deep breathing when in fear-inducing situations; understanding that paranoia might be based in a part that feels fear and shame; understanding different states and changing relations to these; placing feelings in the context of history; developing a more complex understanding and relation to early caregivers; learning to accept oneself and develop a more positive attitude towards a younger self but also to take steps to care for the self in the present and future.

Specific work with post-traumatic symptoms

Several approaches drawing on CBT have been developed for working with trauma, and some of these have been evaluated in the context of psychosis (Rhodes, 2022). A contribution of Schema Therapy is to develop methods, including imagery, that can address the impacts of trauma indirectly, that is, not to focus principally on reliving the events but rather trying to help the client to feel what it might be like to give the younger self what they needed from a caring figure at that point in time. The framework of modes is key in allowing a shared conceptualisation of extreme negative states and building the caring adult mode which can facilitate a re-appraisal of painful emotional and interpersonal responses, and address how the client's needs can be met in the present and future. We illustrate this approach in the following case and other examples are given in Rhodes (2022).

Hamza

Hamza presented with severe protracted depression and many psychotic symptoms, including persistent persecutory ideas of being attacked by others; for example, someone might attempt to poison him or run him over in a car, or push him under a train; he also heard voices, which he sometimes described as his own thoughts, though sometimes he was not sure. He sometimes felt extreme and unusual sensations in his arms and other parts of his body, which felt like the presence of an animal or insect, although he tended to realise later that this explanation was unlikely. He also recounted suddenly feeling as if he was in a childhood situation on the street of a foreign town. As a child and teenager Hamza had undergone physical and emotional forms of abuse by family members and sexual abuse by a group of strangers in his neighbour-hood: his symptoms were consistent with a sort of dissociative psychosis.

In spite of these difficulties, Hamza had managed to achieve some qualifica-tions in his later teenage years and various forms of employment. The latter, however, had recently collapsed due to extreme depression and the impacts of his other symptoms. The therapy developed with Hamza proceeded in phases, starting with a solution-finding and resource-building phase to achieve some stabilisation, then moving on to self-esteem work as outlined by the Padesky (1994), and only then turning to focus on states of the self and a mode concep-tualisation. In the following we will describe specific moments of our work.

When first asked the future focused question: 'what would your life be like without these problems,' Hamza said at first that it really wouldn't be him with-out them. He was then able to go on to say that he would be transformed, and in fact came back the next week to say it would really be a sort of 'rebirth.' He explained that he would be able to develop good relationships with family members, look after his health and be free to do what he wanted. Adding detail, he said that he could talk properly with his father, take up classes at the gym and return to a martial arts practice. Encouragement was given in sessions to progress in returning to healthy activities, and he made incremental steps in these directions, particularly in returning to exercise. When discussing beliefs about self and others, Hamza said he was 100 per cent convinced he was weak and worthless, and that other people were manipulative, selfish and perhaps even 'evil.' He said that he would prefer to be strong and confident, and for others to be honest and non-manipulative. Initially he had zero conviction that he was strong or confident but did allow that some people could be honest and non-manipulative. He was asked to look out for examples supporting his pre-ferred beliefs.

After the stabilisation and self-esteem phases, we assembled a narrative overview of Hamza's history of trauma and abuse, as well as strengths, resist-ance and resilience (Rhodes & Jakes, 2009). The aim was not to go into any detail but to form a succinct overview of major events. This phase ended with a clear emphasis on how Hamza had survived and got out of these situations, and how he was now progressing in his life. We return to working indirectly with trauma in the following mode work.

Hamza's mode conceptualisation was informed by discussion of his states of self and his responses to the mode questionnaires. The latter strongly emphasised the modes of vulnerable child, punitive parent and detached self-soother, with a suggestion at a moderate level of an angry child. He also scored very highly on not being able to access the contented child or contented adult modes. He articulated subjectively that he felt he had a fearful paranoid state and one that was very anxious and obsessed; one that was filled with self-hate (he added, 'at least in the past'); and the one he hoped to be moving towards, which is a state of being 'balanced.' When describing how anxious he felt he said it was like a 'white box' filled with tensions, had pulsating sides, and that was about to explode. When asked about the state of detachment, he described this as a sort of 'mist.' In the following, however, we will focus particularly on direct work with the vulnerable child. When asked to envisage his younger self, Hamza had the image of sitting outdoors on a street pavement alone, leaning forward, at a distance from a group of men. Nothing in particular was happening in this scene; he said that the young boy was sad, felt little confidence, was insecure and on edge. When asked what he felt towards the child, he said that he would like to give an apology. In the following session, we were able to explore what he thought the apology was about; he said he would like to apologise to the child for not growing up well and not helping himself better. We then proceeded to use mental imagery so that Hamza could feel what it was like to make this apology to his vulnerable child self. The next week he reported no negative consequences of this work or distress. Hamza still wanted to apologise further to his child self in several more imagery sessions, and we returned to this image until there became a more balanced exchange between the two. The aim in working with the child is most frequently to give compassion or somehow help the child. Apologising could be considered negative or at least not obviously helpful to the young child, but it appeared that in the situation, and with such extremity of experiences, this was what Hamza could achieve at the time, and it seemed to have a positive effect. The apologies could be seen as a way of reconnecting the adult self with the younger self and in a way declaring that he would now take care of himself.

Hamza's vulnerable child part was further addressed via a memory from his time at school, when a gang of boys shouted insults at him. He was encouraged to step into the mental image as an adult, and he reported that he stood in the way between the young child and the boys; he then looked straight at the boys and gave a hard stare. He told them that he would get the headmaster, and they ran off. When asked what the young Hamza needed, he said for the adult self to take his hand and lead him to a peaceful place looking at the sea. The adult was encouraged to ask the child self if he knew that he was now a big grownup and doing well in the world. He then showed the younger self various good things in his life, in particular his flat in London. Hamza reported feeling very moved after this piece of imagery.

A connected element of the work with Hamza involved asking him to explore what his persecuted self-state would look like, and, in fact, if he could demonstrate in the room how that mode behaved. It was striking when he demonstrated showed how he could be sitting, for example, at a table, his eyes moving side to side but keeping his head static and slightly down. His enactment demonstration looked like he was in a state of dread where he was expecting to be attacked. An exploration of the meanings and feelings of such shifting states of self facilitated the adoption of body focused strategies such as slow breathing, as well as the use of positive imagery, particularly to reassure his fearful self.

The therapy over time proceeded in blocks of sessions with gaps of several months. Later phases focused on using imagery to speak to his family members. Eventually, he was able to make many small steps to reclaim his life and return to work as his depression levels fell. As with many cases of psychosis with severe trauma histories, I found that his level of anxiety and persecutory ideation fluctuated over time; however, as therapy progressed he was increasingly able to carry out various sorts of self-care actions and to take up the position of the adult caring mode. He also eventually embarked on a new intimate relationship.

Conclusion

Clinical work by ourselves and others demonstrates that a version of Schema Therapy can be useful for those diagnosed with psychosis; the work, as stated, needs modification in various ways, for example to take account of the client fluctuating in out of states of persecution and also to work around more severe and disturbing trauma histories. Given certain precautions, significant improvements in multiple domains can be achieved, and without a strong focus on rational disputation of specific delusions or hallucinations. The clients described here moved away from preoccupation with psychotic content, experienced less depression and anxiety, and in general coped in better ways with everyday life.

References

Arntz, A., & Jacob, G. (2013). *Schema Therapy in practice*. Wiley-Blackwell.

Briedis, J., & Startup, H. (2020). Somatic perspective in Schema Therapy: The role of the body in the awareness and transformation of modes and schemas. In G. Heath, & H. Startup (eds), *Creative methods in Schema Therapy: Advances and innovation in clinical practice*. Routledge.

Fisher, J. (2017). *Healing the fragmented selves of trauma survivors*. Routledge.

Padesky, C. A. (1994). Schema change processes in cognitive therapy. *Clinical Psychology & Psychotherapy*, 1(5), 267–278.

Rhodes, J. (2022). *Psychosis and the traumatised self*. Routledge.

Rhodes, J., & Jakes, S. (2009). *Narrative CBT for psychosis*. Routledge.

Schwartz, R. C. (1995). *Internal family systems therapy*. Guilford.

Young, E., Klosko, J. S., & Weishaar, M. E. (2003). *Schema Therapy: A practitioner's guide*. Guilford Press.

Chapter 9

Bipolarity and Schema Therapy

Introduction

In this chapter we will summarise the wide range of difficulties experienced by those diagnosed with bipolar disorder and explain some of the ways in which Schema Therapy might connect particularly well with several of these difficulties, potentially providing a very meaningful contribution in conjunction with other established treatment methods. The chapter will then outline the application and adaptation of Schema Therapy for bipolarity, and illustrate this with several in-depth case studies of such therapy.

Aspects of bipolar conditions with relevance to Schema Therapy

People with diagnoses of bipolar disorder suffer from the specific effects of mania and hypomania (Mansell & Pedley, 2008) but perhaps even more so from long-term and repeated experiences of depression (Mansell et al., 2005). Episodes of depression are often associated with negative life events, although not in all cases. In addition, milder depressive experiences commonly continue to occur in between episodes (Benazzi, 2004), especially in those with a younger age of onset, longer illness duration and more episodes of depression. Benazzi spoke of 'inter-episode mood lability,' while Tsapekos et al. (2021) used the term 'residual depressive symptoms,' arguing these were the strongest predictor of overall functioning; they also noted that executive dysfunction was associated with occupational difficulties. Given the complexity of these impacts, it is not surprising that individuals suffer long-term consequences in their interpersonal and emotional lives.

In addition to the specific impacts of mood fluctuations, it is also the case that individuals with bipolarity tend to have suffered a range of other difficulties, both at present and in the past. These difficulties include histories of abuse and trauma, attachment disruptions, maladaptive schemas, and issues with identity and relationships. Abuse and trauma in early years is thought to be a major contributing factor to the distress and dysfunction of those with bipolar

DOI: 10.4324/9781003350583-9

conditions (Garno et al., 2005): a review of 19 studies of childhood found that adversity was 2.63 times more likely to have occurred in those diagnosed with bipolar disorder in comparison to non-clinical controls (Palmier-Claus et al., 2016). Gilman et al. (2015) also demonstrated an increase of risk for mania in those with childhood adversity and, in addition, that various negative events in adult years predicted onset and recurrence of manic episodes; they noted that childhood adversity potentiated the effect of recent stressors on adult mania.

In addition to the difficulties described above, many clients also report a serious challenge to their sense of identity, particularly if they have experienced a very dramatic first episode of mania; Farr, Rhodes, Baruch and Smith (2023a) noted that: 'some mourned the loss of their exceptional manic self, and attempted to relapse into mania, while others struggled with the loss of who they had been prior to their episode.' They reported that participants described diverse states during manic phases, which included feeling exceptional, but also angry and persecuted. Farr, Rhodes and Smith (2023b) emphasised the importance in the recovery period of finding purpose through diverse activities and goals, yet also noted that such changes could involve a compromise for some participants, perhaps having to give up valued experiences, particularly in regard to being high or seeking pleasure. Clearly recovery is not only about managing symptoms but in fact facing a wide range of problems and often pursuing new ways of living. These observations suggest that it is important for therapy, and related services, to consider the narrative of what has happened, how the person can move forward and with what sense of self: often they will need to adjust former assumptions and targets, and while this can involve a loss, it is also an opportunity for new ways of living, not least of which might be a more caring and compassionate attitude to self and deeper knowledge of one's many states.

Hawke, Provencher and Parikh (2013) argued that Schema Therapy is well suited for bipolar clients given the findings of early trauma, the effects of life events and cognitive appraisals, and the diagnostic overlap between bipolarity and borderline personality disorder (Zimmerman & Morgan, 2013). Research has in fact indicated that those with bipolarity score highly on measures of early maladaptive schemas. In contrasting participants with bipolarity to healthy participants, Khisravi et al (2017) reported high scores on a range of schemas, including emotional deprivation, mistrust/abuse, social isolation and defectiveness. Hawke and Provencher (2012) compared the scores for those with bipolarity, unipolar depression and anxiety: when comparing bipolar participants with unipolar, they noted that the former showed stronger schemas of approval/recognition-seeking, as well as entitlement/grandiosity. They suggested that schema patterns indicating membership of the bipolar group comprised high scores on approval/recognition-seeking and low scores on emotional inhibition and abandonment. We suggest that the therapy described in this chapter can in fact be suitable to help with such a range of difficulties.

Several therapies have been designed specifically for bipolarity, addressing different aspects of its specific features. Such therapies include cognitive behaviour therapy (Lam et al., 2010), family therapy (Miklowitz, 2010) and interpersonal and social rhythm therapy (Frank et al., 2005). There is often a focus on achieving regular sleep patterns (Sorensen et al., 2007) and other physiological features such as diet and relaxation. The use of imagery for patients with bipolarity (Holmes et al., 2019) has been explored, especially with a view to targeting experiences of anxiety. Our aim in this chapter is to outline how Schema Therapy might well complement other therapies for bipolarity and, in particular, might help those with long-term interpersonal emotional and social difficulties. Initial findings of acceptability and therapeutic benefit have been reported by several small-scale studies of short-term (ten to fifteen sessions) Schema Therapy protocols (Ghaderi et al., 2016; Erfan et al., 2019); the approach we illustrate here is potentially longer and more complex, depending on the client need.

It is certainly not the case that all clients with a diagnosis of bipolarity show social and emotional difficulties, but it is certainly a very important feature for a substantial number and, in particular, for those for whom a simple course of therapy for managing mood fluctuations and developing a healthy lifestyle is not sufficient. There is a need for therapies which work with long-term emotional and interpersonal concerns, and Schema Therapy is precisely an approach formulated for working with these issues.

Outline of therapy

Initial phase and stabilisation

Often a client will be referred for therapy who already has received a diagnosis of a type of bipolarity; of course this may or may not be something accepted by the individual and can become relevant during therapeutic discussions (Miklowitz, 2018). Whether such diagnoses are accepted, or another term suggested by the client, the approach outlined here emphasises exploring how the person sees their own present and long-term difficulties, as well as their goals and hopes for the future. Orientation around the client's goals is in line with recovery focused approaches, as outlined by Jones et al. (2015).

The sort of information explored at this stage involves the following: the goals and hopes of the client; levels of anxiety, depression, and possibly assessment for mania; any social or interpersonal difficulties; the individual's occupational and leisure activities, and how they feel they are managing in all of the various areas relevant to their lives, for example at home, at work, with friends and partners. If this early stage assessment suggests that there are very specific concerns such as the misuse of drugs and alcohol, or PTSD, then the relevant therapies might be suggested as appropriate before Schema Therapy.

In line with existing therapies for bipolarity, such as those outlined by Lam et al. (2010), and Holmes et al. (2019), we propose a first phase focused on the client's current day to day life, putting together a relapse prevention plan and establishing emotional stabilisation to whatever extent possible. To achieve these aims, the therapist can use techniques from cognitive behaviour therapy, behavioural activation, dialectical behavioural therapy and also from solution focused therapy (Rhodes & Jakes, 2009) which gives special attention to meaningful personal goals and coping resources. In addition, it is very useful to draw on physiological techniques for anxiety management and emotional stabilisation, which could include breathing exercises, progressive muscle relaxation and other body-focused strategies (Fisher, 2017).

In cases where the client is particularly depressed or manic at the beginning of therapy, it might be important, with their agreement, to focus on coping with their current mood state in the first instance. Dealing with depression can often involve behavioural activation and may draw on various resources using solution orientated questions. Working with mania requires a wide range of responses; if a patient is very manic then it becomes increasingly unlikely that they will attend therapy sessions, and if they do, lack of focused attention can impede progress. It may be most appropriate to engage further sources of support, including other professionals involved, as well as trusted friends or relatives, in implementing a previously developed relapse prevention programme. The latter might involve certain personal coping strategies, potentially seeking medical advice and taking precautions in any areas known to be potentially damaging, such as handing over credit cards for temporary safekeeping. The more involved phase of therapy can be postponed, with client agreement, until a point where mood is once again more balanced.

Schema Therapy-focused assessment

For many clients with bipolarity, versions of the above stabilisation strategy might be all that is required and all that the client wishes to pursue. Not all clients with bipolarity have significant interpersonal and emotional difficulties, and certainly not all are interested in pursuing therapy for these areas. However, for those who do wish to focus on emotional and interpersonal issues, and given a Schema Therapy approach is feasible and agreeable, the next stage can comprise an augmented assessment specific to this model.

Clients with bipolarity, when not particularly manic, can present very much like any other clients with social difficulties, in which case the full range of assessments, techniques and targets of the standard Schema Therapy protocol can be appropriate. These will not be detailed here, since they are catalogued in the main Schema Therapy textbooks. The assessment will usually include the use of questionnaires to assess schemas and modes, observation of the client's interactions in sessions, discussion of interpersonal difficulties in the present and in the past, and the use of imagery to explore difficult emotional situations. These diverse sources of information all contribute to a formulation developed collaboratively with the client.

It is our clinical observation that with some bipolar clients it can be quite difficult at first to clarify what exactly their emotional and social problems are: a long and changing list may be given, or the client may struggle to describe these at all. This can be linked with avoidance and a sense of self stigma but also may reflect unfamiliarity with these types of discussions; here the questionnaire measures can help to note features that may not be described spontaneously. Another issue might be that some clients may not wish to articulate personal difficulties or quite often are ambivalent about recognising problems; however, over time and with discussion, it is usually possible to focus on specific areas relevant to therapy.

It is usually advisable to fully explore schemas and modes as they function and manifest in the present before addressing past issues, particularly if there are histories of interpersonal abuse and trauma. In general the approach taken in Schema Therapy to trauma is indirect, whereby an important emphasis is addressing the unmet needs of the person around the time of the trauma rather than engaging in direct reliving of trauma memories. In the rest of this chapter we will present detailed clinical work which illustrates such an approach.

Case illustration: Alex

Introduction

Alex had been diagnosed with bipolar disorder type I in his late thirties, and he had come to therapy several years later; he had taken several months off work following a manic episode, which had been followed by a period of depression. By the time of his first therapy session, he reported that he was somewhat high again, but just coping; the main effect of this in the room was that he spoke very rapidly, and it was difficult to maintain any specific focus during the first few sessions. He did, however, turn up for his appointments, and we were able to discuss his life and to list several problems that he suffered from: these included depression, anxiety and the recent destructive mania at work. He reported that when feeling very high he became 'paranoid' about others at work, and in extreme situations sometimes heard a voice or a distorted perception of the voices of others; he was, however, aware in our sessions that these voices were generated in some ways by his own mind. He described feeling that he was a failure in life due to having been divorced more than once and was experiencing work difficulties. He reported a reasonable relationship with his father and stepmother but a very abusive one with his stepsister. His biological mother was now living abroad, and he rarely saw her. When his parents had divorced, he had found this very distressing. He said that at school for a time he had been considered a 'geek,' but eventually decided to become strong by learning martial arts. In spite of his multiple difficulties, Alex was well engaged in therapy and willing to talk freely and carry out homework.

Stabilisation and relapse prevention

The first phase of therapy involved developing a relapse prevention plan and dealing with the immediate effects of being high. The high state soon declined and was followed by depression, which then became the new focus of the work. The details of his relapse prevention plan for the state of being high were quite simple, though effective, and included: communication with his GP or other medical staff, taking medication and seeking help from a friend, specifically to take his credit cards for safekeeping until the mania settled. In states of depression, it was conspicuous that negative thoughts and feelings would trigger extensive rumination, withdrawal from work and sometimes drinking excessive amounts of alcohol. These responses were liable to unintentionally make Alex feel even worse, so he was encouraged to pursue enjoyable and engaging activities such as long-distance walking, which could prevent rumination by keeping his mind engaged in the present, to resist drinking alcohol and to try to keep up social contacts as much as possible. We explored the deeper themes of depression in later phases; at this early point he was not able to clearly articulate what these might be.

Schema Therapy

Alex had made it clear from the first session that he did not want to have 'another course of CBT,' by which he meant challenging thoughts with rational evidence using worksheets. He accepted, however, the idea that some long-standing patterns of emotions and relationships, as well as his attitude towards himself, might have been impacted by past events, and he was interested in the idea of using a Schema Therapy approach to look at these.

In terms of schemas the most conspicuous ones were of mistrust/abuse, self-sacrifice and unrelenting standards, followed by abandonment; in addition, there were issues of emotional deprivation, social isolation, subjugation, approval seeking and punitiveness. On the questionnaire that asked him to assess schemas with regard to his parents, he added a column for his sister; the scores on that were extremely negative concerning mistrust/abuse, being defective, failure and subjugation. On the mode questionnaire, his highest scores were for vulnerable child, punitive parent, compliant surrender, detached self-soother and lack of the contented child self.

The imagery work described below occurred alongside developing a narrative linking key moments of Alex's life: this included difficulties at school, work, his marriages but also the difficult events of his family life, in particular, a step-sister who mistreated him in various ways; she had sometimes been violent and on some occasions sexually abusive. His parents had not believed him when they were told about what was happening. He had rarely seen his biological mother since his parents' divorce, but she had been very critical of him. We did not do any direct reliving of these events but constructed an overview, which helped to guide and contextualise the specific elements of the intervention.

Imagery work and initial exploration of states

We brought together the results from the questionnaires, the comments that Alex had made on a diary sheet regarding the states he experienced during the week and our in-session assessment of experiences from the past and present. In discussion of states, he was well aware of sometimes being very angry, of being distressed, of feeling worthless and a self-critical state which was sometimes expressed as a sort of disgust. Alex was encouraged to imagine how these states would look, how they might be visualised; we checked whether any mode was concerned or worried about this process of accessing parts. He acknowledged a concern about 'opening gates' to feelings of distress: this led to a plan around managing these. As we continued, Alex described a critical part with 'folded arms' and a face expressing disgust, which looked, he thought, somewhat like his father. His manic state was likened humorously to 'the Hulk,' while anger was envisioned 'like a tiger' in the 'pit of his stomach.' A particularly striking image he gave during the initial exploration was of his child self, who he saw at the 'bottom of a quarry,' abandoned, in darkness and lost; we returned to this important image in later sessions. In the following, we will mainly focus on working with the vulnerable child, and subsequently with the mode of compliant surrender.

In line with the usual sequencing of imagery work in Schema Therapy, we preceded from an initial tentative encounter with an image of a child self from the past, through to interactive scenarios in which dialogues were initiated to explore what was happening and to show understanding and care. Events surrounding early adversity and trauma were addressed later, and finally we turned towards how Alex could relate to the child part in the present.

Depression, the critic and vulnerable child

As the work progressed, we turned to address Alex's thoughts and feelings related to depression. These included criticising himself and in relation to this he returned to the image that resembled his father expressing disgust. In the presence of this image, Alex reported feeling embarrassed, and then had another image of his child self curled up in a ball. Alex felt warmth towards this latter image, so we were able to explore the child's feelings. The child spoke about being attacked by his stepsister, said that she was a 'monster,' and explained how he was not being helped. These feelings and meanings seemed central to Alex's repeated depressions, and we returned to them several times over the course of therapy.

The vulnerable child

With the aim of getting to know his young self, Alex gave an image of a boy of about ten years old sitting in his room at a little desk, absorbed in some logic puzzles, his books neatly arranged. Adult Alex felt caring towards the young boy, noting that he looked sad but also wary. A dialogue was started: the young self said he had been through 'shit' and that his mother and father didn't listen. When asked what help was needed, he replied that he wanted his parents to 'kick out' his stepsister. After this imagery, Alex remembered how after that time he pursued getting very strong, and he was tearful remembering this.

In the next session, Alex reported that he thought that the feelings he some-times experienced in the morning were similar to those of his ten-year-old self. In further imagery work, we came back to the image of the child down a quarry. When Alex as the adult spoke to him, the young boy said: 'you've forgotten me.' This began a phase aimed at meeting the needs of the child in the image. When the boy in the quarry said 'no one stopped the abuse,' the adult Alex said 'we can stop it now.' We asked: 'what do we need to understand?' The young Alex then explained how he had been attacked from behind while sitting on the floor. Alex was then able to imagine himself at 18 fighting his sister and throw-ing her out of the house; he was also able to picture a scene in which his father saw the abuse happening and showed great anger. Further images were simple positive ones, such as seeing his young self happily playing with toy cars.

Depression in the morning

We returned to exactly what happened on the days when Alex felt depressed, stayed in bed and did not go to work. He had noticed the feeling of dread and of feeling as if he was about to be attacked, and he observed that the feeling of being trapped now was similar to how he had felt as a child (this aspect had been articulated in earlier sessions). We hypothesised that the dread might be an expression of the vulnerable child mode being reactivated in the present. He was then able to use imagery to engage in a caring way with his child and adult selves in the present, emphasising current safety.

Compliant surrender mode

In exploring how the compliant mode affected his life, Alex expressed that this turned up particularly in relationships, where he ended up feeling exploited; this typically involved paying for everything when dating someone, despite thinking that this was not fair. In one piece of imagery work, the compliant part was asked why it was giving in to the demands of others: in response he frowned, and said that he wanted an easy life, and that complying felt like helping and caring. He added that if he did not keep being compliant, then perhaps others would not like him; he could be left alone, and then would feel worthless. When the origins of the mode were explored, it became clear that it had started in dealing with Alex's stepsister, as a way of surviving the abuse. Clearly there was a strong motivation to protect himself. Articulating these concerns began the process of reconsidering how Alex would like to be in the future, including his relationship and how not to be too compliant. He practised in imagery how he could whisper in the ear of his complaint self, reminding him of the impact of continuing to give in to demands, and encouraging a more assertive stance. A plan was developed to note the earliest warning signs in a new relationship that indicated possible exploitation and to practise assertively asking for equal contributions and mutual support.

Outcomes

By the end of therapy, Alex was back at work full time; he no longer felt the need to take days off to stay in bed when feeling a dread of the day, and reported in general not feeling depressed or high. He continued to function well several months later. Many factors can contribute to therapeutic change, but the most conspicuous with Alex was how he began to develop a new understanding of his variable states and related difficult feelings but also, and crucially important, that he took up a stance of actively looking after himself when such feelings emerged, that is, he took up the caring adult stance to the suffering of the vulnerable child who felt trapped and in danger.

Case illustration: Ira

Introduction

Ira had a diagnosis of bipolar disorder type I, and had experienced long periods of depression, during which she would withdraw to her flat, not eat properly and sometimes engage in self-harming behaviour. When manic, she would walk or run through the streets without end, spend large quantities of money and sometimes engage in causual sexual encounters; at such times she had an extreme sense of power, saying that she felt 'invincible.' She would also engage in behaviours she called 'without measure,' in particular regarding things that she might say to others. There was a pattern of developing a preoccupation with a specific person, usually a man of high status who she knew through work; she would then want to be in his company all the time, and she might make inappropriate comments such as the person being wonderful. Such behaviour, on a couple of occasions, had led to terminations of employment. Ira sought therapy after a very difficult year, during which she lost a job she particularly enjoyed; at this time she was clearly depressed, having withdrawn from spending time with other people. She was very cooperative in therapy and willing to explore different areas as needed.

Phases of therapy

The phases of therapy proceeded as follows: first a period focused on Ira's immediate depression, mainly using ideas from behavioural activation and augmented with the use of solution focused questions to explore those things which had worked in the past to help her to survive or cope with negative moods; these activities turned out to include running, swimming and seeing friends. The second phase explored the specific problem of obsessive behaviours towards others, an exploration of her family history and life, and bringing together the results of the schema and mode tests into a developmental formulation. The therapy continued with a focus on social relationships, self-care but also imagery work, particularly for the vulnerable child self and punitive parent mode.

All of this was in the context of seeking to build a collaborative understanding and to express concern, interest and care. One recurrent element of the work was to suggest alternatives to extreme self-attacks and expressions of hopelessness. Some topics were quite practical, for example, relapse prevention and the development of intentional self-care practices. Other work looked at the advantages and disadvantages of Ira's idolising and obsessive behaviour, some of this being as simple as asking what she really believed would happen if she got the full attention of someone who she wanted to be with; it was striking that she had not ever thought through what could happen if her interest was reciprocated.

Family history

Ira had lived during childhood with her father, mother, sister and grandmother. The dominant impression of the family overall was one of distance, summed up by the image of them all having dinner together, as they did on a regular basis, yet Ira never seeing her father and mother actually speaking to each other. Her father abandoned the family when Ira was a young teenager, and she did not see him for some years. The reasons for this were not discussed with Mary by any of the adults in the family, and she had felt powerfully that it would not be acceptable to ask her mother about it. She had to move schools, and then found herself to be culturally different from her new classmates; she subsequently became a target for bullying. In her adult years, she dropped out of university and drifted through several jobs, which she considered not to match her full capacity or intelligence. She did not settle down in any romantic relationship.

Schemas and modes

The schema questionnaire highlighted difficulties in the areas of emotional deprivation, abandonment, social isolation, defectiveness but also entitlement, insufficient self-control and approval seeking. Her modes included self-aggrandiser, punitive parent, detachment, compliance and vulnerable child.

We discussed many examples from her life indicating activations of the various modes. Illustrating the punitive mode, she said she was 'disgusting' and 'could not bear' herself, adding that her body was 'ugly.' Her mode of self-aggrandising did not take the form of boasting as such but rather a preoccupation with those she saw as having high social status at work, symbolising an effort to try to show that she was in fact level with those of senior status and superior to others doing the same work as herself. The vulnerable child mode was linked with feeling disconnected from others and a sort of undeveloped idea or picture of what would happen if a person who she idolised actually did give her their full attention.

Formulation

Ira suffered distance and disconnection from her father and mother; she had also felt herself to be different from the other children at school. The trauma of being abandoned, not receiving care, not feeling loved and appreciated, led to the formation of schemas of disconnection. As a way of coping, she developed strategies of detachment, of not showing affection but also overcompensating strategies of extreme attachment to distant others, and in general a way of behaving that sometimes involved seeking a sense of status. Her early experience of rejection also resulted in a sense of self-disgust and ferocious self-attacks in the form of criticism by the punitive mode. In short, her early life had led her to feel unlovable, fundamentally flawed in some way, and in the effort to cope with this she pursued a yearning for ideal love and attention from what was essentially an imaginary figure who could not actually give her love and care.

The father in imagery

As outlined in Young et al. (2003), we explored in imagery a scene of distress based on interactions with early caregivers. One scenario was meeting her father after years of absence; in reality, when they had met, she had expressed little to him about her feelings and suffering. She imagined in the session what she would have liked to say and how she would have liked him to respond to her. Next, we focused on what would have met her needs; she asked him why he had not written, why he had left. She imagined that he could have said that he had read all her letters, and that he had missed her.

The self as invalid

When asked to visualise a version of herself in distress at present, Ira described this as 'a dirty machine, rusty and not working.' Asked how she felt toward the image, she expressed disgust. This sort of attitude towards a part of the self poses an obstacle for direct strategies involving interaction between parts; to work around this, Ira was encouraged to picture storing the rusty machine in a dedicated room, then to create a new image of herself as an adult human in distress. This time, she pictured herself as an 'invalid,' injured and debilitated, feeling 'hollow.' Ira was asked: 'if this image was of a friend, how would you want to care for this person?' She was then able to express care towards the image of the damaged figure.

Bullies at school

Ira remembered how she would save up her pocket money during school years to buy treats such as ice cream, but almost every time one of the other girls would demand her money and take it from her. We discussed what it would have been like to stand up to the bullies, and she went through preferred inter-actions in imagery. This process seemed to prompt Ira to share a recent episode from work where someone had come up to her and said direct unpleasant things about her appearance. She explained that normally she does not respond in such situations, but she was able on this occasion to see that the comments had been completely unacceptable. With encouragement, she disclosed the event to HR, resulting in the other staff member being moved to a different part of the workplace. This was the first time that Ira had ever taken such action to protect herself. Chair work was also used to explore and practise how she could speak to this person if encountered again.

The lonely child

Ira was able after some time to envisage herself as a child: she saw a girl around the age of four or five sitting alone on the bathroom floor. As an adult now, she felt anger at this situation, as well as a sort of 'pity.' When asked what 'pity' looked like, she said: 'someone in a soft white veil.' This was a useful clarifica-tion, especially given that pity might be experienced as a negative and detached feeling, but what Ira used the word to mean on this occasion was benevolent and involved certain gentleness. Having explored her different reactions, she was able to return to the child image and expressed a feeling of being 'sisterly' imagining how the young self could show the adult Ira the books that she was reading, and how they could sit and look at them together. She noted during this work: 'I did not think I was like abused children,' but now she was able to see how she had been mistreated and had suffered from neglect, subsequently being able to remember these events without blaming or attacking herself.

Outcomes

One very significant outcome was that, perhaps for the first time, Ira was able to choose to stop pursuing a man with whom she had felt obsessive toward recently and to stop these actions deliberately. She recovered in her mood and took up a new job, focusing on behaving in new ways, such as avoiding making personal comments towards others at work. After several months in a follow-up session, she reported that she was still working, doing self-care, seeing friends and had not had any relapses; two years later she reported that she had maintained this progress.

Case illustration: Geoffrey

Introduction

Geoffrey was taken to a psychiatric ward during a manic episode, in which he had become preoccupied by various issues of power; at one point he thought that the world was under a form of invisible control, and that he needed to write out all of the ways this could be solved, which he spent many hours doing. He also reported that the world looked different than it did before in terms of colour and perspective, everything somehow seeming 'unreal.' He had in fact suffered from various problems for many years, including severe anxiety, depression, aggression with others and struggles with drug use. Despite these difficulties, he had completed a first degree. He reported historical emotional and physical abuse from his mother, and his family had in fact been under investigation by social services on more than one occasion. His mother and father had divorced while he was in his early teens.

Initial sessions and focus

It was difficult in initial sessions to maintain a focus, with Geoffrey speaking of many problems, which included: difficulties in communicating with others, concerns about how he was perceived by others and a great preoccupation regarding whether there had been an incorrect diagnosis or other diagnoses were possible. It took several sessions before we began to clarify what to focus on, which eventually became: communication with others, aggression and a wish to discuss the contribution of the past to his life. However, we also agreed that first we needed to focus on a written relapse prevention plan, which Geoffrey engaged with in great detail. We also found a range of activities he wished to embark on and considered his long-term future. To the future-focused question regarding how things would be without the current problems, he said that he wouldn't feel anxious 'with 1,000,001 things over his head,' he would return to further study and then get a job that was fun and enjoyable, he would be energised, seeing friends, avoiding arguments with his family, and in himself feeling confident, strong, happy and at ease. We compiled a list of strengths and successes that had occurred throughout his life so far, and these included winning athletic events, learning another language, being good at coming up with ideas and finishing his first degree. He kept the list, which he could revisit at times when he felt doubtful or put himself down.

Self-states and formulation

When first asked what he thought his diverse states might be, Geoffrey mentioned self-doubting, anger, impatience with others, feeling down, self-punishing, not being a good person and feeling like 'a burden.' He scored very highly on many schemas and modes: besides a high score on mistrust and abuse, there were also prominent entitlement, impulsivity, and punishment; these themes were very conspicuous as shown on the schema questionnaire concerning his mother and father. In terms of modes, very high-scoring ones included the enraged child, vulnerable child, detached protector, and overcompensator modes of self-aggrandisement and bully and attack. In addition, there were also prominent modes of punitive parent and demanding parent.

Over time we developed a formulation which noted how certain key cognitions, modes and schemas emerged from the way that Geoffrey had been treated as a child, and particularly how he experienced a fearful state of vulnerability, which was overcompensated for by explosive and aggressive behaviours. We considered extensively how he interacted with others in the present, how he might jump to conclusions, and how he could avoid being drawn into arguments and disputes with family members. The rest of this case illustration will focus on work done with angry and vulnerable child modes.

Angry mode

Geoffrey was asked to visualise himself in a state of anger: he said that he would be frowning, his nostrils flared, leaning forward and giving the attitude of 'who do you think you're talking to?' When asked what he felt towards this image, he said that it depended: sometimes he felt grateful for it, but at other times ashamed and disappointed. We then explored an image of shame, in which his head was lowered and his shoulders rounded. After gaining some distance from the feeling of shame, a conversation was started in imagery with the angry part. When asked what it did in Geoffrey's life, it replied that it protected him; if it stopped doing that, then Geoffrey would embarrass himself, would come across as weak, and would feel put down and inferior. The angry part was asked if it realised some of the negative effects it created; it retorted that it did not care and did not see the relevance. When asked how Geoffrey could change to limit negative consequences, the angry part said he would have to act with more confidence and begin to interpret people's actions in a more flexible way, but would also need to value his own opinion and not to be so defensive about it. These discussions were part of a long-term exploration regarding anger, the interpretation of others' actions, the expression of ideas and in general how to avoid outbursts. This approach was well received by Geoffrey, and it seemed effective in helping him to interact with others and particularly his family in a more relaxed fashion. Using chair work, he demonstrated how he could put these ideas into practice with different people.

Abuse and the child self

There had been many episodes of emotional and physical abuse in Geoffrey's childhood: the aim of our work, however, was not to look at these in detail or carry out reliving but to generate an overview and then to attend to unmet needs using imagery work. Geoffrey was able to recount an occasion, for example, when he and his mother had been walking home from shopping, and he had become impatient. His mother had not seemed to respond in any remarkable way to his complaints, but when they got home, she suddenly beat him. In the imagery work, we were able to bring his father in to actively protect him and prevent this attack. The therapist also entered the imagery, and was able to express a professional view to the mother, outlining the harm that she was doing and how utterly unnecessary it was; this being followed by expressing care to the child self and asking what else would bring comfort.

Outcomes

Over several months, Geoffrey made major changes, moving away from his mother's house to live alone and starting a postgraduate course. The new course suited his skills, which tended to be practical and organisational. As planned, he focused on regulating anger and thinking flexibly in social interactions, as well as on fostering improved communication using turn taking and active listening. During this time, Geoffrey no longer felt depressed, and his anxiety levels fell to below clinical levels. He recognised that he would need to pursue self-acceptance and continue to work on managing anger and conflict in interactions with others.

Concluding comments

While some clients with diagnoses of bipolarity do not report serious social difficulties, clearly a substantial number do. Interpersonal and emotional difficulties are a source of distress in themselves but also interact in complex ways with the manifestation of bipolar mood symptoms. For those with long-term social difficulties, Schema Therapy, or adaptations of it, appear to be an appropriate and acceptable approach. The work described here represents an exploration of the application of Schema Therapy with this group, and the initial results seen in specific clinical work are promising. We hope that in the future there can be larger evaluations of the impact of this type of therapy for individuals diagnosed with bipolar disorders. We believe that most bipolar clients are fully able to use complex therapies such as Schema Therapy and have the potential to benefit in a very lasting way from such an intervention.

References

Benazzi, F. (2004). Inter-episode mood lability in mood disorders: Residual symptom or natural course of illness? *Psychiatry and Clinical Neurosciences, 58*(5), 480–486.

Erfan, A., Ghezelbash, S., Kazemian, M., & Noorbala, A. (2019). The effectiveness of emotional Schema Therapy on impulsivity and mood symptoms of women with bipolar disorder. *Journal of Research in Behavioural Sciences, 17*(3), 388–399.

Farr, J., Rhodes, J. E., Baruch, E., & Smith, J. A. (2023a). First episode psychotic mania and its aftermath: The experience of people diagnosed with bipolar disorder. *Psychosis,* 1–11.

Farr, J., Rhodes, J. E., & Smith, J. A. (2023b). Recovering from first episode psychotic mania: The experience of people diagnosed with bipolar disorder. *Early Intervention in Psychiatry, 17*(8), 807–813.

Fisher, J. (2017). *Healing the fragmented selves of trauma survivors.* Routledge.

Frank, E., Kupfer, D. J., Thase, M. E., Mallinger, A. G., Swartz, H. A., Fagiolini, A. M., … & Monk, T. (2005). Two-year outcomes for interpersonal and social rhythm therapy in individuals with bipolar I disorder. *Archives of General Psychiatry, 62*(9), 996–1004.

Garno, J. L., Goldberg, J. F., Ramirez, P. M., & Ritzler, B. A. (2005). Impact of childhood abuse on the clinical course of bipolar disorder. *The British Journal of Psychiatry, 186*(2), 121–125.

Ghaderi, D., Maroufi, M., & Ebrahimi, A. (2016). Comparing the effectiveness of Schema Therapy with cognitive-behavioural therapy on improving quality of life and modifying dysfunctional attitudes in patients with bipolar disorder type I and II in Isfahan. *Recht & Psychiatrie, 724*(2247), 410–420.

Gilman, S. E., Ni, M. Y., Dunn, E. C., Breslau, J., McLaughlin, K. A., Smoller, J. W., & Perlis, R. H. (2015). Contributions of the social environment to first-onset and recurrent mania. *Molecular Psychiatry, 20*(3), 329–336.

Hawke, L. D., & Provencher, M. D. (2012). Early maladaptive schemas among patients diagnosed with bipolar disorder. *Journal of Affective Disorders, 136*(3), 803–811.

Hawke, L. D., Provencher, M. D., & Parikh, S. V. (2013). Schema Therapy for bipolar disorder: A conceptual model and future directions. *Journal of Affective Disorders, 148*(1), 118–122.

Holmes, E. A., Hales, S. A., Young, K., & Di Simplicio, M. (2019). *Imagery-based cognitive therapy for bipolar disorder and mood instability.* Guilford Publications.

Jones, S. H., Smith, G., Mulligan, L. D., Lobban, F., Law, H., Dunn, G.,… & Morrison, A. P. (2015). Recovery-focused cognitive–behavioural therapy for recent-onset bipolar disorder: Randomised controlled pilot trial. *The British Journal of Psychiatry, 206*(1), 58–66.

Khosravi, S., Ebrahimi, M., Shayan, A., Havasian, M. R., & Jamshidi, F. (2017). Investigation of early maladaptive schemas in patients with bipolar disorder compared to healthy individuals. *Journal of Pharmaceutical Sciences and Research, 9*(6), 771.

Lam, D., Hayward, P., & Jones, S. H. (2010). *Cognitive therapy for bipolar disorder: A therapist's guide to concepts, methods and practice* (Vol. 101). Wiley-Blackwell.

Mansell, W., Colom, F., & Scott, J. (2005). The nature and treatment of depression in bipolar disorder: A review and implications for future psychological investigation. *Clinical Psychology Review, 25*(8), 1076–1100.

Mansell, W., & Pedley, R. (2008). The ascent into mania: A review of psychological processes associated with the development of manic symptoms. *Clinical Psychology Review, 28*(3), 494–520.

Miklowitz, D. J. (2010). *Bipolar disorder: A family-focused treatment approach.* Guilford.

Miklowitz, D. J. (2018). *The bipolar disorder survival guide: What you and your family need to know.* Guilford Publications.

Palmier-Claus, J. E., Berry, K., Bucci, S., Mansell, W., & Varese, F. (2016). Relationship between childhood adversity and bipolar affective disorder: Systematic review and meta-analysis. *The British Journal of Psychiatry, 209*(6), 454–459.

Sorensen, J., Done, D. J., & Rhodes, J. (2007). A case series evaluation of a brief, psycho-education approach intended for the prevention of relapse in bipolar disorder. *Behavioural and Cognitive Psychotherapy, 35*(1), 93–107.

Rhodes, J., & Jakes, S. (2009). *Narrative CBT for psychosis.* Routledge.

Tsapekos, D., Strawbridge, R., Cella, M., Wykes, T., & Young, A. H. (2021). Predictors of psychosocial functioning in euthymic patients with bipolar disorder: A model selection approach. *Journal of Psychiatric Research, 143*, 60–67.

Zimmerman, M., & Morgan, T. A. (2013). Problematic boundaries in the diagnosis of bipolar disorder: The interface with borderline personality disorder. *Current Psychiatry Reports, 15*, 1–10.

Young, E., Klosko, J. S. & Weishaar, M. E. (2003). *Schema Therapy: A practitioner's guide.* Guilford.

Index

Pages in *italics* refer to figures and pages in **bold** refer to tables.

Aas, M. 9, 79
abandonment 2, 20–21, 23, 25, 44
abuse 21, 66; acceptance of 29; childhood 29, 33, 82; sexual 32–33, 97; substances, of 32, 41, 132–133, 146
adaptive behaviour 21
Addington, D. 7
Addington, J. 7
adult mode 67
aggression 24, 30, **37**, 157; verbal 49
Ainsworth, M.S. 94–95
Airey, N.D. 97, 102
alienation 21, 23, 96
Allison, E. 66
anger 25, **37**, 134; child, in *see* angry child mode; control of 25; mode of 3, **16**, 23–24; outbursts of 24; paranoia and 27; psychosis and 27; triggering of 26–28; uncontrollable 50
angry child mode 3, 74
angry mode 3, **16**, 23–24, 28, 35, **37**, 47
anxiety 3, 20, 87, 95; reduction of 119
Arntz, A. 15, 17, 21, 24, 43, 47, 72, 78–82, 113–115, 118, 124, 133
Arseneault, L. 7
assessment 11, 84, 86, 94, **99**, 104, 106, 116, 128, 146–147, 150
assumptions 68
attachment 94; disruptions 7, 9; disturbances of 1, 7; theory of 91, 94, 106
attack, self 4, **16**, 20, **37**, 40–41, 128, 153–154
avoidance 29, 55, 64; conflict, of 30–31; emotions, of 32; *see also under* modes

bad me 19; *see also* self-criticism
Bailey, T. 92
Bakos, D.S. 6
Bamelis, L.L.M. 6
Barkus, E. 112
Bartlett, F.C. 73
Baruch, E. 145
Bee, P. 94
behaviours 16, 21, 37, 114; adaptive 21; adult 6; aggressive 157; controlling 139; obsessive 153; self-destructive 4
Benazzi, F. 144
Bennett-Levy, J. 118
Berry, K. 91–92, 95, 106, 112, 116
betrayal 21
bipolarity 8, 62, 70; disorder 9, 36, 78, 144; misconceptions of 8; modes, in *see under* modes; Schema Therapy and 78, 158
blame, self 17, 40, 42, 44
Blankenburg, W. 66
Bleuler, E. 60, 63, 69
Boyda, D. 96
Bonoldi, I. 7
Bortolon, C. 96
Bowlby, J. 73, 94
Brand, R.M. 93, 113
Braun, V. 10
Briedis, J. 85, 130
Brown, G. 96
borderline personality disorder (BPD) 120
Bucci, S. 112, 116
bullying 5, 16, 22, 27, 120
Buswell, G. 91–92

Cairns, A. 94
Carr, S. 91, 95
certainty 66
Chadwick, P. 19
chair work 81, 84, 155, 157–158
child self 82, 114–115, 118–119, 129, 139, 142, 149–151, 153, 158
childhood: abuse 29; adversity 21, 23; trauma 7, 9, 19; unmet needs 20, 23–24, 119
Citak, C. 9
Clarke, R. 10, 21, 93
circadian rhythm, regulation of 8
Cognitive Behavioural Therapy (CBT) 1–2, 77, 80; psychosis, for (CBTp) 7–8, 93
Cohen, L.H. 92
Compassion Focussed Therapy (CFT) 8, 83
compassionate self 62
compliance 29, 59; consequences of non-31; paranoia and 30; voices and 30; see also compliant surrender
compliant surrender 15, **16**, 28–31, 34–36, **37**, 52–54, 57, 138, 150–152; psychosis and 31; see also surrenderer
compulsive distraction 32
conflict 29, 47, 52, 54, 133, 158; avoidance 5, 9, 30–31
confrontation 5–6, 81
consequences 57; non-compliance 31; self-imposed 38
continuum of self-states 58, 70–72
controllability 25–26, 49
coping 34, **37**; detached 56; modes 4, 28, 34, 52, 54–55; schema therapy and 5
core belief 8; negative 7
Corstens, D. 83
criticism 52; self 15, 19, 40–41, 56, 62
Crowe, M. 8
Cutajar, M.C. 7

Dana, D. 74
Danquah, A.N. 95
de Bont, P.A.J.M. 112
de Leede-Smith, S. 112
defeat of self see self-defeat
defensiveness 6
delusions 64, 67, 95, 97, 132
demanding mode 4, 36, **37**, 40, 59, 112, 133
demanding parent 4, 112, 132, 157
dependence 44

depersonalisation 32
depression 6, 36, 42, 44, 48, 50, 56–57, 62; descent into 59, 65, 150; post-natal 102
desperation 20
detached: mode see detachment; protector 5, 15, **16**, 28–29, 32–36, **37**, 46, 54–57, 59, 73, 113, 132, 137
detachment **16**, 32–33, 59; mode of see detached protector
Dimaggio, G. 83
disconnection 22, 32–33, **37**, 55; modes, of 65–66
disorders: bipolar 9; personality 2, 6
dissociation 32–33, 63, 119; management of 124
dissociative identity disorder (DID) 112
distraction, compulsive 32
distress 2, 4, 150
drug abuse 32, 41, 132–133, 146
Dualibe, A.L. 8, 78

early: life experiences 86; trauma 7, 9, 19
Edwards, D. 92
ego-dystonia 20; see also paranoia
emotion: avoidance of 32–33; disruption of regulation 7; needs, unmet 7, 119; reactions 23; regulation 7; states of 21; struggles 8
Engledew, Z. 10
Erfan, A. 146
erotomanic delusion 60–61
Erten, E. 9
Eye Movement Desensitisation and Reprocessing (EMDR) 93, 113

Farr, J. 61–62, 145
fear 3, 19, 21, 26, 30, 59, 68–69
Feeney, B.C. 95
felt security 95
Fisher, J. 63, 72–73, 82, 92, 130, 147
Fonagy, P. 66
fragmentation 58, 62–64, 67, 70
Frank, E. 146
Freeman, D. 8

Garno, J.L. 145
Ghaderi, D. 146
Giesen-Bloo, J. 6
Gilbert, P. 62, 72, 93
Gilman, S.E. 145
Gipps, R. 66, 68

Gould, R.A. 7
Grant, P. 92
guilt 20, 50, 133
Gumley, A.I. 7, 78

Hackmann, A. 82, 91, 118
Haddock, G. 97
hallucinations 22, 68, 95, 97
harassment 16, 19, 27
Hardy, A. 7, 78, 112, 116
harm: others, to 26; self 15, 32, 34, 152
Harnic, D. 8, 78
Harper, S.F. 8, 96
Hawke, L.D. 145
healthy adult (mode) 6, 62, 73
Heath, G. 80
Heim, G. 63
helplessness 3, 20–22, 33, 42
Heriot-Maitland, C. 8, 83
Herman, J.M. 83
Hett, D. 9, 79
Holmes, E.A. 91, 114, 118, 146
humiliation 21, 43, 138
Humphrey, C. 7
Hutton, J. 95
hypomania 61, 65

illusory social agents 61; see also
    psychosis
imagery 81, **98**; difficulties with therapy
    of 105; father in 154; negative 82;
    person-specific 85; psychosis and 92;
    rescripting 113–114, 116–117; Schema
    Therapy and 150; therapeutic 92,
    102–*103*, 150
imagery therapy for psychosis (iMAPS)
    93, 97, **99**, 106
impulsive mode 3
inferiority 21, 41
internal dialogue 20; see also voices
internal leadership 62
interpersonal struggles 8
Irons 83
isolation 20–23, 36, 44; mania and 44–45
Ison, R. 93, 113

Jacob, G. 15, 17, 21, 24, 43, 47, 78,
    80, 133
Jakes, S. 131, 135, 141, 147
Janet, P. 63, 69, 73, 83
Ji, J.L. 91
Johns, L.C. 112

Jones, S.H. 146
Jung, C. 63

Keen, N. 93
Kefeli, M.C. 8
Khosravi, S. 146
Körük, S. 6
Kosslyn, S.M. 92

Lam, D. 8, 146
Lazarus, G. 3–4, 10
Lincoln, T.M. 7
Livingstone, K. 7
loneliness 3, 21, 33, 44, 55
Longden, E. 83, 112, 116, 124
Luyten, P. 66
Lysaker, J.T. 83
Lysaker, P.H. 83

Madill, A. 112
Main, M. 94–95
maladaptive mode 34, 96
mania **37**, 39, 56; episodes of 59; hypo 61,
    65; isolation and 45, 57; states of 61
manic moods 36, 42, 59, 61
Mansell, W. 8, 65, 144
Martland, N. 92
McCarthy-Jones, S. 112
McEvoy, P.M. 112
McKay, M.T. 7
mediation 27
medication 26, 30
memory disruptions 7
Mental Health Act 30
mental health: deterioration of 39;
    stigma 34; struggles with 28; system 30
Miklowitz, D.J. 146
Mikulincer, M. 95
mistreatment by others 24, 48, 51, 53
mode concepts, schema 2, 35
modes 73–74; adult 67; angry 3, **16**,
    23–24, 28, 35, 47; angry child 3, 74;
    bipolarity, in 70; child 3; coping 4,
    28, 34, 52; impulsive 3; maladaptive
    34, 96; mapping of 6; psychosis, in
    14–35; punitive 20, 35; schema
    concepts of 2, 35; vulnerable 3, **16**,
    20–21, 35, **37**, 42, 47
moral standards 4
Morgan, T.A. 145
Morina, N. 113
Morrison, A.P. 92–93

Morriss, R.K. 8, 78
Moskowitz, A. 63–65, 69, 79
multi-self 6, 8–9

National Collaborating Centre for
    Mental Health (NICE) 7
negative core beliefs 7; see also
    self-negativity
neglect, self 41
Newman-Taylor, K. 95, 98, 124

obsessive-compulsive disorder
    (OCD) 131
Ociskova, M. 9
Ogden, P. 63
Osório, F.L. 8, 78
overcompensating 5; mode of 28, 34
Özabacı, N. 6

Padesky, C.A. 141
Palmier-Claus, J.E. 145
paranoia 16, 19, 22, 24, 26, 31, 34, 102;
    anger and 27
parent modes: demanding see demanding
    parent; dysfunction of 4
Parikh, S.V. 145
Paulik, G. 82, 93, 112–113, 115, 124–125
Pedley, R. 144
Peeters, N. 6
Peters, E. 7–8
perfectionism 4
personality disorder 2, 6
person-specific imagery 85
Pilton, M. 116, 124
Pitfield, C. 95
polyvagal theory 74
Porges, S.W. 74
post-traumatic stress checklist
    (PCL-5) 104
post-traumatic stress disorder (PTSD)
    92, 112–113
protection 16, 29, 61, 74; self, of 29
Provencher, M.D. 145
psychopathology 72
psychosis 19, 26–27, 70; anger and 27;
    behavioural states 20; compliant
    surrender and 31; experiences of
    19–20, 22, 34; imagery and 92; modes,
    in see under modes; onset of 23;
    schema therapy application to 7, 60,
    78, 95–96; symptoms 7, 60; trauma
    and 7

Pugh, M. 81
punishment 4; self 17, 41–42
punitive: mode 15, 16, 20, 35, 37, 40;
    parent 4

qualitative research 1, 9, 11, 72, 96–97

racism 22
Rafaeli, E. 3–4, 10
rage see anger
Ratcliffe, M. 66, 69
regulation, emotional 7; disruption of 7
rejection 21, 46–47, 50, 52, 54
Renner, F. 6
Rhodes, J.E. 60, 66, 68, 71–72, 79, 82, 87,
    89, 131, 135, 140–141, 145, 147
Rowan, J. 72, 82

sadness 3, 20–21, 50
Schäfer, I. 92
Schema Therapy 57, 140; aims of 62, 72,
    77; assessment 147; bipolar disorder,
    applications for 78, 144, 158; coping
    and 5; imagery and 150; mode concept
    2; mode framework 2; model 2; origins
    1–2; psychosis, application for 7, 64–65,
    78; stages of 80–81; trauma and 79
schemas 59; negative 60; therapy see
    Schema Therapy
schizophrenia 63–64
Schmucker, M. 114
Schulze, K. 92
Schwartz, R.C. 62, 64, 72, 74, 85, 130
Searle, J.R. 65–66
self: aggrandisement 60–61, 157; attack 4,
    16, 20, 37, 40–41, 128, 153–154; blame
    17, 42, 44; child 82, 114–115, 118–119,
    129, 139, 142, 149–151, 153, 158;
    criticism 15, 19, 40–41, 56, 62; defeat
    1–2; harm 15, 32, 34, 152;
    improvement 4; injury 15, 32; multi 6,
    8–9; negativity 7; see also negative core
    beliefs; protection 29; punishment 17,
    41–42; sense of 18, 42; states of see
    states of self; submissive 52; unified 62
sense of achievement 20
separation 21–22, 36; see also alienation;
    isolation
Serruya, G. 92
sexual abuse 32–33, 97
shame 21, 59
Shapiro, F. 93

Shaver, P.R. 95
Sheaves, B. 93
Shiel, L. 61
Smith, K. 93, 145
social: difficulties 87; stigma 23;
    withdrawal 32, 56
Solomon, J. 94–95
Sood, M. 78, 83, 95
Sorensen, J. 146
Stain, H.J. 7
Stanghellini, G. 66
Stanton, K.J. 7, 78
Staring, A.B.P. 116
Startup, H. 80, 85, 130
states of self 65; continuum of 58, 70–72
Steardo, L. 8
Steel, C. 82, 93, 112–113, 115, 124
stigma 24, 26; mental health 34; social 23
Stone, H. 64, 83
Stone, S. 64, 83
Strachan, L.P. 112–115
subjugation, resisting 51, 53–54
submissive self 52
substance abuse 32
suffering 34
Sundag, J. 96
supernatural powers 23
surrenderer 29, **37**; *see also* compliant
    surrender
survival 28, 32; behaviours 30
symptomatology 79; psychotic 7

Taylor, C. 8, 82, 93–94, 96–97, 100, *101*,
    117–118
telehealth 125
thematic analysis (TA) 10, 35
therapy 147; imagery focused 92,
    102–*103*; multi-self 62; schema *see
    under* schemas; trauma and 88
Thrift, O. 83
trauma 66; early 7, 9, 19; environments
    of 32; interpersonal 7; psychosis and
    7; schema therapy and 79, 88

triggering anger 26–28
Trower, P. 19
trust 21, 66
Tsapekos, D. 144

undisciplined mode 3
unfair treatment 29, 48, 104
unhappiness 20, 54
unified self 62
unshared reality 22–23

van den Berg, D.P.G. 93, 116
van der Hart, O. 63–65, 67, 79, 82
van Os, J. 112
Van Vleet, M. 95
Van Winkel, R. 7
Varese, F. 7, 92, 112, 116
verbal hallucinations 61; *see also* voices
victimisation 16
violence 21–22, 24, 26, 50
voices **16**, 22–24, 26–27, 64, 69;
    compliance and 30; critical 61; hearing
    of 22, 26, 30, 35, 112–113, 116; *see
    also* internal dialogue
vulnerable child mode 3, 16, 20–21, 35,
    37, 42, 44, 47, 64, 70, 151
vulnerability 3, 15, 21–22, 45–46, 50, 52,
    59–60, 70, 96, 112, 157

Waterman, M.G. 112
Weertman, A. 79, 81–82, 114, 118
Whitehead, H. 10
withdrawal 64; social 32, 56
Wittgenstein, L. 66
Wrobel, A.L. 9, 79
Wykes, T. 8

Young, J.E. 2–5, 7, 10, 15, 20, 23, 28, 32,
    34–36, 40, 43, 47, 58, 60, 71–72, 77,
    80–81, 86, 93, 95–96, 132, 154

Zimmerman, M. 145

For Product Safety Concerns and Information please contact our EU
representative GPSR@taylorandfrancis.com Taylor & Francis Verlag GmbH,
Kaufingerstraße 24, 80331 München, Germany

Printed and bound by CPI Group (UK) Ltd, Croydon, CR0 4YY
08/06/2025
01897005-0016